Higher Ground

MICHAEL J. LEAMY

Copyright © 2012 Michael J. Leamy

All rights reserved.

ISBN: 1505557569
ISBN-13:9781505557565

Unless otherwise marked, Scripture quotations are taken from the KJ3 Literal Translation Bible, First Edition, Copyright 2006-2010. Used by permission of the copyright holder, Mary V. Green.

Scripture quotations marked ESV are from The ESV Bible (The Holy Bible, English Standard Version) Copyright 2001 by Crossway, a publishing ministry of Good News Publishers. Used by permission.
All rights reserved.

DEDICATION

We discover an unbroken proclamation of the truth of God's Word spanning the generations of humanity from our Lord's sojourn on Earth through the time of our own pilgrimage. God has chosen to use faithful believers as His chosen vessels, who have planted and watered, while God Himself provided the increase. As the Apostle Paul writes, ***"So, then, you are no longer strangers and tenants, but you are fellow citizens of the saints and of the family of God, being built up on the foundation of the apostles and prophets, Jesus Christ Himself being the cornerstone, in whom all the building being fitted together grows into a holy temple in the Lord, in whom you also are being built together into a dwelling place of God in the Spirit."*** (Eph 2:19-22) One body, one building, one generation spanning nearly 2000 years, the assembly of believers has grown through the process Paul outlined for his son in the faith, Timothy: ***"And what things you heard from me through many witnesses, commit these things to faithful men, such as will be competent also to teach others."*** (2Tim 2:2)

Our Lord uses many lives to shape and sharpen each one of us, to lead each one of us into a deeper understanding of the Scriptures, as His Spirit in our mentors resonates with His Spirit in us, and His indwelling Spirit leads us deeper into the Word. As He does this work to the praise of the glory of the grace of God, any dedication of our feeble efforts must be in the same direction, with humble appreciation to those who have faithfully taught us and prayed for us.

The support, proofreading efforts and cups of tea provided by Lynda Leamy are greatly appreciated. Heart-felt thanks go to Pastor Jerry Conklin of Lewis and Clark Bible Church for his faithful teaching of the Scriptures, his encouragement and sharpening chats during the writing process.

To the glory of His grace!

CONTENTS

	Acknowledgments	i
1	Higher Ground	1
2	Widowmaker	11
3	Rescued	19
4	Gardening	24
5	Who's There?	30
6	Got Milk?	39
7	Ripple Effect	45
8	Voles in the Tater Patch	52
9	Too Many Supervisors	59
10	Storms	65
11	Butterflies	73
12	Protozoa	81
13	Black Line	88
14	Drifting	96
15	Lingering Lights	102
16	Pay Streak	110
17	There is a Way That Seems Right	116
18	Greedy Birds	122
19	Salt Water	131

20	Life or Death	139
21	Bee Stings	147
22	Chameleons	155
23	Rip Currents	161
24	Sound Waves	171
25	Moles	179
26	Refreshing	187
27	Cormorants	193
28	The Fungus Among Us	199
29	Led Astray	205
30	Flash Flood	211
31	Tickling Trout	219
32	Bracken Fern	227
33	Greater Glory	236
	About the Author	247

ACKNOWLEDGMENTS

No work is a solo effort. Even the majestic works of God are collaborative efforts, involving all three Members of the Godhead. All three are actively working, whether in creation, salvation, justification or sanctification, God the Father, God the Son, and God the Spirit work to accomplish the purpose, the decree of God.

Knowingly or unknowingly, many have contributed to this work. If you see yourself here, it is because you know the author, or perhaps it is because you are generalized into an event that segues into a scriptural theme. If your spiritual toes have been stepped upon, perhaps the Spirit is saying that you needed it. The author denies any intention of offending anyone. So, read and be edified. Be encouraged. Be admonished. Be growing.

1

HIGHER GROUND

A rocking sensation roused me from predawn sleep. Dull-headed, I struggled to focus on my surroundings. We sleep on a platform bed, so it could not be my wife turning over or getting up. Besides, it was the house and not the bed that was creaking. Then I became aware of a deep rumble that accompanied the movement of the whole house. Earthquake! It lasted for about half a minute, and the motion ceased. I went back to sleep. My wife missed the excitement. She slept through it. We live in a house on a hill. We dwell on higher ground.

In recent years, officials have posted warning signs in low-lying coastal areas. The signs are stark visuals, showing a stick figure scrambling up a slope as waves break at his feet, waves that threaten to engulf him. The text is equally terse: ENTERING TSUNAMI HAZARD ZONE. The signs, the sirens, the emergency broadcasts will all convey the same message: flee to higher ground. All the disaster preparation and planning, done in such a high-profile manner, have a purpose of present caution, as well as a goal of preconditioning the mindset of coast dwellers to react immediately to a powerful earthquake. Signs not only warn of the hazard, but they also designate escape routes and gathering points.

Flee. Flee this way. Flee to here. The message is reinforced on the Oregon coast by the arrival of debris from the tsunami that devastated the Japanese coast. It was driven home by the news footage that showed real-time destruction as the leading edge of the surging water gathered boats, trucks, buses, automobiles and buildings with which to batter and crush everything in its path, careening across broad lowlands, tearing down what it could not inundate, stalling out as the land rose, and finally rushing seaward dragging victims and captives with it. In some areas, this roiling juggernaut pushed over six miles inland. In other parts of the country, where the lowlands were not so wide, its momentum carried the surge as high as the four hundred foot elevation on the flanks of the mountains.

There was a tragic statistic attached to the event in Japan. There were severe pre-shocks, giving advance notice that there was about to be a major earthquake. These occurred over a span of several days before the quake itself, which has been rated as the strongest earthquake recorded on Earth. Just before the major quake, sensors triggered a public alert system. Of those who received the alert, just over half took it seriously, and fled toward higher ground. The rest? The death toll was over fifteen thousand confirmed dead, with over two thousand more missing. Near a quarter of a million buildings were flattened. Three times that many were seriously damaged. Video footage shows the horrific, inevitable end that took those who realized too late the danger that was descending upon them.

The warning sounded on both sides of the Pacific Ocean. As on previous occasions, even after news footage of the devastation in Japan, the tsunami warning prompted many on the west coast in the United States to flock to the beach from over a hundred miles inland. In northern California, three were swept out to sea when, brimming with bravado, they stood on the wet sand at the edge of the surf to photograph the wave. Two escaped. The other washed ashore hundreds of miles north.

It is not just along the coast that we find those who charge headlong into trouble. The major rivers of the world meander through hundred-year flood plains that are dotted with farms and homes, towns and cities. Floods come, taking houses and livestock and lives. Survivors move right back to the same location once the waters recede. Each time a major flood occurs on a hundred-year flood plain, the name only indicates that sometime within the next hundred years, another major flood will occur. It will come, perhaps next month, or next year, or even with the next storm, and that will only start another hundred-year cycle.

What prompts this mindset? Why do so many ignore or scoff at warnings, running headlong into the ways of danger and disaster? A close friend came up with a design for a T-shirt that presents the mindset in visual form. He took the idea of the tsunami warning sign, and turned the stick figure around so he was running down the cliff toward the waves, with a surfboard under his arm.

We find the same willful insistence on the chaotic maelstrom of ever-changing human philosophy, the crashing waves of false teaching and the deceptive breezes of empty religiosity. Believers in the Lord Jesus Christ are called, even urged to higher ground. There is a stark contrast between the values, purposes and methods of this world, and those of God. ***"For My thoughts are not your thoughts, nor are your ways My ways, says Jehovah. For as the heavens are high from the earth, so My ways are high from your ways, and My thoughts from your thoughts."*** (Isa 55:8-9) The rebellious, self-willed thoughts of man reject the higher ways of God. In this passage, God has His plan and work of salvation in view. Man, in his lower views, demands the way of tolerance, the broad-minded dismissal of difference between the holy and the profane as the basis of acceptance. Our Lord Jesus Christ underscored the distinction between the ways of God and those of man: *"Go in through the narrow gate; for wide is the gate and broad is the way that leads to destruction, and many are the ones entering in through it. For narrow is the gate, and constricted is the way that leads away into life, and few are the ones finding it."* (Mat 7:13-14) When presented with this analysis of man's proposed avenues of admittance into God's holy presence, it is all humanity, not just Israel, that squeals. *"But the house of Israel says, The way of the Lord is not fair. Are My ways not fair, O house of Israel? Is it not your ways that are not fair?"* (Eze 18:29)

God calls His own, His chosen ones, to that higher ground, that higher place, whether it shows up in His word as a mountain, or simply an upper room. Those are symbolic. The reality is Christ. Paul writes, *"I press on after a mark for the prize of the high calling of God in Christ Jesus."* (Php 3:14) Ponder the *high calling of God*. It is not merely an occupation in the brief span of years we are here on this Earth. Paul pointed this fact out to the believers at Thessalonica. *"But we ought to thank God always concerning you, brothers, beloved by the Lord, because God chose you from the beginning to salvation in sanctification of the Spirit and belief of the truth, to which He called you through our gospel, to obtain the glory of our Lord Jesus Christ."* (2Thes 2:13-14) This obtaining is a process, and the One accomplishing it is God Himself. Peter gives us an insight into the process that we call life: *"Now the God of all grace, the One calling you to His eternal glory in Christ Jesus, you having suffered a little, Himself will perfect, confirm, strengthen, establish you."* (1Pet 5:10) Enigmatically, the processes Peter mentions are at once sequential and simultaneous. As each new step is begun, the previous continue. What, then, do we find in that higher place to which we are called?

God knows our needs, and the first is knowledge. His thoughts are higher than ours. We need His instruction. The higher ground is the place where we receive the knowledge of His will. Notice His call to Moses at Horeb, or Mount Sinai: ***"And Jehovah said to Moses, Come up to Me to the mountain, and be there. And I will give to you the tablets of stone, and the Law, and the commandments which I have written, to teach them."*** (Exo 24:12) Centuries later, Emmanuel, God with us, continued the teaching, again on higher ground: ***"But seeing the crowds, He went up into the mountain, and seating Himself, His disciples came near to Him. And opening His mouth, He taught them…"*** (Mat 5:1-2)

There is power in the Word of God. The knowledge of His will, and submission to His purpose by His grace, opens the way to the next need being met. Speaking both physically and symbolically of Jerusalem on the heights of Israel, God promises to do the needed healing work. ***"Behold, I will bring health and healing to it, and I will heal them and will show them the abundance of peace and truth. And I will cause the captivity of Judah and the captivity of Israel to return, and will build them, as at the first. And I will cleanse them from all their iniquity which they have sinned against Me; and I will pardon all their iniquities which they have sinned against Me, and which they have rebelled against Me."*** (Jer 33:6-8) That national healing of Israel is future. The need, though, both for them and for everyone, is now, and is of a spiritual focus. In the days of His flesh, Jesus ministered to the physical needs that weakened and crippled people. ***"And moving from there, Jesus came beside the Sea of Galilee. And going up into the mountain, He sat there. And great crowds came to Him, having with them lame ones, blind, dumb, maimed, and many others. And they flung them down at the feet of Jesus. And He healed them; so that the crowds marveled, seeing dumb ones speaking, maimed ones sound, lame ones walking, and blind ones seeing. And they glorified the God of Israel."*** (Mat 15:29-31) Each physical need Jesus met on the mountain has its spiritual counterpart. He alone can open spiritual eyes, restore the spiritually wounded, enable a God-honoring walk, and supply sound words to communicate His message.

Those He has called to His presence for instruction, those He has cleansed and healed, He consecrates for His service. To Moses on the flanks of Horeb, He gave an assurance: ***"And He said, I will be with you, and this shall be the sign for you that I have sent you, when you bring out the people from Egypt: You shall serve God on this mountain."*** (Exo 3:12) We see the literal fulfillment of that word in the life of service of Moses. A parallel scene unfolds centuries later. We read of Jesus, ***"And He went up into the mountain, and He called near whom He desired. And they went to Him. And He made disciples of twelve, that they might be with Him; and that He might send them to proclaim..."*** (Mark 3:13-14)

The higher ground is the place of perspective. ***"And Jehovah said to Moses, Get up into this mountain of Abarim, and see the land which I have given to the sons of Israel."*** (Num 27:12) On the bank of the Jordan, he would have seen only a fragment. John needed an even higher viewpoint. He was not shown the expanse of the land, but the scope of the ages. ***"After these things I saw. And behold, a door being opened in Heaven! And I heard the first voice as a trumpet speaking with me, saying, Come up here, and I will show you what needs to happen after these things."*** (Rev 4:1) Down through the ensuing centuries, that needed higher perspective has been given within, by the indwelling Guide, God's Holy Spirit, as He applies God's written Word to the heart of the believer, as He opens our understanding.

Higher ground is the place of prayer. In Moses' case, he came down the mountain to pray, in humility. To the people under his charge, he recounts, ***"And I fell down before Jehovah, as at the first, forty days and forty nights; I ate no bread and drank no water; because of all your sins which you had sinned, in doing that which was evil in the eyes of***

Jehovah, to make Him angry. For I was afraid because of the anger and the fury with which Jehovah had been angry against you, to destroy you. And Jehovah listened to me at this time also." (Deut 9:18-19) Jesus, on the other hand, in communion with His Father, went up the mountain. *"And having dismissed the crowds, He went up into the mountain alone to pray. And evening coming on, He was there alone."* (Mat 14:23) But in the depths of His humiliation, He was down the mountain, in the Garden. *"Then Jesus came with them to a place called Gethsemane. And He said to the disciples, Sit here, until going away, I shall pray there. And taking along Peter and the two sons of Zebedee, He began to grieve and to be deeply troubled. Then He said to them, My soul is deeply grieved, even unto death. Stay here and watch with Me."* (Mat 26:36-38) There is no higher calling for the believer than that of bowing in prayer, whether individual or corporate, as modeled by our Lord.

Indeed, the higher ground is the place of sacrifice, as Abraham learned. He had waited long for the promise of the Lord. Promise received, he was called upon by God to release that for which he had waited and prayed. *"And He said, Now take your son, Isaac, your only one whom you love, and go into the land of Moriah. And there offer him for a burnt offering on one of the mountains which I will say to you."* (Gen 22:2) It was there in the place of sacrifice, that God provided His substitute to be offered in the place of Isaac. He provided His perfect Sacrifice in the same place centuries later. Jesus, the Lamb of God, *"...went out bearing His cross, to the place called Of a Skull (which is called in Hebrew, Golgotha)..."* (John 19:17) *"And when they were come to the place, which is called Calvary, there they crucified him, and the malefactors, one on the right hand, and the other on the left."* (Luke 23:33) For believers, walking as He walked leads us to that same higher ground place of sacrifice: *"By this we have known the love of God, because that One laid down His life for us; and on behalf of the brothers we ought to lay down our lives."* (1John 3:16)

We find yet another higher ground reality in the assurance our Lord offered his own: His presence. It is His purpose that He who is the Light of the world be revealed in each of His own by the indwelling Holy Spirit. His glory is revealed in us as we are yielded to and responsive to the Spirit. For Moses, the glory was physical: *"And Moses went up into the mountain. And a cloud covered the mountain. And the glory of Jehovah dwelt on the mountain of Sinai. And the cloud covered it six days. And He called to Moses on the seventh day from the midst of the cloud...And Moses came into the midst of the cloud, and he went up into the mountain. And Moses was in the mountain forty days and forty nights...And it happened as Moses was going down from Mount Sinai, the two tablets of the testimony being in Moses' hand as he went down from the mountain, Moses did not know that the skin of his face had become luminous through His speaking with him."* (Exo 24:15-16, 18, 34:29) The residual glory of the presence of God required Moses to veil his face.

The glory of the presence did not adhere to the three disciples who accompanied Jesus on the mount of transfiguration. That was not the purpose. *"And after six days, Jesus took Peter and James, and his brother John, and brought them up into a high mountain privately. And He was transfigured before them, and His face shone like the sun, and His clothing became white as the light. And, behold! Moses and Elijah appeared to them, talking with Him. And answering, Peter said to Jesus, Lord, it is good for us to be here. If You desire, let us make three tents here, one for You, one for Moses, and one for Elijah. While he was yet speaking, behold, a radiant cloud overshadowed them. And, behold, a voice out of the cloud saying, This is My Son, the Beloved, in whom I have been delighting; hear Him."* (Mat 17:1-5) His presence is revealed in the changed life of the believer, as seen in Peter and John when they were called before the Council in Jerusalem: ***"But beholding the boldness of Peter and John, and having perceived that they are untaught and uneducated men, they marveled. And they recognized them, that they were with Jesus."*** (Acts 4:13)

His physical presence ended on a mountain. But His promise to come again for His own implanted a longing in every believer. He had commissioned them, and as He did so, He ascended:

"And saying these things, as they looked on, He was taken up, and a cloud received Him from their sight. And as they were intently looking into the heaven, He having gone, even behold, two men in white clothing stood by them, who also said, Men, Galileans, why do you stand looking up to the heaven? This Jesus, the One being taken from you into the heaven, will come in the way you saw Him going into the heaven." (Acts 1:9-11) The renewed assurance made the higher ground the place of anticipation. The pull of a higher home was reinforced in John's vision: ***"And he carried me in spirit onto a great and high mountain, and showed me the great city, holy Jerusalem, coming down out of Heaven from God..."*** (Rev 21:10) The glory of His presence is the destiny of His own. It is our longing, as well as His will: ***"Father, I desire that those whom You have given Me, that where I am, they may be with Me also, that they may behold My glory which You gave Me, because You loved Me before the foundation of the world."*** (John 17:24)

Until we stand in His presence, the higher ground is the place of communion. But the higher place is the upper room, the place of intimate fellowship. It started before Calvary, when the time of the Passover came. ***"And that one will show you a large upper room which he has spread. Prepare there. And having gone, they found as He had told them, and they prepared the Passover. And when the hour came, He***

reclined, and the twelve apostles with Him. And He said to them, With desire I desired to eat this Passover with you before My suffering." (Luke 22:12-15) He washed their feet. He served. He sang with them. When they left for the place of prayer, and the place of betrayal, He encouraged His own. He challenged them, and us, to the fellowship of the love of God. ***"I give a new commandment to you, that you should love one another; according as I loved you, you should also love one another."*** (John 13:34) On the road to Gethsemane, He reiterated that challenge that only God's grace can accomplish: ***"This is My commandment, that you love one another as I loved you."*** (John 15:12) That is the way of the higher-ground sacrificial love of God that actively and consistently seeks the best interest of the object of that love. That is the high calling of God in Christ Jesus.

2

WIDOWMAKER

My stomach stiffened in knots as I stared at the chunk of cedar that pinned my chainsaw and my stocking cap to the frozen ground. Blood oozed from my skinned forehead and nose. It was that close.

Life is often a matter of inches or seconds. That cedar pole was about thirty feet long, and at the point that lay against my shoes, it was about six inches in diameter. Winter-soaked and frozen, that log would have split my head like a melon. Instead, it gave me a rug burn as it pulled the wool over my eyes and nose, ripping the knit cap from my head, and tearing the still-running chainsaw from my hand.

The segment of life that flashed through my mind was recent, a matter of months, not decades. After the three years I had spent teaching in a small Christian school in the Idaho panhandle, I had been told that, due to financial difficulties, the school would soon be closing. I was advised to seek another position. The words were gentle in their urgency. The private school simply was not financially viable.

My wife and I enjoyed the scenic area in which we were living. After three years in a chaotic public junior high school setting on the Oregon coast, we had been in a similar situation. The teaching position had been closed. We moved from a climate with two seasons. It was either the rainy season, or the rain was coming. Idaho offered four seasons, with plenty of activities appropriate to each one. We had decided to stay in Idaho, where we had purchased a home. We would simply find another means of support.

My wife and I had been told of a teaching position that was available in a private school in Oregon. However, it was on the coast, and, even though the door was open, we had told the Lord we would never live on the coast again. The year we moved to Idaho, we had endured the wettest autumn and winter in decades. The rains set in in early November, and with one Pacific storm after another, it rained almost constantly from then until the end of March. We recorded only two days without rain during that period. So, with that gloomy weather memory combined with the unpleasant workplace experience, we told the Lord, "No." He had other plans.

A friend who was a forester for a timber company operating in Idaho mentioned he had access to salvageable cedar, and that shake bolts were selling for four hundred dollars per cord. Two men could cut, split and load two cords per day, easily. I had a chainsaw, and bought a two-ton flatbed truck that would handle the abundant harvest that would fund our stay as we settled into our own long-range plan.

We went to work. Our first weekend out was less productive than we had anticipated. My friend was only available on Saturdays, and the salvage sites were only open to me when he was there. We managed one chord of shake bolts that trip, and when we sold that load, a third of it was rejected. The second weekend was more productive, but the working conditions were miserable. A cold, drenching rain gradually changed to huge, wet snowflakes. We got our two chords loaded, and drove out through three inches of slush that threatened to slide the truck off the logging road and into the ravine. The slush came in handy, though. The seller of the truck had patched a hole in the muffler with baling wire and tar paper, which caught fire as we were driving out of the forest. We doused the fire, which was just behind the gas tank, stripped away the remains of the tar paper, and rumbled the rest of the way home.

At last, with the muffler patched, we were back in the woodland, at another clear cut where the loggers had left dozens of cedar snags standing. It was the third snag that I cut that pinned my hat and saw to the ground.

To this day, I do not know where the pole came from. I had looked at the snag, about sixty feet tall, from all angles, and calculated the best direction of fall. It was about two and a half feet in diameter just above the root swell, tapering to about a foot and a half where it had snapped off. There were no branches, and if it had a second top, I missed it.

I had made a western undercut, then back cut to it, leaving about a one-inch hinge. It was so perfectly balanced that it did not pinch the saw. I pulled the saw out, stepped back, and pushed the snag off balance with one hand. It started to fall, and I backed out of the way. My friend saw the widowmaker coming and opened his mouth to shout a warning. No sound would come. If it had, I would have stepped forward to turn toward him.

Sometimes we get so set on our own purposes, our own ideas, our own plans, that the Lord simply allows us to pursue them, and fail. Indeed, as Miles Stanford notes in his book, <u>The Green Letters</u>, it is God's purpose that we, as believers, put our confidence in Him, and depend on Him alone. He states that it is the ministry of the Holy Spirit to lead in God's purpose, and if we become self-confident, He will orchestrate our failure, that we might learn both our weakness and foolishness, and His wisdom and power.

Consider Elijah's plight. God had demonstrated His power at Mount Carmel. He had infused Elijah with His power, enabling an old man to out-run a horse-drawn chariot. Then, Elijah received a message from the queen, saying, "You're a dead man." His focus changed from the powerful God who had called him, to his own thoughts, plans and fears. He ran. This time, though, it was in his own frail strength, in his own purpose to save his own skin. Exhausted, he groveled under a broom tree, and begged God to take his life. For perspective, he had run in God's power for seventeen miles, and then fled in his own waning strength for another hundred miles before he collapsed. He was at the end of his own ability, but not at the end of his self-will.

At this point, God gave him something to think about, when he regained his focus. For now, it merely refueled him for the journey to the end of himself. *"And he lay down and slept under a certain broom tree; and behold, an angel touched him and said to him, 'Get up, eat!' And he looked, and behold, at his head was a cake on burning stones, and a jar of water; and he ate and drank, and turned and lay down. And the angel of Jehovah returned a second time, and touched him, and said, 'Get up, eat, for the way is too great for you.'"* (1Kings 19:5-7) Elijah had been sent to Israel. Threatened by Jezebel, he had run for his life and had escaped her jurisdiction, and was now at the southern extreme of Judah. However, refreshed by God's provision, which for the moment he took for granted, he pursued his self-willed way for another two hundred miles, to Mount Horeb, or Sinai. *"And he came there to the cave, and lodged there; and behold, the Word of Jehovah came to him, and said to him, 'What are you doing here, Elijah?'"* (1Kings 19:9) Elijah ran from wallowing in self-pity under the tree, to hiding in a cave, perhaps fleeing from the face of the Lord? The self-willed mind may think so.

Consider Jonah: *"And the Word of Jehovah was to Jonah, the son of Amittai, saying, 'Rise up, go to Nineveh, the great city, and cry out against it; for their evil has come up before Me.' But Jonah rose up to flee to Tarshish from the face of Jehovah. And he went down to Joppa, and he found a ship going to Tarshish. And he gave its fare and went down into it in order to go with them to Tarshish, from before the face of Jehovah."* (Jonah 1:1-3) Note the stark parallel. Jonah, sent to Nineveh, fled toward Spain, hiding in the bowels of a ship.

David records the futility of such self-willed efforts to escape the purpose of God: *"Where shall I go from Your Spirit? Or where shall I flee from Your face? If I go up to Heaven, You are there; if I make my bed in Sheol, behold, You are there! If I take the wings of the morning, dwelling in the uttermost part of the sea, even there Your hand shall lead me; and Your right hand shall seize me. If I say: Surely the darkness shall cover me; even the night shall be light around me. Even the darkness will not be dark from You, but the night shines as the day; as is the darkness, so is the light."* (Psa 139:7-12)

Back to Elijah. Visualize the scene in the cave this way, with staging notes:

God: What are you (points to Elijah) doing here? (indicates cave; emphasis on words 'you' and 'here')

God does not ask this question for information. He knows. His purpose in asking the question is to point out the futility and inappropriateness of the situation. In the Garden of Eden, He asked a similar question, with a like purpose: *"And they heard the sound of Jehovah God walking up and down in the garden at the breeze of the day. And the man and his wife hid themselves from the face of Jehovah God in the middle of the trees of the garden. And Jehovah God called to the man and said to him, 'Where are you?'"* (Gen 3:8-9) In a variety of circumstances down through the ages, stated or implied, that question has come to those who have turned from the purpose of God to follow their own ideas: "What are **you** doing **here**?"

What does God get in reply? Excuses offered up as rational reasons for dereliction of duty. They may contain a dose of truth, but they lose their validity in the light of disobedience. Listen to Elijah:

"What are **you** doing **here**, Elijah?" *"And he said, 'Being zealous, I have been zealous for Jehovah the God of Hosts, for the sons of Israel have forsaken Your covenant; they have thrown down Your altars, and they have killed Your prophets with the sword, and I am left, I alone, and they seek to take my life.'"* (1Kings 19:10) All of the elements of Elijah's excuses were valid, except his perception that he was the only one left. Their being true, though, did not validate Elijah's present disobedience. They were instead Elijah's attempt to justify his insistence on his own way.

God had an object lesson for him. *"And he said, 'Go out and stand on the mountain before Jehovah.' And, behold, Jehovah passed by, and a great and strong wind tearing the mountains and breaking the rocks in bits before Jehovah! Jehovah was not in the wind. And after the wind was an earthquake, but Jehovah was not in the earthquake. And after the earthquake was a fire, but Jehovah was not in the fire; and after the fire came a still, small voice."* (1Kings 19:11-12) Three natural extremes that result in devastation and tragedy, allowed by God, forces that show us our frailty, and the pointless futility of self-reliance, yet they did not touch Elijah. Demonstrations of power, reminders of God's power, and yet the Scriptures make it clear that God was not *in* any of them. He was not in the natural chaos on Horeb, nor was He in the circumstances Elijah had cited. But, in that demonstration, He reminded him that none of them had destroyed

Elijah. God was not in the wind that buffeted the ship in which Jonah fled, nor in the waves beneath which he sank, nor in the great fish that swallowed him. God was not in the cedar pole that lay at my feet. These were merely situations God allowed, or orchestrated, and used to reclaim the spiritual attention of His chosen messenger.

Attention refocused, what then? There came *"...a still, small voice."* To Elijah, He said, "Go back where you belong." To Jonah, "Go where I sent you." God's Spirit speaks quietly. If we resist, He waits. He guides even through the pathways of struggle and failure, until we are ready to yield, and to respond. For Adam, for Elijah, for Jonah, indeed for each of us, there is always that choice between the way of the flesh, and the way of the Lord. Paul admonishes us, *"But I say, Walk in the Spirit, and you will not fulfill the lust of the flesh."* (Gal 5:16) Circumstances shout instructions. Carnival hucksters, they cry enticements to draw us in the way of the flesh, arguments that seems so logical, so right, so righteous. God's Spirit guides through a still, small voice, bringing to our meditations the necessary portions of Scripture. Circumstances cry, "Act!" The Spirit urges, "Yield." Paul writes, *"Neither present your members as instruments of unrighteousness to sin, but present yourselves to God as one living from the dead, and your members instruments of righteousness to God."* (Rom 6:13) We will eventually be brought to the place of yielding. How much agonizing fear we endure, how much mental chaos, how much disquieted spirit, we determine by our persisting in our self-willed way.

We will eventually reach the point of crying, "I can't!" He can then calm us with His quiet "I can! I will!" We will be maneuvered by the Spirit into the realization that our way is the way of failure. When we yield to His guidance, we can go grudgingly, as Jonah did, and miss the blessing of obedience. Or, we can, as Paul did, see the open door of obedience, and find blessing in spite of circumstances. *"And a vision appeared to Paul during the night: a certain man of Macedonia was standing, entreating him and saying, 'Passing over into Macedonia, help us!' And when he saw the vision, we immediately sought to go forth into Macedonia, concluding that the Lord had called us to announce the gospel to them. Then having set sail from Troas, we ran a straight course into Samothrace, and on the morrow into Neapolis, and from there into Philippi, which is the first city of that part of Macedonia, a colony. And we were in this city, staying some days."* (Acts 16:9-12) In Philippi, Paul encountered a mixed bag of circumstances. He was presented with opportunity and opposition. He was received, and rejected. He was beaten, and yet blessed in seeing souls saved.

We arrived at the Oregon coast for an interview, and were met by a downpour of rain and hail that the windshield wipers could not clear. We had to sit in the car in the parking lot for nearly a quarter of an hour, trapped by the roaring water and wind, the rumble of thunder and the frequent flashes of lightning.

Thirty-seven years later, we look back on the blessings and trials, the opportunities and opposition, and the grace and growth in the way of obedience here on the coast where we still find ourselves waiting out sudden squalls and lashing storms. But the circumstances of weather or trial do not eclipse the blessing of His way.

3

RESCUED

Our neighbor raised pigs. She had built a pigpen fenced with field wire, which proved to be inadequate to contain the growing hogs, who discovered while rooting at the base of the fence that the wire would lift up and slide over their backs if they just followed their snouts. After several roundups, she added hog panels around the inside of the field wire. That held the pigs in until their appointed time to move into the freezer.

The pigs were gone, at last. The fertile mud dried, and weeds took over. The pen now became both a feeding ground and a bedding ground for a doe. Deer like the weeds that grew and blossomed in the pen. The blackberry vines and salal that grew along the four foot high fence made a deer-friendly covert that excluded dogs that wandered through the neighborhood. The hog panels had horizontal bars welded to the verticals so that the higher up the fence went, the farther apart the bars were. Near the bottom, the openings were a foot wide, but only two inches high. Halfway up, the openings were six inches high, and at the top, eight inches. The doe could easily leap into the pen, and out again, choosing any of half a dozen trails for her escape.

The security of the pen became a liability the next spring. The doe had a single fawn, and, for a month, the baby could wriggle through the openings with little difficulty. Daisies grew abundantly in the rich soil, and, since the fawn was spattered with white spots, she blended in with the sunny flowers and their shadowed background. I called her Daisy.

The doe and fawn came and went at will. Mother would leap over the fence, and baby would worm her way in or out, and the two would wander.

Fawns can grow quite a bit in a month. One evening, I saw the two of them in the pen. The doe leaped out, and waited for the fawn, who found she did not fit through the mesh anymore. She lunged, trying to force her way through, but her shoulders caught. She tried several times, growing more frantic. She began trying different points along the sides of the pen, but, though her head went through easily, her body was just too big to fit.

Then, disaster. Her head pushed through the hog panel, and through the field wire, near a fence post. Her effort to force her way through had pushed the wire away from the post just enough to let her head pass through, but then, the wire slipped back, pinning her neck between the wire and the post. She was trapped, snared by the system that would yield when she pushed, but tighten when she pulled. Without aid, she would die.

I had heard that a doe would abandon a fawn if it had human scent on it. Whether or not that was true, I would soon know. I climbed into the pigpen and approached the struggling fawn, talking to her as I got close enough to touch her. I gently ran my hands down her ribs, just behind her shoulders. She shrank from my touch, crouching, and uttered a soft bleat that brought the doe bounding from the brush. She stopped just the other side of the fence from me. Now I had two to talk to, trying to soothe both an upset mother and a frightened baby. I raised up, still talking to the two of them, and as I made myself appear as big as I could, the doe retreated.

The fawn was still struggling to pull back, so I nudged her forward with my knee against her tail. It was difficult to force enough space between the wire and the post, but I was finally able to fold her ears back and button her head back out of the trap. I scooped her up in my arms as she pulled back through the hog panel. After my wife and neighbor got a close-up view, and gave her a quick caress, I set the fawn over the fence. She just stood there, until I clapped my hands, startling her down the trail, where her mother waited, about twenty yards away. The doe sniffed her all over, and, apparently satisfied, gave her a quick slurp on the face, and led her away. An entire week passed before I saw the two of them together again. The doe moved the nursery. But, Daisy survived, and thrived. She is a grandmother, now. Her lesson is instructive.

Looking into the mirror of God's word, we see ourselves in the place of that fawn. We are clearly portrayed as having been trapped, ensnared by our own striving after our own way. We, too, were in the place of death, doomed to perish, unless a Rescuer intervened on our behalf. We, like Daisy, cringed and cried out at the touch of our Rescuer, and struggled against His freeing work. As believers in our Lord Jesus Christ, we stood amazed at our liberty in Him, scarcely daring to take that first free step on the pathway of righteousness.

His word tells us the unseen details of our rescue: "**For man does not know his time. Like fish that are taken in an evil net, and like birds that are caught in a snare, so the children of man are snared at an evil time, when it suddenly falls upon them.**" (Eccl 9:12 ESV) Like Daisy, we were comfortable in the values and behaviors of the world around us, the system into which we were born. We were of the world, and, as the Scriptures tell us, we were children of disobedience, and therefore, children of wrath. We were caught in a trap, but did not notice, until that moment we discovered our helplessness. In that instant, the fruitless struggle began.

The struggle to escape takes many forms. Some turn to whatever dulls the conscience, or desensitizes the mind, if only for a moment. Substances, religious ritual, philosophy, frivolity, asceticism, supposed good deeds – we try them randomly, and each gives a brief delusion of relief. But, like Daisy discovered, progress is minimal, and pulling back is impossible, and only tightens the snare. The struggle to escape intensifies.

God has a simple beseeching of grace: "***...do not turn aside after empty things that cannot profit or deliver, for they are empty.***" (1Sam 12:21 ESV) "***...and call upon me in the day of trouble; I will deliver you, and you shall glorify me.***" (Psa 50:15 ESV)

What a contrast! The one who is ensnared looks frantically around, seeking relief from helpless helpers, those things that are powerless to save. At the same time, God calls the captive to look to the One who is higher, who is able to deliver. Of the captive, God says, "**When he calls to me, I will answer him; I will be with him in trouble; I will rescue him and honor him.**" (Psa 91:15 ESV) Note the eternal purpose in this verse. It starts with deliverance, continues with ongoing deliverance, and culminates in final and eternal deliverance. We are set at liberty in Christ Jesus. The believer is drawn to the Lord by God Himself: "***All that the Father gives me will come to me, and whoever comes to me I will never cast out. No one can come to me unless the Father who sent me draws him. And I will raise him up on the last day.***" (John 6:37, 44 ESV) Drawn to Him, His Spirit inclines our heart to believe, in the faith He implants. Christ Jesus delivers, having said, "***...and you will know the truth, and the truth will set you free. So if the Son sets you free, you will be free indeed.***" (John 8:32, 36 ESV) Set free outside the prison that bound us, oppressed us and enslaved us, we discover, "***We have escaped like a bird from the snare of the fowlers; the snare is broken, and we have escaped!*** (Psa 124:7 ESV) Free in Christ! Free to serve, to follow, to obey. Free, and yet, as the old hymn, "Holy God, We Praise Thy Name" expresses it, "*Spare Thy people, Lord, we pray; by a thousand snares surrounded. Keep us free from sin today; and never let us be confounded...*"

I set Daisy free into a hostile world. She was free to go, but at risk. Her world held coyotes, dogs, bobcats, bears and a cougar. It was a world filled with claws and fangs, and she had neither. In the spiritual realm, we find ourselves in the same situation. Our Lord told his disciples, "***Go your way; behold, I am sending you*** out as lambs in the midst of wolves." (Luk 10:3 ESV) *"I have said these things to you, that in me you may have peace. In the world you will have tribulation. But take heart; I have overcome the world."* (John 16:33 ESV) Paul wrote to Timothy, *"Indeed, all who desire to live a godly life in Christ Jesus will be persecuted..."* (2Tim 3:12 ESV), yet we walk in the assurance that *"the Lord knows how to rescue the godly from trials..."* (2Pet 2:9 ESV) Paul looked beyond the trials, temptations and dangers of this life, keeping in view the eternal destiny, when he wrote to Timothy, *"The Lord will rescue me from every evil deed and bring me safely into his heavenly kingdom. To him be the glory forever and ever. Amen."* (2Tim 4:18 ESV) In his first epistle, Peter wrote of the things that are our secure possessions now, although we do not yet enjoy the full benefit of them: **Blessed be the God and Father of our Lord Jesus Christ! According to his great mercy, he has caused us to be born again to a living hope through the resurrection of Jesus Christ from the dead, to an inheritance that is imperishable, undefiled, and unfading, kept in heaven for you, who by God's power are being guarded through faith for a salvation ready to be revealed in the last time. Therefore, preparing your minds for action, and being sober-minded, set your hope fully on the grace that will be brought to you at the revelation of Jesus Christ.** (1Pet 1:3-5, 13 ESV)

The living hope set before us is an earnest expectation, not yet realized. The inheritance is ours, but is stored up for us. The salvation is ours now, but the knowledge of its fullness is beyond our comprehension now. Even the understanding of the depth of grace is waiting, with the others, to be revealed with the appearing of our Lord and Savior, when we *"meet the Lord in the air, and so shall we always be with the Lord."* (1Thes 4:17 ESV)

4

GARDENING

Winter hobbles slowly offstage, exiting stage left. He turns, and gives a sunny smile, that for all of its brightness, is still distant and cold. Spring is waiting in the wings, and, as Winter smiles a cold farewell, she sends her radiance before her, giving an apparent warmth to Winter's hesitant departure. Spring peeps around the curtain, and the audience stirs in anticipation. But, Winter turns and coughs his icy breath across the stage, even as Spring draws back, awaiting her proper cue. A disappointed audience sits back, expectation tempered by frigid reality.

Such is the gardener's plight. Here on the Oregon coast, February is often peppered with sunny days, intermingled with frost. The pattern continues into March, and sometimes into April.

Mix in the soaking downpours and soggy mist that keep the soil saturated, and you have the perfect setting for the old gardener's planting lament: One for the root rot, one for the crow, one for the cutworm, and one to grow. Warm days of winter encourage gardeners to get out their tools. Those with large plots drag out the tiller, and those with smaller spaces pull shovels and rakes out of storage.

The large-garden tiller folk work up aching arms and shoulders as they struggle to start the machines that should have been winterized months before. Once the engine sputters to life, they further abuse muscles and joints in the wrestling match of mud stirring that must pass for soil preparation.

Those who garden on a smaller scale work up their aches by digging a never-ending series of shallow wells. Each shovelful reveals the slow seeping flood of a high water table, but with an endless scoop-and-splatter process, they, too, complete the rite of hasty futility.

As the sun descends toward the horizon, these who want to fulfill their annual pledge of getting an earlier start on planting squish the first rows of seeds into the ground. Surely this year, the warmth will continue. Why, one year, it was warm and sunny during the whole month of February, and half of March! Perhaps this year...

Others simply skip the preparation step. Planting is done on unbroken soil, and compost or mulch is spread over the top. The mulch will hold back the weeds, and hold in the warmth and moisture, and gardening will be a simple wind-up-and-watch operation. It says so in the book.

Recently, one of those winter days dawned sunny, warm and very promising. We stopped by the farm and garden supply store for some fence hardware we needed for a project. It was the store's busiest day of the year. Gardeners, those eternal optimists, were carting out starts, seeds and soil amendments, spending money that the shop owners knew they would spend again, fulfilling the adage, "plant early, plant twice." Or three times. Or, in a bad weather year, maybe four times. But, in wisdom or in folly, the planting goes on.

In His earthly ministry, our Lord used the rituals of spring planting, as well as harvest, to illustrate spiritual realities. In one parable, He pointed to a distant farmer who was striding across his field, broadcasting seed. His robe gathered into a basket and filled with seed, he would walk back and forth across the ground, holding the hem with one hand, and with the other, taking a fist full of seed and flinging it alternately to the left and to the right. As he did, some of the seed would land on the pathway that led along between his field and the roadway. People preferred to walk there to avoid the exhaust emissions of the vehicles of that day. Emissions then tended to splatter on the ground, rather than linger in the air. That wayside soil, trampled hard by the passing of many feet, was as hard as pavement, and formed a continuous bird feeder.

Other seed fell on shallow soil. Much of the land that was farmed lay over shelving stone that bulged through the surface of the ground, leaving soil-less areas, and areas with a thin film of dirt over the emerging stone. The stone had been simply left in place. The thin film of surface soil would hold little moisture, and beneath the strengthening sun, would parch quickly.

Other seed fell in the steep-sided washes and gullies that were choked with thorn bushes. The brush had not been cleared, and the washes had not been filled.

Much of the seed, though, fell on ground the farmer had carefully prepared. It was broken up, softened, opened to both seed and moisture. The unprepared soil areas were fruitless. The sowing effort was adequate. But, birds don't break up the wayside soil, they simply eat the seed. While the seed has an outward appearance of life in the shallow soil, the appearance fades, and the deadness is all that remains. The same is true among the weeds. Overshadowed and strangled by competing worthlessness, the seeds show the appearance of life, only to wither, absorbed by the weeds. In the old gardener's saw, only one fourth of the seed is productive. But as the Lord pointed out in the parable, the issue in not with the seed, but rather with the soil.

Hear the Lord's words: *"The seed is the Word of God."* (Luke 8:11) The seed is all good. The Word of God is pure, living, powerful, and eternal. In the Psalms, David describes it this way: *"The law of the LORD is perfect, reviving the soul; the testimony of the LORD is sure, making wise the simple; the precepts of the LORD are right, rejoicing the heart; the commandment of the LORD is pure, enlightening the eyes; the fear of the LORD is clean, enduring forever; the rules of the LORD are true, and righteous altogether."* (Psa 19:7-9 ESV) Expand David's descriptions of the written word, and you find the same is true of the Living Word, exponentially increased. The seed of God's word has no expiration date or "best by" date. It contains no duds.

The delivery of the seed was timely and direct. *"But when the fullness of time had come, God sent forth his Son..."* (Gal 4:4 ESV) Jesus prayed, *"For I have given them the words that you gave me, and they have received them..."* (John 17:8 ESV) There was, and is, no problem with the supply system.

There was no ambiguity in the mission: *"You did not choose me, but I chose you and appointed you that you should go and bear fruit and that your fruit should abide..."* (John 15:16 ESV) *"But you will receive power when the Holy Spirit has come upon you, and you will be my witnesses in Jerusalem and in all Judea and Samaria, and to the end of the earth."* (Acts 1:8 ESV) *And He said to them, "Going into all the world, preach the gospel to all the creation."* (Mark 16:15 ESV)

For the believer, then, it is a mission of planting. As believers, we have a stewardship responsibility for the seed of the Gospel of Christ that has been entrusted to us. We, like the farmer in the parable, stride through the field of life, broadcasting seed. We are surrounded by a variety of soil conditions. As with the farmer of old, our planting is not selective. The preparation of the hearts of people is not our concern. God alone can do that work. Neither are we to test the soil, and decide whether or not to plant. God looks on the heart, and the Word of God probes and discerns. Ours is a ministry of planting and watering, of evangelism and discipleship. The heart work belongs to God alone. Paul wrote, **"I planted, Apollos watered, but God gave the growth. So neither he who plants nor he who waters is anything, but only God who gives the growth."** (1Cor 3:6-7 ESV)

Think about our Lord's commission to His own: **"Going into all the world..."** Ours is a daily ministry of life, to be carried out without usurping our Lord's authority, without resisting His guiding, **"That ye may be blameless and harmless, the sons of God, without rebuke, in the midst of a crooked and perverse nation, among whom ye shine as lights in the world, holding forth the word of life."** (Php 2:15-16 ESV) In our going, we encounter hard hearts, shallow hearts, crowded hearts, and prepared hearts, all dark, all desperately needing the light of the Gospel. **"In their case the god of this world has blinded the minds of the unbelievers, to keep them from seeing the light of the gospel of the glory of Christ, who is the image of God."** (2Cor 4:4 ESV) God has chosen to use believers as the agency through which the seed of the Gospel is to be sown. Hear Paul's admonition to Timothy: **"...preach the word; be ready in season and out of season; reprove, rebuke, and exhort, with complete patience and teaching. For the time is coming when people will not endure sound teaching, but having itching ears they will accumulate for themselves teachers to suit their own passions, and will turn away from listening to the truth and wander off into myths."** (2Tim 4:2-4 ESV)

Preach the Word. Sow the seed. Life is in the Word. Power to save is in the Word. "The unfolding of your words gives light; it imparts understanding to the simple." (Psa 119:130) Remember that it is God who gives the increase, who causes the growth. ***"For God, who said, 'Let light shine out of darkness,' has shone in our hearts to give the light of the knowledge of the glory of God in the face of Jesus Christ."*** (2Cor 4:6 ESV) Or, as we read in the early history of the church, ***"...the Lord added to their number day by day those who were being saved."*** (Acts 2:47 ESV)

5

WHO'S THERE?

    People trudged by twos and threes out through wrought iron gates of the small military cemetery. The service had been brief, and the crowd small. They chatted as they emerged, then regrouped as they dispersed to their various vehicles. Those drivers farthest from the gate jockeyed their cars back and forth, trying not to run up or down the embankments that flanked the inadequate parking area. Turned at last, they edged down the graveled road, dodging potholes, and making room for the next rank to follow their examples.

    When the hearse and military van with the color guard pulled out, the last to leave, I drove my truck up the hill, through the gate, and parked in the cemetery. It was my responsibility to lower the casket and close the grave. I serve as sexton for several historic cemeteries in our county, as well as some in neighboring counties, and across the state line, as well. I suppose you could say that I'm the last one on Earth to let you down.

The afternoon sunshine had made the truck and the handles of my tools unbearably hot. I was glad the site itself was in the shade of the giant, old spruce trees that lined the short road into the cemetery. I got the wheelbarrow and shovels out of the truck, and trundled them up the slope. The historic cemeteries in our area are somewhat fragile, and some of them are quite steeply sloped, so no power equipment is usable without risk of damage. I was restricted to the poor man's steam shovel, and the poor man's dump truck.

After lowering the casket into the grave, and moving my gravesite equipment down to the truck, I picked up a scoop, and paused to mop my face before beginning to move the sand back into place. I was about to undo all of yesterday's labor. I sighed. There is a certain solemnity to the closing of a grave, a reminder of the brevity of life, of our own mortality. I scooped up the first shovelful of sand, and tossed it into the grave. Loose sand is still heavy. It hit the casket with a thud of finality.

"Hello?"

I froze, halfway through a thrust of the scoop for more sand. A quavery voice of the elderly called out. It sounded as if someone was answering the telephone, or trying to get my attention. The inflection was ascending, questioning. I slowly straightened, and looked around. I was the only person in the cemetery. There was no one in the parking area outside the gate.

With a frown, I scooped up more sand, and threw it into the grave.

"Hello?"

The instant the sand thumped on the casket, the same quavery voice rang out. I scanned the houses beyond the cemetery grounds. It was early afternoon on a school day, and nobody was at home. I slowly turned, searching in a full circle around the graveyard. I was the only one in the neighborhood.

I listened for a full minute, and, hearing nothing, I hesitantly reached for a third shovelful. I paused, then tossed it in. Thud.

"Hello?"

As soon as it hit the casket, I heard the same voice. I looked down into the hole for a moment, then shook my head. I stabbed the scoop into the pile of sand, and headed down the walkway and out the gate. As I started down the hill along the row of homes, looking for anyone who might need help, I heard the voice behind me.

"Hello?"

I whirled around, searching back up the slope toward the cemetery. In one of the huge Sitka spruce trees, a raven ruffled his feathers, bobbed his head, and called, "Hello?" in the same elderly voice I had been hearing. Then, with a burst of child-like laughter, he flew away. I returned to my mournful task, wondering who all that raven could mimic.

We are surrounded by voices in a busy world. The larger the crowd, the louder the cacophony, and the less intelligible the messages bombarding us. We are inclined to generalize them into background noise. In Old Testament times, there were those who tended to do the same with the Voice of God, but not all. We have to think back to that age through the doorway of Hebrews 1:1, where we read, **"Long ago, at many times and in many ways, God spoke to our fathers by the prophets..."** (ESV)

In many ways included dreams, visions, visitations and voices. In many of the scriptural records, we are merely told **"...the word of the LORD came to"** whichever prophet is writing. How it came to the prophets, we are not told. We do know that Joseph, Jacob, Pharaoh, and others dreamed dreams, in which the message of God came to them. Moses was drawn to a bush that was in flames, but not burned to the ground. When he went to investigate, the Voice of God spoke to him from the fire. When the last of the judges, and the first of the prophets, Samuel, was a child in the temple, the Voice of God called to him with no visible presence. The Preincarnate Christ, termed the Angel of the LORD, visited Abram, wrestled with Jacob, met Joshua at the walls of Jericho, and encountered others, speaking face to face with them. An angel of the LORD spoke to Zachariah the priest, and to Mary, and to Cornelius the centurion in person, and to both Joseph and the magi in dreams. God spoke in an audible voice to the children of Israel from Mount Sinai, those present at the baptism of Jesus, to Peter, James and John on the Mount of Transfiguration, and to Jesus at the feast in Jerusalem. Indeed, in many ways God spoke in the past.

The response was as varied as the method of communication. Some worshiped. *"And it happened, when Joshua was beside Jericho, that he lifted up his eyes and looked. And, behold! A Man stood in front of him, and His drawn sword was in His hand. And Joshua went to Him and said to Him, Are You for us, or for our foes? And He said, No, for I now come as the Commander of the army of Jehovah. And Joshua fell on his face to the earth and worshiped. And he said to Him, What does my Lord speak to His slave? And the Commander of the army of Jehovah said to Joshua, Take your shoe off your foot, for the place on which you are standing is holy. And Joshua did so."* (Jos 5:13-15)

Some were stunned. *"And I, Daniel, alone saw the vision. For the men who were with me did not see the vision. But a great trembling fell on them so that they fled to hide themselves. Then I was left alone, and I saw this great vision, and there remained no strength in me. For my glory was turned within me into corruption, and I kept no strength. Yet I heard the sound of his words. And when I heard the sound of his words, then I was on my face, stunned, and my face was toward the ground."* (Dan 10:7-9)

Some recoiled in fear. *"And all the people saw the thunders, and the lightnings, and the sound of the ram's horn, and the smoking mountain. And the people looked, and they trembled, and they stood from a distance. And they said to Moses, You speak with us, and we will hear. And let us not speak with God, that we not die."* (Exo 20:18-19)

Some doubted. *"And Jehovah said to [Gideon], Because I am with you, you shall strike Midian as one man. And he said to Him, Please, if I have found grace in Your eyes, then You shall do for me a sign that You are speaking with me."* (Jdg 6:16-17) *"And Gideon said to God, If You are to deliver Israel by my hand, as You have spoken, behold, I am placing the fleece of wool on the grain floor; if the dew is on the fleece only, and dryness on all the ground, then I will know that You will deliver Israel by my hand, as You have spoken."* (Jdg 6:36-37)

Some rejected the message, and attributed the sound to something else. Jesus raised His eyes and prayed, *"Father, glorify Your name. Then a voice came out of the heaven: I both glorified it, and I will glorify it again. Then standing and hearing, the crowd said that thunder occurred. Others said, An angel has spoken to Him. Jesus answered and said, This voice has not occurred because of Me, but because of you."* (John 12:28-30) *

Some believed and obeyed. *"About the ninth hour of the day, he saw plainly in a vision an angel of God coming to him, and saying to him, 'Cornelius!' And he was staring at him, and becoming terrified he said, 'What is it, Lord?' And he said to him, 'Your prayers and your alms went up for a memorial before God. And now send men to Joppa and call for Simon who is surnamed Peter. This one is lodged with one Simon, a tanner, whose house by the sea. He will tell you what you must do.' And when the angel speaking to Cornelius went away, calling two of his servants and a devout soldier of those continually waiting on him, and having explained all things to them, he sent them to Joppa."* (Act 10:3-8)

Our Hebrews 1:1 focus in these methods and responses were all *"Long ago."* The thread of thought continues, however: *"...but in these last days he has spoken to us by his Son, whom he appointed the heir of all things, through whom also he created the world."* (Heb 1:2) Once the written body of Scripture was finished, the means of communication was changed. Visions, dreams, audible voices, visitations, and other former methods of conveying His message ceased. God's message came through His Son, the Living Word, as He conveyed His written word through His chosen, yielded, Spirit-guided instruments. Paul speaks of that transition to God's choice of His written word: *"Love never fails. But if there are prophecies, they will be caused to cease; if tongues, they shall cease; if knowledge, it will be caused to cease. For we know in part, and we prophesy in part; but when the perfect thing comes, then that which is in part will be caused to cease."* (1Cor 13:8-10)

Our Lord Himself told His disciples of the ministry of God's Holy Spirit in bringing about that which is perfect: *"I have yet many things to tell you, but you are not able to bear now. But when that One comes, the Spirit of Truth, He will guide you into all Truth, for He will not speak from Himself, but whatever He hears, He will speak; and He will announce the coming things to you. That One will glorify Me, for He will receive from Mine and will announce to you."* (John 16:12-14) God's Spirit, through the pen of the apostle Peter, underscores that ministry: *"knowing this first, that every prophecy of Scripture did not come into being of its own interpretation; for prophecy was not at any time borne by the will of man, but being borne along by the Holy Spirit, holy men of God spoke."* (2Pet 1:20-21) Paul adds, *"All Scripture is God-breathed and profitable for doctrine, for reproof, for correction, for instruction in righteousness, so that the man of God may be perfected, being fully furnished for every good work."* (2Tim 3:16-17)

It is the Word of God, not dreams, visions, feelings or voices that brings salvation. Saved by the grace of God, the born-one hungers for the nourishing truth of God's Word. It is the the Scriptures, written Word of God, not extra-biblical sources, that give wisdom from God, that show direction for life, and that reveal Gods will. The believer, immersed in Christ by the Holy Spirit of God, is guided as the Spirit of God applies the Word of God to the heart of the man or woman of God. God may confirm His purpose for us using other believers, or circumstances. He gives wisdom and discernment to guide us in applying the principles of Scripture. But these are never His primary means of communication. They are only used by God to confirm what the Scriptures affirm. Fellow believers may admonish us, encourage us, and instruct us from the Scriptures, but it is the Scriptures alone that are profitable for direction in life.

Counsel is valuable. *"Where no counsel is, the people fall: but in the multitude of counsellors there is safety."* (Pro 11:14) *"Without counsel purposes are disappointed: but in the multitude of counsellors they are established."* (Pro 15:22) However, counsel must be prefaced by "God's Word says," rather than by "I think…" Even when God uses fellow believers, His communication flows through the same process: *"For this reason, do not be foolish, but understanding what the will of the Lord is. And "do not be drunk with wine," in which is debauchery, but be filled by the Spirit, speaking to yourselves in psalms and hymns and spiritual songs, singing and praising in your heart to the Lord, giving thanks at all times for all things in the name of our Lord Jesus Christ, even to God the Father, having been subject to one another in the fear of God."* Eph 5:17-21) *"Let the Word of Christ dwell in you richly, in all wisdom teaching and exhorting yourselves in psalms and hymns and spiritual songs,*

singing with grace in your hearts to the Lord." (Col 3:16) Even when God uses other members of the body of Christ to speak into our lives, His Spirit uses His Word through His own.

Solomon gives a pointed admonition that underscores the vital need for the indwelling Word of God: ***"Keep your heart with all diligence, for out of it are the issues of life."*** (Pro 4:23) The values programmed into our core, our control center, must be from Scripture. David's admonition in Psalm 1:1 is pointed and restrictive: ***"Blessed is the man who has not walked in the counsel of the ungodly, and has not stood in the way of sinners, and has not sat in the seat of scorners."*** We are awash in a sea of voices in this world. The majority are, like the raven, able to deceive, to mislead. Many false teachers twist the Scriptures, presenting pseudo-gospels and false christs rooted in human philosophies. Those who profess to be believers, having learned the language of the saved, mimic the message with subtle changes. Paul raises a caution flag for our day, warning ***"But evil men and pretenders will go forward to worse, leading astray and being led astray."*** (2Tim 3:13) Their deceiving messages fill the shelves of Christian bookstores, and fill the airwaves of Christian radio and television. They find a ready audience: ***"For a time will be when they will not endure sound doctrine, but according to their own lusts, they will heap up to themselves teachers tickling the ear; and they will turn away the ear from the truth and will be turned aside to myths."*** (2Tim 4:3-4) Demonic laughter rings with each successful deception.

Peter knew he was about to be put to death. As he prepared to put off his 'tabernacle,' he wrote of his personal experiences with our Lord during His earthly ministry, but subordinated experience to the written Word of Truth: ***"For receiving honor and glory from God the Father such a voice being borne to Him from the magnificent glory, "This is My Son, the Beloved, in whom I have been delighted," even we heard this voice being borne out of Heaven, being with Him in the holy mountain, and we have the more established*** *prophetic Word, in which you do well to take heed, as to a lamp shining in a murky place, until day dawns and the Light-bearing One rises in your hearts..."* (2Pet 1:17-19)

6

GOT MILK?

Hunger brings its own urgency. Prolonged hunger brings increasing urgency. Among the very young, demand is nearly constant, and time trudges on leaden feet, in the minds of those who wait. This fact was underscored humorously by a pair of fawns I observed.

Mother deer take time away from their offspring, time for themselves. They train their fawns early on to seek cover on command, and to stay put. How, I have not yet observed. But, they select as lairs for their little ones thickets, brush tangles, or some other places where the fawns can lie unseen, resting, napping, or just tucked away while mother deer fills her own stomach, or suns herself while keeping watch for threats to her young. I have learned to recognize the watchful posture of the resting doe, and to know that somewhere within signal range, she has hidden speckle-sided young ones.

Even when the fawns are able to keep up with the doe, and eat the forbs she finds so delightful, she will still put them down for a while. As they make the transition to solid food, the urge to nurse is still strong.

That is where the humor arose. The fawns I observed had been napping in a brushy margin of the meadow. They were now a little over three months old, and had grown quite strong. Their mother had eaten her fill, and had rested in the warmth of the summer sun, chewing her cud as she watched me work. When I eventually moved to a different location, she got up, stretched, and came to check on me, to be sure I posed no threat. She kept looking back over her shoulder. I did not see any detectable sign, or hear any sound from her. But, when she seemed satisfied that I was ignoring her, she turned, and stood looking toward the brush.

The scotch broom wiggled a little, and first one fawn, and then the other, slipped out into the sunshine, and stopped. It seemed like a full five minutes that all three players stood immobile, except for questing nostrils. Then, at no signal I could perceive, the twins came racing across the meadow toward their mother. They reached her at a dead run, one on each side, and dived under her flanks for a snack, simultaneously butting her udder with such eagerness that her hind quarters rose upward, and her hind hooves came off the ground. The fawns were allowed to nurse for a few minutes, and then the doe stepped over each little neck and walked away. The trailing fawns held on for a step or two, desperate for a few more sips. When the doe turned to pull away, they followed with outstretched noses questing for a new hold, until, forestalled by the doe's evasive moves, they contented themselves by licking the milky foam from their muzzles.

Hunger and thirst are strong motivators. Extreme hunger or thirst will drive a person to desperate attempts to satisfy those agonizing needs. A person will eat or drink things that in other circumstances would be repulsive.

In more comfortable situations, we are generally selective in our choices. Our palate and our preferences govern our consumption. In addition, we develop an unseen internal list of favorites. From that department of special desires, cravings arise, and sometimes, these are insatiable. Marketers take advantage of this fact, including in their products substances that make us want more.

For the believer, we find a spiritual counterpart for physical appetites. Just like those fawns, the believer has a God-given need for the Word of God. The need is stimulated by God Himself, through His truth. ***"As newborn babes, desire the sincere milk of the word, that ye may grow thereby: If so be ye have tasted that the Lord is gracious."*** (1Pet 2:2-3 KJV) The Literal Translation uses the expression, ***"the pure soul-nourishing milk,"*** underscoring our need for and dependence upon spiritual food.

Notice the last part, found in verse 3: ***"If so be ye have tasted that the Lord is gracious."*** This is where we find the stimulation. I was raised on a farm, where we had a small herd of milk cows. When the calves were born, we separated them from the cows, and fed them after we had milked. We had to train them to drink, first from a pan, and then from a bucket. To do this, we took a pan of warm milk into the pen, dipped two fingers in milk, and then slipped our fingers into the calf's mouth. The taste of the milk stimulated a nursing response. We would then push the calf's nose down into the milk, and hold our fingers a little bit apart, to allow the milk to be drawn into the hungry mouth. We could then slip our fingers out, slowly, and the calf would continue drinking, and empty the pan.

The taste stimulated the desire. So it is with us. The taste of the Word of God brings us to the Living Word, our Lord Jesus Christ. That taste creates within us a craving for more. That craving causes a newborn to suckle on almost anything, nourishing or not. A calf will attempt to nurse on another calf's ear, or on a farmers fingers. A human baby will do the same on its own thumb, or a pacifier. This craving for more presents a double-edged challenge.

The first is a vulnerability to false teaching, and the opposite edge in the need for, and sometimes the lack of, consistent discipleship. The first is for the one being drawn to the Savior, or to the new believer. The second is for the one instructed in the Word. Notice Peter mentioned desiring the **"sincere milk of the Word."** That word **sincere** alludes to a dishonest potter's practice of rubbing sand and bees wax into a crack in a vessel to make it appear sound. The shrewd shopper would look into a clay pot in the sunlight. The light of the sun would shine through the wax, revealing the falsehood.

Ingredient lists of food packaging abound with "imitation" this and "artificial" that. The same is true in the spiritual realm. God offers a spiritually healthy alternative to the fatal fakes: **"Come, everyone who thirsts, come to the waters; and he who has no money, come, buy and eat! Come, buy wine and milk without money and without price. Why do you spend your money for that which is not bread, and your labor for that which does not satisfy? Listen diligently to me, and eat what is good, and delight yourselves in rich food. Incline your ear, and come to me; hear, that your soul may live..."** (Isa 55:1-3 ESV) What a glorious concept is bound up in that word, delight. It evokes the enthusiastic enjoyment of those fawns. While the beauties of creation delight the eyes, and savory foods delight the palate, it is the Lord and His Word that delight the soul and spirit.

The Word admonishes us, **"Delight yourself in the LORD, and he will give you the desires of your heart."** (Psalm 37:4 ESV) An enthusiastic enjoyment of the Lord Himself opens the way for Him to fill our hearts with the desires that He delights to fulfill. Of the one so delighting, David writes in Psalm 1:2, **"...his delight is in the law of the LORD, and on his law he meditates day and night."** (ESV) An enthusiastic enjoyment of God's Word nourishes the inner man as wholesome food nourishes the body. In Psalm 119, David writes 176 verses,

174 of which mention the Word of the Lord, using a variety of terms. Ten times in that psalm, he uses that word, delight, in relation to God's Truth.

Speaking to wayward Israel through Amos, the prophet, God shows us the depth of the desire in the one who has tasted that the Lord is good: ***"Behold, the days are coming," declares the Lord GOD, "when I will send a famine on the land-- not a famine of bread, nor a thirst for water, but of hearing the words of the LORD. They shall wander from sea to sea, and from north to east; they shall run to and fro, to seek the word of the LORD, but they shall not find it."*** (Amos 8:11-12 ESV) Physical hunger and thirst, unsatisfied, bring desperation. So, too, does spiritual starvation. We met a woman from the Philippines, a believer, who had come to the United States. She attended church, but she told us, "I cannot follow the teaching. My English is slow." She labored through the English Bible. We contacted a Gideon in our church, and were able to give the woman a Tagalog New Testament. She opened it, embraced it, and wept tears of joy, jumping up and down in the parking lot.

The prophet Jeremiah was similarly blessed. ***"Your words were found, and I ate them, and your words became to me a joy and the delight of my heart, for I am called by your name, O LORD, God of hosts."*** (Jer 15:16 ESV) Job's view of God's spiritual nourishment was as intense: ***"I have not departed from the commandment of his lips; I have treasured the words of his mouth more than my portion of food."*** (Job 23:12 ESV)

The craving for spiritual nourishment can be satisfied only by Christ Jesus, the Living Word. The human philosophies are but empty husks, devoid of life-sustaining value to the soul and spirit. The savory-seeming concoctions of the purveyors of false religion are poison. These things take up space without filling, without satisfying. Our Lord said, ***"Blessed are they who hunger and thirst after righteousness! For they shall be filled."*** (Mat 5:6) Filled with what? Christ Himself, and His word. ***"Jesus said*** *to them, I am the Bread of life; the one coming to Me will not at all hunger, and the one believing into Me will not thirst, never!"* (John 6:35)

7

RIPPLE EFFECT

Sunbeams chased the shadows from the treetops. Peace held court in the cloudless sky, commanding the breezes to sit and stay, guarding the doorway of morning. Calmness spread her glassy mantle over the bay. It was the perfect opening of a glorious May day that promised more of summer than of spring. The tide was at high slack. Not a duck stirred a wake. Even the fish sulked near the bottom of the channel.

I shattered the stillness. The rock I chose weighed about seven pounds. With a side-armed grenade toss that strained aging muscles, I hurled the stone. It spun in an arching trajectory, out over the willows and reeds along the shore, and slapped the morning awake with a loud ker-PLUNK. Croaking startled dismay, a great blue heron leapt into the air, and flopped on ungainly wings toward the far shore, over a quarter of a mile away.

I hurried up onto the knoll above the bay, to watch the effect of my experiment. I had tried before to send ripples all the way across the bay, but each time, my rock had been too small. The wavelets diminished, and faded away to glassy smoothness before they reached mid-channel. Surely this time, judging by the loud splash, there would be enough energy to generate a wave that would last, and perhaps reflect, returning to my side of the bay.

I watched the expanding circles. Pilings at the low-tide line divided the pie into wedges. Gulls flew above the bay, and their perfect reflections danced and distorted as the charging ripples, rank upon rank, hurried toward a distant beachhead. This time, I watched them dash ashore. Taken by the suddenness of the assault, the rushes waved a startled surrender. Occupied among their captives, the ripples did not return. Their effect, though, had been easy to measure, at least to the careful observer.

No matter how small or grand the scale, the radiating cause and effect relationship operates inexorably. The day was indeed more summer than spring. The temperature soared to near ninety degrees, a rarity in May for our coastal community. A hundred miles inland, hotter temperatures prevailed. The heat sink of asphalt and concrete superheated the air, sending it spiraling aloft, and that reached over the Coast Range, drawing moist air from over the ocean inland. A thickening line of fog lurked over the beach, and, as evening approached, it slipped up the river in a flanking attack, then rushed in to overpower summer, and reestablish spring. It felt like winter.

As cyclical as tides and weather patterns, relationships ebb and flow in the seasons of our daily lives. A kindness sends ripples of pleasure through our circle of friends. An offense has a chilling effect that slices through warm companionship. Appreciation and affirmation bind us together. Neglect and indifference strain the bonds. Antagonism and offense sever them.

We find the pattern of ripples radiating outward, reflecting and returning within the body of believers. The Scriptures speak of all true believers as the body of Christ. Within the body, there is a bond of connectivity that holds us together, and gives a sensitivity to one another. Paul writes, ***"For as in one body we have many members, and the members do not all have the same function, so we, though many, are one body in Christ, and individually members one of another."*** (Rom 12:4-5 ESV) That phrase, *members one of another*, emphasizes the interconnection between the parts. We can readily identify with a reality Paul mentions to the believers at Corinth: ***"If one member suffers, all suffer together; if one member is honored, all rejoice together."*** (1Cor 12:26 ESV) Every believer either has or will physically experience the truth of that assertion, especially the suffering part. In a moment of inattentiveness, I crushed the tip of my left ring finger. The bone was fragmented and the nail was torn off. A bolt of pain shot through me, and my whole body reacted. My right hand grasped my left wrist. My knees buckled. My back alternately bowed and arched. My jaw clenched, and my eyes slammed closed. My vocal cords got involved in loud but inarticulate sympathy with the rest of my suffering self. It took me a little while to get to the place of rejoicing and thankfulness.

Painful experiences illustrate for us a reality of Scripture. Paul reveals an overarching principle of God He has ordained for the church. Scripture reveals that principle in various facets of the Christ life of which we are an integral part in this world.

If we center for a moment on the image of the physical pain of a crushed fingertip, and expand it to include a broader view of suffering, a purpose for suffering emerges in that principle. Every experience shapes us, and prepares us to minister to the other members of the body.

Consider Paul's instruction to the believers at Corinth: ***"Blessed be the God and Father of our Lord Jesus Christ, the Father of mercies and God of all comfort, who comforts us in all our affliction, so that we may be able to comfort those who are in any affliction, with the comfort with which we ourselves are comforted by***

God." (2Cor 1:3-4 ESV) God Himself, who is the originator and only true source of comfort causes that initial splash of comfort in the life of the suffering saint. That in-pouring of grace and love is not heaped upon us to be hoarded. Rather, it generates a disturbance in the status quo of suffering that ripples outward through the body of Christ. Seeing God's faithfulness as He bears us through our suffering deepens the roots of His gift of faith within us, strengthening and purifying it, that we, in our turn, might comfort another believer whose suffering mirrors our own. The comforted believer, then, yielded to the indwelling Holy Spirit, becomes the arms of God to embrace, the hands of God to uplift, the lips of God to encourage. This purpose of God gives ministering direction to the admonition of Paul in Romans 6:13b, where he writes, "***...present yourselves to God as those who have been brought from death to life, and your members to God as instruments for righteousness.***"(ESV) Implements in the hands of God, we are used by the Master Workman for the task for which He has uniquely fashioned us. The ripples of comfort radiate outward as God directs, but Paul points out that those ripples reflect, and sometimes return: "***But God, who comforts the downcast, comforted us by the coming of Titus, and not only by his coming but also by the comfort with which he was comforted by you, as he told us of your longing, your mourning, your zeal for me, so that I rejoiced still more.***" (2Cor 7:6-7 ESV)

We observe the same pattern in God's purpose of evangelism. Consider the wide ranging effect that emerges in our Lord's prayer in John 17: "***Now they know that everything that you have given me is from you. For I have given them the words that you gave me, and they have received them and have come to know in truth that I came from you; and they have believed that you sent me.***" (John 17:7-8 ESV) The message, the words, the Truth radiates from God the Father to God the Son, and from the Son to the disciples. But, that is not the end of the purpose of God.

God sent His Son to personify Light and Truth in this dark

world. He is the Living Word of God. He taught the disciples, conveying to them the words the Father had given to Him to give to them. Our Lord, speaking of His own, says to the Father, ***"As you sent me into the world, so I have sent them into the world."*** (John 17:18 ESV) To the disciples, he said, ***"You did not choose me, but I chose you and appointed you that you should go and bear fruit and that your fruit should abide..."*** (John 15:16a ESV) That resounding splash of Truth could not be confined. Our Lord's parting words to His disciples were, ***"But you will receive power when the Holy Spirit has come upon you, and you will be my witnesses in Jerusalem and in all Judea and Samaria, and to the end of the earth."*** (Acts 1:8 ESV)

The radiating wavelets find their practical illustration in the admonition Paul writes to Timothy: ***"You then, my child, be strengthened by the grace that is in Christ Jesus, and what you have heard from me in the presence of many witnesses entrust to faithful men who will be able to teach others also."*** (2Tim 2:1-2 ESV) The Gospel of Christ has indeed rippled down through the centuries to us today, and it is our stewardship to convey it to others, fulfilling our role in the prayer of our Lord: ***"I do not ask for these only, but also for those who will believe in me through their word..."*** (John 17:20 ESV)

The power of prayer surges through the body of Christ with a global impact, much like the tidal rise and fall in the oceans. In response to the direction of the Son through the Spirit, according to the need, endless waves of prayer wash over believers around the world. When my son's firstborn went from birth to life support in intensive care within a matter of hours, a veritable tsunami of prayer came in from individuals and churches across the country, from Europe, from the South Pacific, from around the world. Paul writes of the ripples of prayer to the believers at Corinth: ***"You also must help us by prayer, so that many will give thanks on our behalf for the blessing granted us through the prayers of many."*** (2Cor 1:11 ESV)

Scripture sparkles with brief insights into those currents that spread through the body of believers according to God's design. David declares in Psalm 23, *"... my cup overflows."* His cup of blessing was filled to point that the blessings slopped over onto those around him, and so it is with us. We are blessed by God so we might bless others.

In writing to the Roman believers, Paul notes **"...the love of God is shed abroad in our hearts by the Holy Ghost which is given unto us."** (Rom 5:5 ESV) Shed abroad, it cannot be contained. The love of God is a sacrificial love, a love that serves, a love that ministers to the deepest needs of the object of that love. It is the connective tissue of the body of Christ that bonds us together. It ripples through us, not just to us.

The comfort of God, the Word of God, the power of God, the love of God, and more course through body of believers like ripples on the bay. There is a glorious image that results. The glassy surface of the bay is stirred by the awakening day. It is not just my stone that splashed. The drowsy morning awakened with jumping fish, diving ducks and fitful breezes, each of which sent its own ripples spreading across the quiet water, intersecting, crossing and breaking the mirror surface into a million points of light, sparkling and dancing in the light of the sun. Such is the testimony of the body of Christ in this world.

The greatest ripple effect is already prepared, waiting its timeless moment of revelation, with the revelation of our Lord and Savior, Jesus Christ, in His radiant glory. That, too, is included in that high priestly prayer of John 17. **"I do not ask for these only, but also for those who will believe in me through their word, that they may all be one, just as you, Father, are in me, and I in you, that they also may be in us, so that the world may believe that you have sent me. The glory that you have given me I have given to them, that they may be one even as we are one..."** (John 17:20-22 ESV)

The unity and the glory He has purposed are impeded by the

residue of Adam we inhabit. But, we have the assurance from Scripture we shall all be changed. God's purpose for the ones He has given as a cherished love gift to His Son is found in Paul's letter to the Roman believers: ***"For those whom he foreknew he also predestined to be conformed to the image of his Son, in order that he might be the firstborn among many brothers. And those whom he predestined he also called, and those whom he called he also justified, and those whom he justified he also glorified."*** (Rom 8:28-29 ESV) Shedding the residue of Adam, we will be made Christlike, conformed to His character. Then, in His presence, His ultimate prayer for His own will find its answer. ***"Father, I desire that they also, whom you have given me, may be with me where I am, to see my glory that you have given me because you loved me before the foundation of the world."*** (John 17:24 ESV) Seeing, we will be enveloped in His glory, glorified. Moses veiled radiance of the residue of the glory of the presence of God. We will, as one body, rejoice in the fullness of His glory, and truly worship in the beauty of holiness.

8

VOLES IN THE TATER PATCH

Consternation turned quickly to despair in Ireland, generations ago. Blight destroyed the potato crop, robbing the poor in Ireland of their staple food supply for winter. Sound potatoes were few, and those were soon reduced to black mush by the destroyer.

My roots are in Ireland, and I felt a surge of empathy for my forefathers over the water, as they say in Ireland. My potatoes were hollow shells.

Late summer and autumn are the days of harvest for gardeners. Some salad veggies flourish and fade quickly, but most of the plantings take time to be fruitful. On the Oregon coast, the last frost is not much of a concern. The weather issue that can delay planting is rain. Soggy ground cannot be worked, and ground that is saturated after it has been worked and planted rots the seeds.

On the other end of the gardening time frame, the fall rains usually set in about the middle of October, and some of the crops are not water tolerant. Soggy gardens grow an abundance of mildew.

The potatoes were the last part of the garden to be harvested. I started at one end of a row, turning the plant over with a fork. While there were a few little potatoes, about the size of a marble, the bigger ones were either fragments clinging to the roots, or hollowed out shells. Toothmarks and tunnels told the tale of destruction. Hungry voles, or meadow mice, had started tunneling at one end of the patch, and had progressed plant by plant, damaging almost every potato cluster in three rows. There was no sign of their presence. The plants thrived because it was the tubers, not the roots, that were systematically eaten by unseen marauders. The patch that should have yielded two hundred fifty pounds of potatoes produced only five pounds that we could use. The appearance of abundance was revealed as worthless in the final harvest. The promised fruitfulness was empty boasting.

How often hidden destruction surfaces at the worst moment. We take a fine wool sweater out of storage, only to discover moths have left their offspring to eat holes in it. We take out a violin, only to find that hair mites have reduced the bow to a fringed stick. Objects stored in the basement or attic have succumbed to dampness-induced mold and mildew. Many unseen destroyers reduce treasures to trash .

Worse, our own efforts can be destructive. My mother once inadvertently poured a cup of salt into her bread dough, instead of sugar. My wife, in cutting out a sewing project, accidentally caught a wrinkle in the fabric with the scissors, and left a gaping hole in a major piece of the garment she was making. An inappropriate choice, a careless action, a thoughtless word or wrong motive can be as destructive as voles in the tater patch.

The same applies in the spiritual realm. All believers in the Lord Jesus Christ are called to lives of ministry. We are admonished by God's Word to serve one another, encourage one another, and to love one another with that love of God that consistently and actively seeks the best interest of the other person. We are told to be careful to maintain good works. Our fleshly minds place the responsibility for choosing, planning and executing those good works upon our own shoulders. We pride ourselves in doing the Lord's work, in working for the Lord. We parade our efforts before others, sanctifying them with a pious "praise the Lord." I recall one person proclaiming, "I saved three people last week!"

We are quick to judge our efforts as holy, righteous and good. There will be, however, a higher, more exacting judgment. Paul writes, *"For we all must appear before the judgment seat of Christ, so that each one may receive the things done through the body, according to what he did, whether good or bad."* (2Cor 5:10) All eternal judgment has been committed to our Lord, and *"...it is reserved to men once to die, and after this, Judgment..."* (Heb 9:27) Jesus Christ will judge His own, that is, all true believers, in the judgment of commendation Paul describes in his letter to the Corinthian believers: *"According to God's grace given to me, as a wise master builder, I laid a foundation, but another builds on it. But let each one be careful how he builds. For no one is able to lay any other foundation beside the One having been laid, who is Jesus Christ. And if anyone builds on this foundation gold, silver, precious stones, wood, grass, straw, the work of each will be revealed; for the Day will make it known, because it is revealed in fire; and the fire will prove the work of each, what sort it is."* (1Cor 3:10-13) Notice the sorting process used in this judgment, and the purifying result. There are two categories of building materials mentioned. Gold, silver and precious stones are enduring, valued and nonflammable. Wood, grass and straw are fast-burning fuels. Gold, silver and precious stones are purified and intensified in their beauty by fire. Wood, grass and straw are consumed.

The *bema* judgment Paul describes is a judgment of reward, not condemnation, where each one receives reward for the things done in the body in this life here on Earth, the things done as a believer in the stewardship that has been committed to us. The judgment of sin is not in view here. Sin was judged on Calvary's cross, when the Lamb of God laid down His life, bearing the judgment of our sins Himself. The phrase, **"whether good or bad,"** has to do with the quality of the things done in the body. The focus is on the building materials in the analogy of life, and the result of the fire proving the work, **"of what sort it is."**

Paul goes on to explain the outcome of the proving work: **"If the work of anyone which he built remains, he will receive a reward. If the work of anyone shall be consumed, he shall suffer loss; but he will be saved, but so as through fire."** (1Cor 3:14-15) The believer's reward will be determined by what remains, not by what is consumed. Salvation is not in question. The believer is in Christ, and the life is built upon Christ, the foundation. Though all else is consumed, the believer's eternal destiny is unchanged, because Christ is not consumed. Christ remains, and so the believer, who is in Christ, also remains, as one escaping through the flames.

What, then, determines the quality of the work? What determines which category of building material will represent a good work done in the body? The work of God is eternal. He has a purpose for each believer. He will accomplish His purpose. Paul tells us, **"...for it is God who is working in you both to will and to work for the sake of His good pleasure."** (Php 2:13) If God is doing the work, what is the role of the believer? Paul answers that as well: **"Neither present your members as instruments of unrighteousness to sin, but present yourselves to God as one living from the dead, and your** *members instruments of righteousness to God."* (Rom 6:13) The yielded believer is an implement in God's hand. God does His work, for His glory, and, at the judgment seat of Christ, the work God accomplished, using the obedient believer, is gold, silver, and precious stones. The believer's fingerprints are burned away by the purifying fire, and yet the believer gets the reward for the work done by God, in His own power, for His own pleasure, to His own glory.

What, then, comprises wood, grass and straw? That answer lies in the answers to other questions. Whose wisdom plans the work, mine, or God's? Whose strength accomplishes the work, mine, or God's? Who receives praise for the work? Who gets the glory, me, or God?

In His earthly ministry, our Lord Jesus gave us an insight into these answers. To His disciples, He said, **"Therefore, when you do merciful deeds, do not trumpet before you as the hypocrites do in the synagogues and in the streets, so that they may be glorified by men. Truly I say to you, They have their reward...And when you pray, you shall not be as the hypocrites, for they love to pray standing in the synagogues and in the corners of the open streets so that they may be seen of men. Truly I say to you, They have their reward...And when you fast, do not be as the hypocrites, with sullen face, for they disfigure their faces so that they may appear to men to be fasting. Truly I say to you that they have their reward."** (Mat 6:2, 5, 16) Notice the underlying principle of motivation, and the attitudes in which good works go bad. We may not blow a trumpet fanfare to draw attention to our service we are doing for God, but we can find other ways to boast. We can make sure others are aware of our piety, our industry for God. We can be so busy working for God, doing the Lord's work, that we are unavailable for Him to use for His own glory.

I once asked a long-time pastor how long it took him to stop working for the Lord, and let God use him for His own purposes.

His answer was immediate: "Seventeen years. Seventeen years of wood, hay and stubble." Every believer is subject to the same well-meaning delusion of good works. How easy it is for us to fall into the pattern of the Scribes and Pharisees. Our Lord said of them, **"And they do all their works to be seen by men. And they make their phylacteries broad and enlarge the borders of their robes."** (Mat 23:5) Again we hear the echoing pronouncement from our Lord: **"Truly I say to you that they have their reward."** Conforming ourselves to their image, we can focus on the appearance of good works, and be as fruitless as the tater patch.

In Paul's day, the juxtaposition of precious and worthless works, centered in the proclamation of the Gospel was evident. **"And the most of the brothers in the Lord, being confident in my bonds, more exceedingly dare to speak the Word fearlessly. Some, indeed, even proclaim Christ because of envy and strife, but some also because of good will. These, indeed, announce Christ out of party spirit, not sincerely, thinking to add affliction to my bonds. But these others out of love, knowing that I am set for defense of the gospel. What then? Yet in every way, whether in pretense or in truth, Christ is proclaimed, and I rejoice in this; yet also I will rejoice."** (Php 1:14-18) God can, and has used the foolishness of men for His own purposes. He used Balaam's donkey to get His message across. He can use our self-focused, self-glorifying efforts for His own glory. But, the wood, grass and straw that redounds to us will go up in smoke.

The yielded, obedient believer has the responsibility of responsiveness to the leading of God's Spirit. God does the planning: **"...for we are His workmanship, created in Christ Jesus unto good works, which God before prepared that we should walk in them."** (Eph 2:10) Consider the beseeching of grace in Paul's letter to the believers at Rome. In the light of the soaring doxology that ends Romans chapter eight, that concludes that nothing can separate the believer from the love of God in Christ Jesus, he writes, ***"Therefore, brothers, I call on you through the compassions of God to present your bodies a living sacrifice, holy, pleasing to God, which is your reasonable service."*** (Rom 12:1) From the platform of the altar, the believer in Christ responds to the guiding Holy Spirit within, following another beseeching of grace from Paul's pen: ***"And whatever you may do, work from the soul as to the Lord and not to men, knowing that from the Lord you shall receive the reward of the inheritance. For you serve the Lord Christ."*** (Col 3:23-24) The work of eternal worth is all of God. It is of His doing, by His power, by His planning, in His wisdom. The same principle applies to us, nearly two thousand years later, as Paul saw in his life in Christ: ***"But by the grace of God I am what I am, and His grace which was toward me has not been without fruit, but I labored more abundantly than all of them, yet not I, but the grace of God with me."*** (1Cor 15:10) When we realize we are implements of righteousness for God to use for His own glory, we bear the fruit He produces. When we flounder in self-effort, we are our own voles in the tater patch.

9

TOO MANY SUPERVISORS

August and September were glorious. Clear skies, warm sunshine, and rainless hours allowed us to start several projects, which we then kicked down the path of summer by turns, then into autumn. I worked a little on each, always progressing, but never seeming to be able to finish any one project.

October came. Here on the coast, mid-October usually brings the first heavy rains. The projects in progress would become challenges, if not impossible, once the weather turned. Our firewood was in the basement, but I had people who could not cut their own wood. That was one of my must-finish, you-can't-kick-it-down-the-road-anymore projects. I had three cords cut, split and stacked in the woods, along a dirt road that would turn to squishy, slippery mud once it got wet through by persistent autumn rains. Friday brought an inch of rain, but it ran off rather than softening the road. .

Saturday morning was dampened by off-and-on drizzle, with the forecast of heavier rain in the afternoon. I managed to back the pickup in to where the wood was stacked. I would toss pieces of firewood into the bed of the truck, and once it was fairly full, I would climb into the back of the truck, and stack the wood neatly. That made room for more to be tossed in, to be stacked in its turn. It was an intermittently noisy operation. In the middle of the process, I paused to stretch my weary back, and noticed a forked-horn buck watching me. He was about 20 yards away, alternately peeking over the top of a huckleberry bush to see what I was doing, and reaching up to nibble leaves from the brush between us. I laughed at him, spoke to him, and started to turn back to my wood tossing. As I did, I noticed another deer, a little farther away. I turned, searching the brush around where I was working. I was surrounded by deer. Seven of them were watching, waggling their ears at me as if to give instructions. A pair of bald eagles, perched in the top of a giant spruce tree, took turns tilting their white heads and whinnying their commands. They were joined by a trio of ravens who, flapping through the grove, croaked their own orders. Everyone had something to say about the work, but not one contributed to it. I had too many supervisors.

I had to laugh. That scenario is so typical of human activity. In so many areas, suggestions pour in from watchers. Often preceded by "If I were you, I'd..." or "I always used to...", conflicting ideas, experiences and processes belittle our efforts. The Monday-morning quarterback always knows more than the coach on the sideline. Such contributions are humorous to the casual observer, but can be vexing to the one doing the work.

That fleshly reality has invaded the assembly of believers. Too often, the pews are filled with supervisors who know exactly how things should be done, how endeavors should be run, and give their opinions rather freely, from a disengaged distance. But, help? No. They are willing to come up with a list of helpers they would highly recommend, or even go and tell their candidate what should be done, and how it should be done. I recall one exasperated worker saying, with a sigh, "I like the way I'm doing it better than the way you aren't."

Our Lord's plan for the growth and functioning of His assembly of believers did not include an inactive majority. Peter spoke collectively of believers when he, by the Spirit, said: *"you also as living stones are being built a spiritual house, a holy priesthood, to offer spiritual sacrifices acceptable to God through Jesus Christ."* (1Pet 2:5) Living stones are not passive. Believers are all priests in a holy priesthood, offering spiritual sacrifices of praise, prayer and the worship of obedience. That obedience includes action as well as proclamation, ministry as well as testimony of life and words.

Upon what are we being built? Paul, in writing to the Ephesian believers, tells them, and us, that we *"...are built upon the foundation of the apostles and prophets, Jesus Christ himself being the chief corner stone..."* (Eph 2:20 ESV) Our Lord is the foundation. The base, or floor of this spiritual house is the teaching of our Lord through the apostles and prophets. It was they who through the bearing along by the Holy Spirit, spoke and wrote what our Lord described in His closing pre-Calvary teachings, when, speaking of the ministry of the Holy Spirit, He said, *"I have spoken these things to you, abiding with you; but the Comforter, the Holy Spirit, whom the Father will send in My name, He shall teach you all things and shall remind you of all things that I said to you... I have yet many things to tell you, but you are not able to bear now. But when that One comes, the Spirit of Truth, He will guide you into all Truth, for He will not speak from Himself, but whatever He hears, He will speak; and He will announce the coming things to you. That One will glorify Me, for He will receive from Mine and will announce to you."* (John 14:25-26, 16:12-14) Paul pinpoints the ones used by our Lord in that foundation ministry: *"Which in other ages was not made known unto the sons of men, as it is now revealed unto his holy apostles and prophets by the Spirit..."* (Eph 3:5 KJV) The ministry of the apostles and prophets ended with the completion of the Scriptures. The apostles died, and, as the scriptures attest, the gift of prophecy was done away. ***"Love never fails. But if there are prophecies, they will be caused to cease; if tongues, they shall cease; if knowledge, it will be caused to cease."*** (1Cor 13:8) These sign gifts, given to authenticate the credentials of the ones used to lay the foundation, ceased once the foundation was in place. There are no new revelations, no prophetic additions to the Scriptures today.

The work of building, however, did not cease. ***"And he gave the apostles, the prophets, the evangelists, the shepherds and teachers, to equip the saints for the work of ministry, for building up the body of Christ, until we all attain to the unity of the faith and of the knowledge of the Son of God, to mature manhood, to the measure of the stature of the fullness of Christ, so that we may no longer be children, tossed to and fro by the waves and carried about by every wind of doctrine, by human cunning, by craftiness in deceitful schemes. Rather, speaking the truth in love, we are to grow up in every way into him who is the head, into Christ, from whom the whole body, joined and held together by every joint with which it is equipped, when each part is working properly, makes the body grow so that it builds itself up in love."*** (Eph 4:11-16 ESV) The reality of Acts 2:47 continues to this day ***"...And the Lord added to the assembly, the ones being saved from day to day."*** The Lord employs believers yielded to His use, by His Spirit, with His Word, to continue the building process. That constitutes the evangelism aspect of the work He is doing.

There is another level of the building process that follows evangelism. It might be termed the finish work. The shepherds, or pastors and teachers, systematically teaching the scriptures prepare the saints for the work of the ministry. That portion of the verse underscores the fact that the saints, all of them, have work to do. The body building itself up in love is the work of discipleship, of training, of caring, and of serving. Our Lord, in His high priestly prayer in John 17, reached out through the age of grace and embraced all true believers. *"I am praying for them. I am not praying for the world but for those whom you have given me, for they are yours. I do not ask for these only, but also for those who will believe in me through their word..."* (John 17:9, 20 ESV) His commission to them includes all true believers, and is not limited to a special clergy class. To His Father, He said, *"As You have sent Me into the world, I also have sent them into the world..."* (John 17:18) To His disciples, He repeated the charge: *"Then Jesus said to them again, Peace to you. As the Father has sent Me, I also send you."* (John 20:21)

Why did the Father send Him into the world? It was to present the character of God in a visible, tangible way. It was to reveal His heart of love. It was to be His expression of grace and truth. Look again at His prayer: *"I have glorified You on the earth. I finished the work that You gave Me to do. I revealed Your name to the men whom You gave to Me out of the world. They were Yours, and You gave them to Me; and they have kept Your Word. For the Words which You gave to Me, I have given to them. And they received and truly knew that I came out from beside You, and they believed that You sent Me. And I made known to them Your name, and will make it known, that the love with which You loved Me may be in them, and I in them."* (John 17:4,6,8,26)

Our Lord Jesus Christ, in His earthly ministry, was the means through which God, in all that God is, became knowable. He glorified the Father. He demonstrated the full character of the Father. He presented the message of the Father. He demonstrated the love of the father.

Our Lord, by His Holy Spirit, has as His purpose for His own the same goal. He made the reality of the Father known through His life, and through His death. His intention for believers is that the reality of Christ Himself be made known in this world through our death to self, and the Christ life in the new creation we are in Him. Through us His love is made known, His word is proclaimed, His character is revealed. God Himself is the hand doing the work. The believer is the glove, supple and yielding, allowing the work to go on unimpeded: ***"...for it is God who is working in you both to will and to work for the sake of His good pleasure. Do all things without murmurings and disputings, that you may be blameless and harmless, children of God, without fault in the midst of a crooked generation, even having been perverted, among whom you shine as luminaries in the world, holding up the Word of Life..."*** (Php 2:13-16) We are light bearers and truth bearers. Christ is the Light, and the Truth. He alone is worthy of all praise and all glory. ***"...and what you have heard from me in the presence of many witnesses entrust to faithful men who will be able to teach others also."*** (2Tim 2:2) Are we getting anything done, by His grace, in His strength, or are we kibitzing?

10

STORMS

Late in November, 2007, the first warning was broadcast: "A strong Pacific storm appears headed toward the North Coast." Fall and winter storms often pounded the beaches and coastal communities with lashing rains driven by gusting winds. The early advisories held nothing ominous, nothing to prompt serious preparation. Residents continued their usual activities, with only casual attention to the reports.

"A cold front is approaching...possibility of snow in the higher elevations..." Again, although it was a little early in the season for snow, it was not unprecedented to have a cold storm after Thanksgiving, and when heavy, wet snow blanketed the coastal mountains, and heavy rains soaked the lower elevations, daily activities continued in rain gear.

"The Pineapple Express is expected to bring strong winds and significant rainfall...heavy surf advisory..." Forecasts took on a more urgent tone. The remains of two typhoons were drawn into the low pressure system that had brought the snow, and was being accelerated by an adjacent weather system. Storms were converging far out in the Pacific Ocean, and the warnings now spoke of possible beach erosion, coastal flooding and power outages. The storm watch became a high wind watch, and then a high wind warning. The advisories, however, did not anticipate the ferocity that would be unleashed over the following 48 hours.

The second storm hit Sunday morning. Sustained winds rose to 40 miles per hour, then 50. Gusts over 80 mph shook the church. Through the roar of the wind, we could hear the screeching sound of the metal roofing grating against the shaft of the screws that held it in place, as it flexed and buckled. The lights flickered, and then went out. Fellowship time was canceled, and once the downed wires across the intersection were cleared, worshipers hurried home to wait out the storm.

The velocity of the wind continued to rise, and for the next 38 hours, the region was battered by sustained winds over 80 miles per hour, with gusts over 100. Heavy rainfall and temperatures in the 60s combined to melt the heavy snow from the previous storm. The soil, already saturated and softened, produce a rapid runoff, mud slides and debris flows. Thousands of acres of mature timber fell before the hammering winds, with trees either uprooted or snapped off, sometimes as high as 60 feet above the ground. Hundreds of power poles blew down, and steel transmission towers collapsed. Roofing and entire roofs were torn from houses. Store windows exploded into the streets. Beaches and waterfront buildings were hammered by waves up to 70 feet high.

When the winds abated, citizens ventured out to survey the

damage. Power poles, power lines and trees lay in the streets, along with signs, patio furniture, and anything else the wind could scatter. All highways into the area were blocked by fallen trees and landslides. Telephone service, including cellphones, was cut off. Cleanup would take months.

The forests sustained the most lingering damage. Officials estimated that some 3,500 acres of timber lay uprooted or broken. It was the pattern of the damage that proved to be both challenging and instructive. On the slopes that faced the ocean, whole hillside stands were flattened. In the breaks between the hills, where the wind was accelerated by the funnel effect, or else deflected by the orientation of the fold, a patchwork of destruction left broken trees at the foot of standing timber.

Beyond the most exposed ridges, a more ominous destruction occurred. There were the typical swaths of destruction between bands of spared timber. But, there were also stands of undamaged trees with the center portion of the grove blown down. Microblasts, wind gusts blowing straight down like hammer blows, shattered the hearts of huge groves of trees, leaving a circle of sentinels watching over their fallen companions.

The predominant species in the coastal band are Sitka spruce and hemlock. The spruce trees, with their shallow root disks, were tipped over. The hemlocks, being weaker in their structure, were more likely to be snapped off above the ground, but they, too, with shallow root systems were uprooted, contributing their entries to the parade of the root wads.

The grove at the back of our property sustained two kinds of damage. A wind gust of around 150 mph struck it a glancing blow, shaving off an edge strip of trees. A microblast hammered the heart out of the remaining stand. But, in the middle of the broken heart of the grove, surrounded by uprooted and broken trees, stood an undamaged Douglas fir tree. What made the difference for that one tree?

The Douglas fir has a taproot system that plunges deep into

the ground. The others had only a shallow grip on the ground. When the chaotic forces around them and buffeting them exceeded their strength, they fell.

For the believer in our Lord Jesus Christ, the well-rooted tree is used in scripture as a symbol of growth, maturity, strength and steadfastness. ***"Blessed is the man who walks not in the counsel of the wicked, nor stands in the way of sinners, nor sits in the seat of scoffers; but his delight is in the law of the LORD, and on his law he meditates day and night. He is like a tree planted by streams of water that yields its fruit in its season, and its leaf does not wither. In all that he does, he prospers."*** (Psa 1:1-3 ESV) David alludes to the strength and fruitfulness of the tree being dependent on being rooted and established where it can imbibe freely of the life-giving water. Our Lord used the water as a symbol of the Word of God, in which David says the believer *"meditates day and night."*

That Douglas fir tree, standing firm in the center of destruction, reflects Paul's prayer for believers: ***"...so that Christ may dwell in your hearts through faith--that you, being rooted and grounded in love, may have strength to comprehend with all the saints what is the breadth and length and height and depth, and to know the love of Christ that surpasses knowledge, that you may be filled with all the fullness of God."*** (Eph 3:17-19 ESV) Rooted and grounded, firmly planted, established. These are terms of a strength that can endure trials, troubles, struggles, disappointments...the storms of life that assail us with a frequency we would rather avoid.

Consider the elements in which we are to be established. The primary essential is that we be established in the unfathomable, incomprehensible love of Christ. He is the embodiment of the love of God, which He pours immeasurably into our hearts, to the overflowing point and beyond, that His love in us might impact those around us. We are to be ***"rooted and built up in him*** *and established in the faith, just as you were taught, abounding in thanksgiving."* (Col 2:7 ESV) We are to be established and growing in Christ Himself, drawing our life and fruitfulness from the Vine, in whom we are branches, cleansed and pruned for His purposes. We are to be rooted and nurtured in **the faith**, a term used in the scriptures to refer to the teachings of the Word of God. The Word of Christ can only dwell in us richly if we dwell in the Word of God, studying the Truth, and taught by the guiding Holy Spirit. *"Then stand firm in the freedom with which Christ made us free and do not be held again with a yoke of slavery."* (Gal 5:1) The knowledge of His Truth gives us a freedom to obey Him, and to serve Him. Ours is a freedom to do as we ought. Notice that we also stand fast, established in thankfulness. Paul wrote, *"In everything give thanks, for this is the will of God in Christ Jesus toward you."* (1Thes 5:18)

"Watch! Stand fast in the faith! Be men! Be strong!" (1Cor 16:13) Standing fast, standing strong, standing in spite of raging storms is our privilege, *"...if indeed you continue in the faith grounded and settled and not being moved away from the hope of the gospel which you heard proclaimed..."* (Col 1:23) We stand steadfast in the hope of the Gospel of Christ, knowing that scripture uses the word *hope* to signify eager anticipation of that which is certain. *"So, then, brothers, stand firm and strongly hold the teachings you were taught, whether by word or by our letter."* (2Thes 2:15)

It is indeed rich ground in which we are planted. We are rooted in the ground of glory, in our Lord Jesus Christ Himself. *"So as, my brothers, ones loved and longed for, my joy and crown, so stand firm in the Lord,"* (Php 4:1) *"through whom also we have had access by faith into this grace in which we stand, and we glory on the hope of the glory of God."* (Rom 5:2) All the elements that comprise the ground of victory find their source, their very stability, in our Lord. They are all by the grace of God, freely bestowed in His Son. Not even the tiniest particle finds its source in us. *"For we are... the ones who worship by the Spirit of God, and who glory in Christ Jesus, and who do not trust in flesh."* (Php 3:3) The arrogance of self-righteousness is the pathogen that produces root-rot in our lives. In that gale of 2007, we lost an ornamental monkey puzzle tree that was over a century old. Its crown exceeded its hold on the hilltop on which it stood, exposed to the hurricane-force gusts that assailed it. It fell, and great was the damage it caused when it went down. What a picture of us, should we dare to proclaim ourselves strong in ourselves, should we think more highly of ourselves than we ought to think. The scripture gives a somber warning: *"So that he that thinks to stand, let him be careful that he not fall."* (1Cor 10:12) It is only by, and in God's grace that we stand. It is all of Him, and none of us. *"Now the God of all grace, the One calling you to His eternal glory in Christ Jesus, you having suffered a little, Himself will perfect, confirm, strengthen, establish you."* (1Pet 5:10)

Not only is our strength, our standing firm, our being rooted and grounded His glorious provision, but also the equipping against the storms of life. The climate in which we stand is hostile, but we have been provided an all-sufficient outfit of storm gear: *"Put on all the armor of God, for you to be able to stand against the wiles of the Devil,"* (Eph 6:11) *"...that you may be able to resist in the evil day, and having worked out all things, to stand."* (Eph 6:13) The storms will come, but we are both established and sheltered in our Lord Jesus Christ. Consider the storms of life Paul weathered: *"Five times I received forty stripes minus one from the Jews. I was flogged three times; I was stoned once; I was shipwrecked three times; I have spent a night and a day in the deep. I have been in travels often, in dangers of rivers, in dangers of robbers, in dangers from my race, in dangers from the nations, in dangers in the city, in dangers in a wilderness, in dangers in the sea, in dangers among false brothers, in hardship and toil, often in watchings, in hunger and thirst, often in fastings, in cold and nakedness..."* (2Cor 11:25-27) And yet, he tells us, *"I have strength for all things in Christ the One strengthening me."* (Php 4:13)

Are we bending before the stormy blast? It is in those very moments that our gracious Lord is strengthening the fiber of faith within us, and driving our roots deeper into all that He is. The trial of our faith is purifying. Paul writes of our security in the wildest of storms that strike in our physical life here on Earth: *"Who shall separate us from the love of Christ? Shall tribulation, or distress, or persecution, or famine, or nakedness, or danger, or sword?"* (Rom 8:35) He faced these, and found our Lord faithful and sufficient in all of them. His conclusion concerning life storms looks beyond their earth-bound potential: *"Even as it has been written, 'For Your sake we are killed all the day; we are counted as sheep of slaughter.' But in all these things we more than conquer through Him loving us."* (Rom 8:36-37) We are more than conquerors, rooted and grounded in Him, in His love, even should these storms usher us into His presence. Paul looks beyond this earthly sphere, peeking into the spiritual realm of eternity, and declared, *"For I am persuaded that neither death, nor life, nor angels, nor rulers, nor powers, nor things present, nor things to come, nor height, nor depth, nor any other creature will be able to separate us from the love of God in Christ Jesus, our Lord."* (Rom 8:38-39) Established in Christ Himself, who created all things, we have confidence that nothing created can uproot us. With that assurance, Paul urges us to be steadfast in spite of tempests: *"So that, my beloved brothers, you be firm, immovable, abounding in the work of the Lord always, knowing that your labor is not without fruit in the Lord."* (1Cor 15:58) Consider the power to which we are commended, in which we stand: *"Now to Him who is able to establish you according to my gospel, and the proclaiming of Jesus Christ, according to the revelation of the mystery having been kept unvoiced during eternal times, but now has been made plain, and by prophetic Scriptures, according to the commandment of the everlasting God, made known for obedience of faith to all the nations; to the only wise God through Jesus Christ, to whom be the glory forever. Amen."* (Rom 16:25-27)

11

BUTTERFLIES

As October gives way to November in the northern hemisphere, caterpillars seem to abound. Black and orange wooly bears, larvae of the tiger moth, undulate across the pavement in an endless daredevil challenge. Western bluebirds yo-yo from perch to ground and back, capturing a seemingly endless feast of neon-green caterpillars. The swarming worm horde is not new, just more obvious in the fall. The garden teemed with foragers all summer, feasting on the broccoli and cauliflower, the roses, and, bless them, the weeds.

We abhor the worms. We dust them, drench them, squish them. We pick them off our plants in a wearying battle to save our harvest. We harvest, and then brine the produce to rid it of the worms. We dislike what they are as well as what they do. We love what they become.

February is fascinating month on the Oregon coast. It usually holds an astounding contrast of juxtaposed winter and summer, with chilling gloom suddenly yielding to bright warmth that sometimes lasts for weeks. The summer-like weather brings the first airborne blossoms. Tiny powder-blue butterflies emerge, the Eastern-tailed Blue. The bright-colored males take full advantage of the few February hours of warm sunshine, gathering on the mud at the edge of puddles for "pond parties," then scattering skyward on gossamer wings at the slightest movement that may portend danger. They are scouts. The sunshine of ensuing months will bring the varied bouquet of moths and butterflies. Cabbage Whites, black and orange Lady Butterflies, yellow Sulphers and Mimosas, the larger, more striking Swallowtails and the tinier Skippers flutter through the sunny afternoons from spring through autumn. Our eyes are drawn to them for their delicate beauty, a fragile loveliness marred by careless contact.

What they are is difficult to reconcile with what they were. The change from Earth-bound creeping destroyers to heavenly beauty involves a fascinating and instructive process. Metamorphosis, biologically speaking, involves a profound restructuring. The caterpillar, lowly worm that it is, experiences a radical transformation, conspicuous and, in most cases, somewhat abrupt, not only in its structure, but in its habitat and its behavior as well. It is a hidden work, from the inside out. The caterpillar will anchor itself in place, either in a cocoon or without one. The movement that characterized the worm ceases. It is at rest. It will appear dead, but inside its skin, a marvelous process seems to melt the structure of the caterpillar, and through a process of cellular re-differentiation, the body parts of the old stage give way to the body parts of the new. A hard chrysalis forms that looks like a mold in which the new creature will be shaped. The skin of the worm, no longer appropriate, splits, and is cast off. As the worm-that-was gives way to the beauty that will be, the veiled color and the promise of splendor to come can be glimpsed through the transparent shell, until the moment when the fullness of glory is revealed.

Webster's Dictionary generalizes the definition of the term *metamorphosis*, terming it "a major change in the appearance or character of someone or something." We can make an apt application of the term in a spiritual sense, as we see in Scriptures the metamorphosis of the sinner to a saint.

We are all born into this world as Earth-bound worms, writhing in the narrow confines of the dank decay of sin, feasting on the worthless husks of wickedness. We don't like the analogy. To be compared to something repulsive, something abhorrent evokes cries of protest and acts of revision. The human self-aggrandizing thought process rejects such convicting descriptions. The hymn "At The Cross" has suffered a series of such changes designed to mollify the ones objecting. The first stanza was deemed demeaning:

Alas, and did my Savior bleed, and did my Sovereign die?

Would He devote that sacred head for such a worm as I?

It underwent an editorial change designed to alleviate such a loathsome characterization. The offensive line was modified to

Would He devote that sacred head for sinners such as I?

In but a short time, complaints impacted the term *sinners*, concluding it to be offensive to the self-esteem. The line, in some hymnals, became:

Would He devote that sacred head for someone such as I?

Of course He would! Why wouldn't He? After all, I'm worth it. I'm a good person. The revision accommodates the feelings of the most sensitive among us. It also minimizes the evaluation of humanity's condition from God's perspective: ***"And Jehovah saw that the evil of man was great on the earth, and every imagination of the thoughts of his heart was only evil all the day long."*** (Gen 6:5) This constitutes an all-inclusive indictment of humanity, in which God concludes all under sin, children of disobedience and children of wrath. As the

Apostle Paul writes, *"...according as it has been written, 'There is not a righteous one, not even one!' 'There is not one understanding; there is not one seeking God.' All turned away, they became worthless together, not one is doing goodness, not so much as one!' 'Their throat is a tomb being opened;' 'they used deceit with their tongues; the poison of asps is under their lips; whose mouth is full of cursing and bitterness. Their feet are swift to shed blood; ruin and misery are in their way; and they did not know a way of peace; there is no fear of God before their eyes.'"* (Rom 3:10-18) Neither our distaste for such an indictment, our denial of its truth, nor our vociferous protestations of our own exemption from the indictment will change God's purpose in bringing it.

God's grace is free to work in the light of the blanket condemnation of His rebellious creation. His gracious plan of redemption was concluded, according to His omniscient foreknowledge, before the world was. He stretched out hands of love at Calvary, and declared, "It is finished!" Now, His grace is worked according to His Word by His Spirit in those marked out for salvation from eternity. **"But we ought to thank God always concerning you, brothers, beloved by the Lord, because God chose you from the beginning to salvation in sanctification of the Spirit and belief of the truth, to which He called you through our gospel, to obtain the glory of our Lord Jesus Christ."** (2Thes 2:13-14) We must be brought to the place of rest before the miraculous metamorphosis from sinner to saint can begin, and yet, bringing us to that place of rest is in itself the beginning of the work of grace in each of us. It is a humbling realization that brings us to agree with God, but it is essential.

We must join David in saying, **"But I am a worm, and no man; a reproach of mankind, and despised by the people."** (Psa 22:6) In this messianic psalm these are the words of the Lamb of God. We must be drawn to Him in the place of humility. Consider the questions posed by Job in his humiliation, when he recognized the personal and universal pervasiveness of sin: *"How then can man be justified with God? Or how can one who is born of a woman be pure? Behold, even the moon, and it is not bright; and the stars are not pure in His eyes; how much less man who is a maggot; and the son of man who is a worm!"* (Job 25:4-6) We must be brought by the convicting work of God's Spirit to cry out helplessly with Paul, *"O wretched man that I am! Who shall deliver me from the body of this death?"* (Rom 7:24)

The place of rest is the place of ceasing from self-effort and self-righteousness. It is the place of *"Be still and know that I am God! I will be exalted among the nations; I will be exalted in the earth."* (Psa 46:10) Be still. Stop striving. Let God be God. It is in that resting quietness that the glorious work of God is done. It is the place in which the Holy Spirit forms within us the chrysalis that Christ Jesus is, as Paul writes: *"My little children, of whom I travail in birth again until Christ be formed in you..."* (Gal 4:19) That Chrysalis is the form to which we are predestined to be conformed.

As the Spirit forms Christ in us, He places us in Christ as a work of grace. *"But of Him, you are in Christ Jesus, who was made to us wisdom from God, both righteousness and sanctification and redemption, so that even as it has been written, 'He that glories, let him glory in the Lord.'"* (1Cor 1:30-31) The very idea of the caterpillar laboring to transform itself into a butterfly is preposterous. Even more preposterous is the notion that we can change ourselves. That work is done in us, and done to us, not by us. The Apostle Paul contends that we are to entrust ourselves to His working, *"...being persuaded of this very thing, that the One having begun a good work in you will finish it until the day of Jesus Christ; for it is God who is working in you both to will and to work for the sake of His good pleasure."* (Php 1:6, 2:13)

Within the chrysalis, the structures and functions that

characterize the caterpillar cease to exist. The structures and functions of the butterfly come into being. In like manner, the same process takes place in the believer: *"So that if anyone is in Christ, he is a new creation; the old things have passed away; behold, all things have become new!"* (2Cor 5:17) Christ Jesus is then the form, the mold in which the new is formed, because it is the purpose of God that we be made like Him:*"because whom He foreknew, He also predestinated to be conformed to the image of His Son, for Him to be the First-born among many brothers."* (Rom 8:29) The concept of the work being done in and to us, and not by us, is repeated in its several facets in Scripture. *"And be not conformed to this age, but be transformed by the renewing of your mind, in order to prove by you what is the good and pleasing and perfect will of God."* (Rom 12:2) Rather than letting the values of this anti-God world system shape us, as we yield to its influence, we are transformed by God's Spirit applying God's Word, as He uses the Scriptures to renew our minds.

The mirror of God's Word becomes the instrument of change. *"But we all with our face having been unveiled, having beheld the glory of the Lord in a mirror, are being changed into the same image from glory to glory, as from the Lord Spirit."* (2Cor 3:18) As we are shown the glory of Christ Jesus in the written word by the Spirit, created in us is the longing for His purity, His holiness, His glory. It is a desire placed within us by the Lord Himself, a desire that He delights to fulfill. The stirrings of Life within the Chrysalis split the old skin of the worm we were, and it is shed, that the glorious work in progress might be glimpsed, though not in its fullness. *"For you have put off the old man, as regards the former behavior, having been corrupted according to the deceitful lusts, and to be renewed in the spirit of your mind, and to put on the new man, which according to God was created in righteousness and true holiness."* (Eph 4:22-24) That, too, is part of the conforming process. To make us Christlike, the Spirit of

God removes that which does not conform to all that Christ Jesus is, and in so doing, conforms our behavior to the purpose of God: *"for we are His workmanship, created in Christ Jesus unto good works, which God before prepared that we should walk in them."* (Eph 2:10) The shedding of the old skin of behaviors, attitudes and habits is the life-long process by which we come *"to know Him and the power of His resurrection, and the fellowship of His sufferings, having been conformed to His death...that as Christ was raised up from the dead by the glory of the Father, so also we should walk in newness of life."* (Php 3:10, Rom 6:4b)

The glimpses of glory being formed in us as we rest in our glorious Chrysalis are but a foretaste of the ultimate purpose of God, *"...who will transform our body of humiliation, for it to be conformed to His body of glory, according to the working of Him to be able even to subject all things under Himself."* (Php 3:21) As Christ is formed in us, as we are conformed to His character by His Spirit, He is revealed in us. He is manifested to those around us. His Spirit testifies to His reality in His own.

In an extended discourse on the changes in process, and the final shedding of this earthly husk, the Apostle Paul takes us from the worm to the butterfly, emphasizing the contrast between the sinner and the saint: *"So also the resurrection of the dead. It is sown in corruption, it is raised in incorruption. It is sown in dishonor, it is raised in glory. It is sown in weakness, it is raised in power. It is sown a natural body, it is raised a spiritual body; there is a natural body, and there is a spiritual body. So also it has been written, "The" first "man", Adam, "became a living soul;" the last Adam a life-giving Spirit. But not the spiritual first, but the natural; afterward the spiritual. The first man was out of earth, earthy. The second Man was the Lord out of Heaven. Such as is the earthy man, such also are the earthy ones. And such as is the*

heavenly Man, such also are the heavenly ones." (1Cor 15:42-48) The transformation is indeed radical. The reality that was is so incompatible with that which is to be as to require the complete eradication of the old. A caterpillar with wings would still feed on the husks of this world, and not the sweetness of Christ Himself. Such a blended creature would make a bumblebee appear graceful.

The change will be complete. Paul continues his discourse: ***"And as we bore the image of the earthy man, we shall also bear the image of the heavenly Man. And I say this, brothers, that flesh and blood is not able to inherit the kingdom of God, nor does corruption inherit incorruption. Behold, I speak a mystery to you: we shall not all fall asleep, but we shall all be changed. In a moment, in a glance of an eye, at the last trumpet; for a trumpet will sound, and the dead will be raised incorruptible, and we shall all be changed. For this corruptible must put on incorruption, and this mortal must put on immortality. But when this corruptible shall put on incorruption, and this mortal shall put on immortality, then will take place the Word that has been written, 'Death was swallowed up in victory.'"*** (1Cor 15:49-54) It is in His presence that His glorious work will be revealed in all His intended splendor. His completed good work in His own will be displayed to the praise of the glory of His grace. As the Apostle John tells us, ***"Beloved, now are we the sons of God, and it doth not yet appear what we shall be: but we know that, when he shall appear, we shall be like him; for we shall see him as he is."*** (1John 3:2 KJV)

12

PROTOZOA

My students tried an interesting experiment. They poured distilled water into a clean quart jar. Then, I had them go out in a field in early spring, and pick a handful of dead grass that had endured the raging storms of winter. They immersed the stems in the pure water, and left it at room temperature for two weeks. The water took on a greenish color, and had a layer of scum on the surface. They took an eyedropper of the mess, squeezed it into a petri dish, and observed it under a dissecting microscope. The water teemed with tiny life forms, swimming about by a variety of means of propulsion. Flagellates, ciliates, rotifers, all single-celled organisms, fascinating in their variety, in their complex simplicity, yet weak in their isolated individuality.

"Don't drink the water!"

These sage words are offered often as parting advice for travelers headed to foreign lands. The *what* of the advice predates the *why*. Antonij van Leeuwenhoek, a Dutch amateur microbiologist, first observed what he termed *animalcules*. Using his secret method of creating ever-smaller lenses, van Leeuwenhoek was able to observe microorganisms, many of them disease-causing pathogens. Ridiculed by officials, he used his microscope to demonstrate that the city's water teemed with life forms invisible to the unaided eye. The response was immediate, decisive, and foolish. Rather than deal with the contaminated water problem, the officials destroyed the microscope.

Sailors had long known of the trouble water could cause. Drinking water was loaded in wooden barrels, stored below decks, and portioned out over the course of the voyage. Hands on the vessel had long noted that a few days out, the cloudy water "...seemed to stir itself." It also stirred the digestive systems of the crew. Debilitated and dehydrated sailors became dead sailors, and the sea became a graveyard.

The solution? Grog. The alcohol in a measure of rum, when added to the sailor's daily ration of water, killed the microscopic population, making the water safe to drink. The remedy was so effective that ship captains found a measure of power in the mere threat of withholding the rum ration, which would condemn an offending crewman to days of misery, if not death.

Like so many discoveries of those who consider themselves modern, grog was simply a rediscovery of knowledge that had been lost. The apostle Paul, writing to Timothy, advised him to "take a little wine for thy stomach's sake." This was not counseling Timothy to substitute wine for water. Instead, it was a prescription for the forerunner of grog. Mix the wine with water, and the water would be safe to drink.

Animalcules abound. Indeed, microorganisms comprise the most populous and varied segment of life forms on earth. Autonomous, self-contained, self-sufficient, they live out a mostly solitary existence, even to the point of multiplying by dividing themselves into two new organisms that separate and continue in their own isolated life, needing no one.

God has not so designed the body of believers in Christ Jesus, our Lord and Savior. Just as He created us as complex constructions of interdependent parts, He has also built the Body of Christ, the Church, of specially-gifted individuals, parts purposed to contribute to the whole. Paul uses this analogy repeatedly throughout his letters to the assemblies to whom he writes. To the believers at Rome: *"For even as we have many members in one body, but all members do not have the same function, so we the many are one body in Christ, and each one members of one another..."* (Rom 12:4-5) Packed into those two verses, God's blueprint for building a body of many parts as a unit emerges with clarity. He demonstrates His wisdom in object lesson form. When we consider ourselves, our own bodies, we can think through the various systems, divided into organs, subdivided into tissues, broken down into individual cells. Each system has its own function within the whole body. Each organ supplies its function to the system, each tissue within the organ, and each cell within the tissue.

When he writes *"and each one members of one another,"* Paul's body analogy emphasizes the truth that no member can function autonomously, because no member of the body performs all functions. There can be no super-saint, go-it-alone, do-it-all-for-you believers, functioning outside the local assembly. Fellowship is up-close and personal. Paul did not write, "greet one another with a holy kissy-face icon."

To the assembly at Corinth, he writes: *"Even as the body is one, and has many members, but all the members of the one body, being many, are one body, so also is Christ."* (1Cor 12:12) The unity of the body Paul emphasizes here opens several threads of thought, all related to the interdependency of the members of the body of Christ. We need each other. Whatever our gifts, and whatever the gifts of others, we are placed as we are by God Himself. *"But now God set the members, each one of them, in the body, even as He desired."* (1Cor 12:18) The fact that He has equipped us to contribute to the over-all functioning of the assembly of believers precludes arrogance of function. *"And the eye is not able to say to the hand, I have no need of you; or again the head to the feet, I have no need of you."* (1Cor 12:21) The capacity of sight is not superior to the ability to feel, to grasp and to caress. Sight fails in darkness. Meditation is not superior to mobility.

He also precludes envy of function. *"If the foot says, Because I am not a hand, I am not of the body, on account of this, is it not of the body? And if the ear says, Because I am not an eye, I am not of the body, on account of this, is it not of the body? If all the body were an eye, where would be the hearing? If all hearing, where the smelling?"* (1Cor 12:15-17) The preparation of the parts is a work of wisdom by the Holy Spirit. *"But the one and the same Spirit works all these things, distributing separately to each as He wills."* (1Cor 12:11) He enables us spiritually according to His purposes. We receive His enablements. We do not ask for them, pray for them, seek them or develop them within ourselves. It is His work. We find an interesting realization that Nebuchadnezzar came to acknowledge in regard to God's sovereignty: *"And all those living in the earth are counted as nothing. And He does according to His will among the army of Heaven, and among those living in the earth. And no one is able to strike His hand or say to Him, What are You doing?"* (Dan 4:35)

Unity of the body of Christ, then, does not imply uniformity. *"But if all was one member, where would the body be? But now, indeed, many are the members, but one body."* (1Cor 12:19-20) Many parts comprise the whole. Each part is necessary to body life within the assembly, and each part draws from the others within that body life. *"But God tempered the body together, giving more abundant honor to the member having need, that there not be division in the body, but that the members might have the same care for one another."* (1Cor 12:24b-25)

There is a sublime richness in the fulfillment of that last phrase. An assembly of believers, yielded to the leading of God's Holy Spirit, well-nourished with His precious Word, lives out abundantly the body-life care of fellow believers. **"And if one member suffers, all the members suffer with it. If one member is glorified, all the members rejoice with it."** (1Cor 12:26) Without envy, we rejoice with those who rejoice. Without embarrassment, we weep with those who are sorrowing.

We find over two dozen *one anothers* in the new testament, beseechings of grace that implore the yielded believer to subordinate self for the benefit of fellow members of the body of Christ. We call these beseechings of grace because it is only by and through God's bestowed grace that we are able to practice them. Our self-serving flesh, should it become dominant, will never stoop to prefer others over our own interests. It is for this reason that the first and most important of these beseechings of grace came from our Lord Jesus Christ Himself: **"I give a new commandment to you, that you should love one another; according as I loved you, you should also love one another."** (John 13:34) It is that sacrificial love of God that consistently and actively seeks the best interest of the object of that love that was embodied in our Lord Jesus Christ. It is **"...the love of God** [that] **has been poured out in our hearts through the Holy Spirit given to us."** (Rom 5:5) That love of God humbles self by the active power of the Holy Spirit, enabling believers to do **"...nothing according to party spirit or self-glory, but in humility, esteeming one another as surpassing themselves."** (Php 2:3) God's grace supplies God's love abundantly. It is **"poured out in our hearts,"** not that we should contain it, but that it should flow out from us. We serve as channels through which that love of God flows, forming the connective tissue of the body of Christ. Paul writes, **"And above all these, love, which is the bond of perfectness."** (Col 3:14)

It is only within that bond of perfectness, God's love, that the rest of the *one anothers* find their perfect expression. Our flesh prefers to be the recipient of them, not the giver. Beseechings to build one another up (Rom 15:2), encourage one another (1Thes 5:11), bear one another's burdens (Gal 6:2), serve one another (Gal 5:13) and forgive one another (Eph 3:32) are focused on those around us, not on ourselves. To practice them without secretly looking for some benefit for ourselves challenges that fleshly aspect of our being. If the flesh intrudes in such patently beneficial activities, how much more in the equally loving activities that are less pleasant. We are called to lovingly admonish one another (Col 1:28), rebuke (1Tim 5:20) and judge (1Cor 5:12). These activities, motivated by love, are just as needful in the assembly. But they are fraught with danger, arenas for destructive displays of fleshly arrogance. No wonder the Scriptures reserve these loving ministries to those acting in response to the indwelling Holy Spirit. ***"Brothers, if a man is overtaken in some deviation, you, the spiritual ones, restore such a one in the spirit of meekness, considering yourself, that you not also be tempted."*** (Gal 6:1) Hazards abound, should our fleshly natures take the lead, for ourselves, the one we confront, and for the body of Christ as well. For this reason, Paul urges believers to be ***"...eager to keep the unity of the Spirit in the bond of peace."*** (Eph 4:3)

The bond of love and the bond of peace presuppose the consistent close association of believers in a relationship that builds mutual trust and openness. It is in such atmosphere believers encourage one another in the Scriptures, disciple one another, strengthen one another, confess to and forgive one another, and grow in grace and the knowledge of our Lord. Paul writes, ***"And let us consider one another, to incitement of love and of good works, not forsaking the assembling together of ourselves, as is the custom of some, but exhorting, and by so much more as you see the Day drawing near."*** (Heb 10:24-25) He precludes the cold isolation of freelancers. It is only in the assembly of believers, in the close-knit body, that our Lord's plan for His own can be fulfilled. Broadcast, podcast, on-line and digital communication cannot substitute for the warmth of fellowship. John wrote, *"Having many things to write to you, I do not intend to speak by means of paper and ink, but I am hoping to come to you, and to speak mouth to mouth, that our joy may be full."* (2John 1:12) What intimacy is implied by that term, mouth to mouth. It is in that degree of intimate fellowship that God's purposed body life flourishes. *"And let the peace of God rule in your hearts, to which you also were called in one body, and be thankful. Let the Word of Christ dwell in you richly, in all wisdom teaching and exhorting yourselves in psalms and hymns and spiritual songs, singing with grace in your hearts to the Lord. And everything, whatever you do in word or in work, do all things in the name of the Lord Jesus, giving thanks to God and the Father through Him."* (Col 3:15-17)

We benefit individually from the body relationship of believers. But Paul makes it clear that the body benefits from the on-going fellowship, as we collectively are to be *"...speaking the truth in love, we may grow up into Him in all things, who is the Head, the Christ, from whom all the body, having been fitted and compacted together through every assisting bond, according to the effectual working of one measure in each part, produces the growth of the body to the building up of itself in love."* (Eph 4:15-16) It might be wise to take note of how many of the protozoans are pathogenic. As God draws those chosen to salvation to Christ Jesus our Lord, He places His saved ones in the body of Christ. *"For we are members of His body, of His flesh, and of His bones."* (Eph 5:30)

13

BLACK LINE

Winter was a distant memory that late-June afternoon. Three weeks into our honeymoon, my wife and I were enjoying the sunshine of a cloudless, dead-calm day on Lake Pend Oreille in Idaho's panhandle. Our twelve-foot open boat seemed especially miniscule on such an expansive body of water. The lake is long, wide, and deep enough that the U. S. Navy built a submarine base at the south end of it, and a naval training base to go with it, back in the early stages of World War II. The submarines were still there, but the base was now a state park.

We had tried fishing. Visions of Bing Crosby's huge Kamloops rainbow trout swam in the back of my mind. My mother's favorite crooner, being a local boy, loved that lake, and loved to fish it as often as he could.

On a smaller scale, my taste buds recalled the kokanee casserole my mother had made with the fish she and my dad had caught the year before. Those little landlocked sockeye salmon rarely reached a foot in length, but they were packed with flavor. The limit on them was twenty-five. But today, they, like their larger relatives, were where we were not. My limit was zero.

We had trolled across near Pearl Island, then southward well off the Green Monarchs on the east side of the lake. Now, headed westward toward our home-away-from-home, a twenty-foot travel trailer, we had idled just past the middle of the lake, cut the outboard motor, and were enjoying the panorama of blue above and below, split by a jagged band of green, black and dun, steep mountains that rose two- to three thousand feet above the lake's surface, and plunged just as steeply to an equal depth below us.

Looking southward along the length of the lake, we noticed the blue of the surface grew noticeably darker, stretching in a black ribbon from shore to shore. A word of advice from my dad drifted through my thoughts, a caution to "get off the lake" if I saw that dark ribbon. The indigenous lore whispered that on such a day, the spirit of the lake grew restless, and tossed in his slumbers, ruffling his covers. I decided to keep an eye on that harbinger of disquietude. However, my bride was more interesting than the horizon, so my watchfulness waned.

The boat began to rock, gently at first, then more insistently. The lake's surface, so calm a few moments before, was now rolling, and not too far to the south, whitecaps feathered the water as far as we could see. The outboard fired on the second pull, and I started westward for our inlet. That put the swells on our port side, and the boat rose to the crest on one swell, teetered, and slid down into the trough, threatening to capsize. I turned, cut the speed to match the advance of the waves, and ran on their backs as much as possible, angling northwestward, not exactly toward home, but toward shore. We held this course until the whitecaps caught us.

It was amazing. The sun was just as warm. There was absolutely no wind. But, the water was wild. My wife and I both slipped down off the seats, and sat on the bottom of the boat to lower the center of gravity. I pushed the tiller over, turning the boat to quarter across the waves, bucking and wallowing southwestward, trying to keep the bow more or less pointed at the distant tree that marked our inlet. Tranquility had turned to turbulence, calm to chaos, and tension made for pounding hearts and shallow breathing. We had a mile and more of churning water to cross. My experience boating in such conditions? None.

Our Lord's disciples, on the other hand, included some experienced fishermen who knew the nature of the Sea of Galilee. That lake was subject to sudden storms that would whip it into a churning cauldron. Mark's Gospel recounts one such experience.

The day had been a busy one, filled with ministry to needy people. *"And evening having come, He said to them on that day, 'Let us pass over to the other side.' And dismissing the crowd they took Him along in the boat as He was. And other small boats also were with Him."* (Mar 4:35-36) It was a simple plan. Mark does not record the weather conditions when they embarked. It may have been fairly calm, or it could have been a bit choppy. But, at His word, they headed out into the lake, a flotilla of small craft moving into open water in the gathering twilight. The scene seemed idyllic, peaceful and restoring. Sailing or rowing, they anticipated a quiet night crossing. It was not to be.

"And a great windstorm occurred, and the waves beat into the boat so that it was filled already." (Mar 4:37) A small boat, buffeted by violent winds and crashing seas, with miles of water between it and shore, and many fathoms under the keel is enough to intimidate the most experienced boater. The helmsman has his attention on the fight for control, but the passengers focus only on the fury around them. Unoccupied, they only feed their fear. Each upward lurch, each downward plunge, each wallow and slosh of incoming water tightens the grip of

anxiety. My wife and I knew the feeling. So did the disciples. But, where was Jesus? *"And He was on the stern, sleeping on the headrest. And they awakened Him, and said to Him, Teacher, does it not matter to You that we are perishing?"* (Mar 4:38) He was with them! The One they had seen work miracles was there, sleeping in the back of the boat.

Their focus, however, was not on the presence of the Lord. His repose should have inspired confidence, as should His words, "...let us pass over to the other side." The disciples were entangled in their own anxiety, as if He had said, "...let us go to the middle of the sea and perish." Although the Shepherd's Psalm was familiar to them, they had forgotten *"Even though I walk through the valley of the shadow of death, I will fear no evil, for you are with me..."* (Psalm 23:4 ESV) Only in their extremity did they appeal to Him.

His response is instructive. *"And being awakened, He rebuked the wind, and said to the sea, 'Silence! Be still!' And the wind ceased, and there was a great calm. And He said to them, 'Why are you so fearful? How do you not have faith?'"* (Mar 4:39-40) His rebuke addressed to the elements was an authoritative command, which they obeyed. His rebuke to the disciples was a series of questions, gently prompting introspection. The first was directed toward their focus on their circumstances: "Why are you so fearful?" The second addressed their spiritual condition: "How do you have no faith?" Matthew's account, in its literal rendition, has a more direct impact: *"And He said to them, 'Why are you afraid, little-faiths?'"* (Mat 8:26) Instead of a description of their spiritual response, He used an appellation to show their spiritual nature: "Little-faiths." Their confidence was in their boats, their experience, their skills – in themselves. When that misplaced confidence was threatened, and, in reality, compromised by overwhelming circumstances, fear seized them.

Notice the result of his rebuke of the elements: *"...and there was a great calm."* The raging wind died away instantly. The heaving waves flattened. The sea, a moment before in tumult, was tranquil. Not so the disciples. ***"And they feared a great fear and said to one another, Who then is this, that even the wind and the sea obey Him?"*** (Mark 4:41) Their terror of perishing gave way to an awe that set their hearts pounding anew, and took their breath away. Their focus was shifted from their peril to the One present with them. The word *fear* in this case is not the terror of impending doom, but rather to reverence, or to be in awe of something or someone. Their response was much like Peter's, when he drew in a net full of fish at our Lord's command: ***"And seeing, Simon Peter fell at the knees of Jesus, saying, Depart from me, for I am a sinful man, Lord."*** (Luke 5:8) This fear both draws our hearts to worship, and causes our flesh to draw back.

What a difference focus can make. We are surrounded by chaotic situations in this world, both on a global scale, and at the personal level. Storms of violence, contention, disaster and disease churn around us, whipping up waves of doubt, fear, uncertainty and despair that threaten to overwhelm us. On the grand scale, reports of political conflict, natural disasters, famine and pestilence break over us in an endless maelstrom capable of disheartening us, and swamping us, spiritually speaking, if we, like the disciples, fix our gaze on the chaos. On the personal level, disappointments, failures, opposition and sufferings can do the same. Like the disciples, we struggle against the issues that surround us, striving in our own pitiful strength and understanding to overcome them. Failing in those efforts, we find ourselves tempted to give up and sink beneath them.

God's Word acknowledges the chaotic forces on both the global and personal levels, and asserts His power and authority over them. He not only knows of them, but He turns them, and uses them for His own glory in our lives. Consider the impact on the global scale of Isaiah 17:12-13:***"Woe to the multitude of many peoples; they roar like the roar of seas; and the crash of nations, they crash like the crash of mighty waters! The nations shall crash like the crashing of***

many waters, but He rebukes it, and it flees far away; yea, it is driven like the chaff of mountains before the wind, and like a rolling thing before a tempest." The final victory is His. Chaos will continue in this world's system, fulfilling the decree of God, who in His time will allow the full revelation of the exceeding wickedness of evil. The roaring and crashing is distracting. It fixates us, mesmerizes us, intimidates us and controls us when our vision is filled with the events of this temporal existence. But, sooner or later, we are driven by fear and drawn by grace to change our focus to the one who is ever with us, who will never leave us or forsake us.

Raging storms can strike on a personal level, as well. Darkening clouds of circumstances billow around us, winds of adversity buffet us, and waves of emotion engulf us. A dear friend recently found herself in just such a tempest. I urged her to change her focus from her situation, to our loving Lord. I cautioned her not to allow the focus on her circumstances to make her cynical. Her message to me was a cry for prayer: *"Not cynical, just wishing. And sad. Now that the tears have started, they won't stop. I've seen one dream after another shattered in irreparable splinters at my feet. Now it feels like I have no dreams left. I'm not sure the last precious dreams can survive without him in them. For the first time it mattered who shared the dreams with me, now....."* Like the storm-tossed disciples, her focus was on the chaotic battering she was suffering. She, however, could not turn to the visible, tangible Savior in the heart-wrenching emotional darkness that surrounded her.

The prophet Micah wrote of just such a situation. ***"Rejoice not over me, O my enemy; when I fall, I shall rise; when I sit in darkness, the LORD will be a light to me."*** (Micah 7:8) Sometimes, we are our own worst enemies. As believers, we can play into the hands of the enemy of our souls, who is out to destroy our testimony, to erode our confidence in our Lord, His love, and His purpose. We stumble. We sit in the gloom of despair generated by our fixation on our circumstances. My wife and I had to run our little boat aground on an exposed point of land, and watch the churning water, waiting for a quietness that would allow us to move on to our place of rest.

To hide her tears, my friend wandered out into a storm of the weather variety that had moved into our area. In the midst of that coastal tempest, she followed the disciples' example: *"He used the wind a little after that too. Once I had at least a marginal amount of sense back in my head, the storm started feeling like a projection of what was in my heart, like my whole life was being caught up in the wind and was being blown and tossed and shredded....and it started to really scare me. Then my cries to Him changed to desperate cries to feel His presence, to know He was there..... suddenly the wind completely stopped, just for a moment, and everything was silent. But then, He really was THERE. The wind came back, just like it had been, but around me it was like a cocoon of warm air that moved around me like an embrace and I could FEEL His arms around me. And I KNEW He was there, I KNEW I was in His hands, safe inside the palm of His hands. Then nothing else mattered....I wish it could be like that always."*

It is possible, but only to those who have learned contentment, who have been exercised by trial into trust. He does not scold when we lose our focus, and then cry out to Him in our extremity. **"For he knows our frame; he remembers that we are dust."** (Psa 103:14 ESV) He knows our weakness. Remember His response when His disciples turned to Him in their terror: **"Then he rose and rebuked the winds and the sea, and there was a great calm."** (Mat 8:26 ESV) He may not altar the circumstances in which we find ourselves. But, He draws our eyes to Himself. He presses us to His loving heart. As my friend expressed it, "Sometimes pain can be a beautiful thing. It drives us back to the Father, to the source of all comfort and cleansing and forgiveness; it brings us back to the place of surrender and rest in the One who is sovereign ruler of all; it leads us back to His everlasting kindness, His everlasting love, and His everlasting arms. It leads us home, back to where we belong."

David took note of the precious rest that awaits us when we are drawn to rest in Him, to rest in His grace, and to rest in His loving purpose. ***"You still the roaring of the sea, the roar of their waves, and the tumult of the peoples."*** (Psa 65:7) Our hearts and minds can know that great calm.

14

DRIFTING

.   Our headlights barely penetrated the white blanket that hung before us, flapping and swirling as it blotted out the pavement, its lines and lanes, and anything outside the small bubble of light we were pushing eastward through a sudden white-out. The Washington Cascade Mountains were behind us, and that passage had been uneventful. It was only after the freeway reached the undulating Palouse that the flakes began to fall. At first, they swirled lazily in the frigid air, hit the road, and crumbled into a fine icy powder. Thicker they swirled, and the billowing powder became a cloud of dancing fairy dust in the headlights. The lower altitude brought flakes that held together when they hit. Large flakes accumulating on the windshield threatened to overwhelm the wipers.

.   The wind hit abruptly. Now, rather than lazy swirling, the snow lashed us as the wind endeavored to push us into the guard rail. We were in what was perhaps the worst vehicle for that storm. Our Volkswagen pop-top camper was lightweight, and presented a broad sail-like wall to the wind that quartered from the left front, inexorably forcing us across the fog line and onto the shoulder, in spite of my counter-steering. We were in a section of the state where there are miles and miles of miles and miles, and little else. There were no trees to slow or block the wind. There were no houses, no towns, and no highway signs telling how near a town might be. Everything was swallowed up in a smothering wall of white.

. We were driving into a gusting wind that quartered across our path, pushing us relentlessly off course. It was a slow battle, as we crept along, alternately steering into the slide to regain control, and then edging back onto the pavement. The newly invented, highly touted plastic chains helped with the forward motion, but it was the front tires, the ones that controlled the direction of travel, that lacked traction.

. The tension of such a battle is exhausting. After a little over an hour of being blown right, and edging left, only to be hit by a stronger gust that caused us to lurch toward whatever field or ravine lay beyond the shoulder of the road, we saw a highway sign the right size and shape to indicate an exit ahead. The name of the town was obliterated by the clinging snow, but the distance, "1 mile," gave us a sense of hope for relief.

. It seemed like the longest mile we have ever traveled, but at last we saw a faint glow in the storm off to our right. We did not have to slow for the exit. It was not much of a town. No service station, no store, but it did have a fly-speck motel, with the "vacancy" sign on. It wasn't inviting, but it was shelter. The room was small, and smelled a bit musty. The bed was old and lumpy and sagged to the middle. It was not where we wanted to be, but it was warm, and would have to do until we could stay on course as we moved on. For the moment, it was good to be somewhere stable, unmoving.

. That experience prompted introspection. Out on the highway, we had been adrift, struggling for direction, and subject to the will of the storm, in a dangerous, potentially deadly situation. The physical experience was disquieting. What about the spiritual? Was I adrift spiritually, as well? Was I firmly established in God's Word, in the faith? Well might we ask those questions, in the light of Scripture.

.   The highway we traveled was solid, well-built and established as the way to reach our destination. But, it was buffeted by forces that conspired to redirect us. The same is true in the spiritual realm. Note the established way, the purpose and the warning in Paul's letter to the Ephesian believers: ***And he gave the apostles, the prophets, the evangelists, the shepherds and teachers, to equip the saints for the work of ministry, for building up the body of Christ, until we all attain to the unity of the faith and of the knowledge of the Son of God, to mature manhood, to the measure of the stature of the fullness of Christ, so that we may no longer be children, tossed to and fro by the waves and carried about by every wind of doctrine, by human cunning, by craftiness in deceitful schemes.*** (Eph 4:11-14 ESV) The apostles and prophets laid the foundation, by God's Spirit both proclaiming and writing our Lord's message to His Church. The evangelists, shepherds and teachers built on the foundation, which Paul pointed out was Christ Himself, not just His message. The goal was the maturity of the believer. The ground of growth was ***the faith, and the knowledge of the Son of God.*** When we see the two words, the faith, in the epistles, it is a term that speaks of the scriptures themselves. They are the means to the knowledge of the Son of God. They are also the preventative for the warning, which introduces a thread of thought that runs through the whole New Testament. Immaturity is characterized by instability, and the forces of the storm of opposition to all that God is, has and does lash the believer and unbeliever alike. Winds of doctrine, human cunning, and craftiness in deceitful schemes have their origin in the prince of this world, whose purpose is destruction. We were all under his power, tossed about by waves of passion. ***"And you were dead in the trespasses and sins*** *in which you once walked, following the course of this world, following the prince of the power of the air, the spirit that is now at work in the sons of disobedience-- among whom we all once lived in the passions of our flesh, carrying out the desires of the body and the mind, and were by nature children of wrath, like the rest of mankind."* (Eph 2:1-3 ESV)

.   The image of being tossed to and fro by winds and waves depicts a helpless vessel adrift in a storm. God's purpose is the opposite. For the believer in the Lord Jesus Christ, growth and maturation lead to the use of more stable terms in Scripture. By God's grace, His Spirit grows us *"...so that Christ may dwell in your hearts through faith--that you, being rooted and grounded in love..."* (Eph 3:17 ESV) The believer is *"...rooted and built up in him and established in the faith, just as you were taught, abounding in thanksgiving."* (Col 2:7 ESV)

.   Rooted, grounded, built up and established are quite the opposite of tossed to and fro and carried about. But, notice where we are to be solidly established. It is in Him, in His love, in the faith, and in thanksgiving. What if we are not so established? What can happen if we do not mature in the written word and the Living Word? Warnings abound in the sacred text. *"But I am afraid that as the serpent deceived Eve by his cunning, your thoughts will be led astray from a sincere and pure devotion to Christ. For if someone comes and proclaims another Jesus than the one we proclaimed, or if you receive a different spirit from the one you received, or if you accept a different gospel from the one you accepted, you put up with it readily enough."* (2Cor 11:3-4 ESV) Here, Paul's focus in on the deceivers and the instruments of deception. They present another Jesus, carefully crafted to approximate our Lord. They proclaim a gospel that pleases the fleshly mind, by a spirit that is not holy. They cater to the desires of the flesh, and of the mind. The response is predictable. Paul writes, *"I am astonished that you are so quickly deserting him who called you in the grace of Christ and are turning to a different gospel--not that there is another one, but there are some who trouble you and want to distort the gospel of Christ."* (Gal 1:6-7 ESV) In this, he shifts the focus to the targets of deception.

. The false message resonates with the unbeliever who seeks to assuage a pricked conscience with religious effort, or religious ritual. Those who are adrift are carried about with the ebb and flow of religious novelty. Paul warned Timothy, *"For the time is coming when people will not endure sound teaching, but having itching ears they will accumulate for themselves teachers to suit their own passions, and will turn away from listening to the truth and wander off into myths."* (2Tim 4:3-4 ESV) Peter spoke of the same danger, and warned true believers that they would be targets of the deceivers: *"But false prophets also arose among the people, just as there will be false teachers among you, who will secretly bring in destructive heresies, even denying the Master who bought them, bringing upon themselves swift destruction. And many will follow their sensuality, and because of them the way of truth will be blasphemed. And in their greed they will exploit you with false words. Their condemnation from long ago is not idle, and their destruction is not asleep."* (2Pet 2:1-3 ESV)

. There is a sinister note in Peter's warning, centered in the word *among*. The greater danger for the believer, and for the true Church, lies in what Paul termed the *brother so-called*, and what our Lord called wolves in sheep's clothing. Paul raised a similar warning in his charge to the Ephesian elders: *"Pay careful attention to yourselves and to all the flock, in which the Holy Spirit has made you overseers, to care for the church of God, which he obtained with his own blood. I know that after my departure fierce wolves will come in among you, not sparing the flock; and from among your own selves will arise men speaking twisted things, to draw away the disciples after them. Therefore be alert, remembering that for three years I did not cease night or day to admonish everyone with tears. And now I commend you to God and to the word of his grace, which is able to build you up and to give you the inheritance among all those who are sanctified."* (Acts 20:28-32 ESV) False teachers would arise from among the very ones recognized as elders in the body of believers. The tares sown among the wheat would bear their evil fruit, distorting the pure gospel. What was true in the first century has grown exponentially through the centuries of church history. The false church, proclaiming a false gospel and a false christ, overshadows the true body of Christ today.

. John affirmed the unregenerate nature of the false teachers. He wrote concerning them, *"They went out from us, but they were not of us; for if they had been of us, they would have continued with us. But they went out, that it might become plain that they all are not of us."* (1John 2:19 ESV) Like Judas, they shared the intimacy of the body they were out to destroy. In truth, throughout church history, persecution of true believers in the Lord Jesus Christ has sprung from the religious fervor of the persecutors. Saul, before his name was changed, fulfilled the words of our Lord, thinking he was doing God a favor in bringing believers to trial and death. Later, he wrote, *"Indeed, all who desire to live a godly life in Christ Jesus will be persecuted..."* (2Tim 3:12 ESV) Believers can expect to be lashed and buffeted by the storm through which they travel. Our refuge is not some uncomfortable fly-speck motel, but rather the Lord Himself, and His precious Word. John wrote, *"Let what you heard from the beginning abide in you. If what you heard from the beginning abides in you, then you too will abide in the Son and in the Father. And this is the promise that he made to us--eternal life. I write these things to you about those who are trying to deceive you."* (1John 2:24-26 ESV)

15

LINGERING LIGHTS

The temperature drops to near freezing. The calendar hovers in the winter portion of the year. The air is damp, and the chill penetrating. Unnoticed, the first snowflake plummets to the ground. Large, wet, half ice, half liquid, it splatters and vanishes. Its passing seems to chill the air even more, preparing the way for the multitude to follow.

Following the vanished scout they come, enormous flakes that swirl and jostle one another in their rush to cover the ground. They cool the air and the ground, and, falling faster than they can melt, they blanket the sleeping Earth with a clinging sheet and lumpy counterpane that draws another multitude with slipping feet and gaping mouths that alternately laugh and scream and lap the falling flakes.

An inch of snow upon the ground, the flakes abruptly cease to fall. Then, indiscriminately scooping hands compress the tatters of the winter quilt into frozen missiles flung, some randomly, and some with stinging accuracy. Dirty snowballs or snowy dirtballs, they fly in their appointed arcs, some to impact, some to miss, but all to vanish, though they leave a memory of their journey.

We find a similar pattern in space. Gigantic compared to their Earth-bound counterparts, but miniscule compared to moons and planets, these dirty snowballs or snowy dirtballs hurtle in their elliptical orbits through our solar system, loop around the sun, and vanish into oblivion. We call them comets.

The body or core of these wanderers has an average diameter of ten miles, and is composed of rock and dust in a matrix of ice and frozen gases. Comets appear first as dim, hazy lights in the night sky, their journey marked by a changing position in relation to the stars. As they approach the sun, they appear brighter, and, as the solar radiation melts the surface of the core, the comets develop a coma, or thin atmosphere, that the solar wind streams away behind the approaching mass, giving the comet an illuminated streamer, or tail of gas, dust and debris. This tail always streams away from the sun, fading as it dissipates, and gives the comet the appearance of a blunt arrow, always pointing in the direction of the sun. Its visible journey is brief in comparison to its time of orbit, but the aftermath of its passage gives a repeated testimony of its brief presence, a testimony that may last for centuries.

Earth's orbit regularly passes through the debris field left by passing comets. Dust particles and larger bits of debris slash into Earth's atmosphere at high speed. Friction generates heat, and in the presence of oxygen, the particles blaze with a momentary brilliance. Meteor showers, visible on a clear night, are in themselves spectacular, but are reminders of a brighter passage, a reminder that portends a return journey of the comet.

In our journey of life, people intersect our course, sometimes briefly, and yet leave lingering memories of their passage. They leave a testimony of their passage in wise or encouraging words, in exemplary behaviors, in honorable passage, or, conversely, in injuries and scars, pain and sorrow. Renewed encounters, or refreshed memories or significant dates or places bring flashes of rejoicing or despair. In our spiritual journey, the message of the comets resonates even more insistently.

Since creation, God has set way points that direct to Himself, and sent messengers, whose testimony has left a record that flashes brilliantly across the sky of our darkest times. The way points are many. ***"The heavens declare the glory of God, and the sky above proclaims his handiwork."*** (Psa 19:1 ESV) The orderly patterns of the celestial bodies in the universe attest to the reality, the wisdom and the glory of God. The vastness of the visible universe, with its mind-numbing distances, declare to the understanding mind the greatness of God and the smallness of ourselves. David writes, ***"When I look at your heavens, the work of your fingers, the moon and the stars, which you have set in place, what is man that you are mindful of him, and the son of man that you care for him?"*** (Psa 8:3-4 ESV) Indeed, once our attention shifts to ourselves, we find innumerable way points. Again, from the pen of David, ***"I praise you, for I am fearfully and wonderfully made. Wonderful are your works; my soul knows it very well."*** (Psa 139:14 ESV) The mind enabled by God's Holy Spirit to perceive not only the complexity of creation, but the Creator as well. To those with a mind blinded to spiritual truths, the testimony of creation gives a general revelation of God's glory, but the alienated mind suppresses that truth. Paul writes, ***"For what can be known about God is plain to them, because God has shown it to them. For his invisible attributes, namely, his eternal power and divine nature, have been clearly perceived, ever since the creation of the world, in the things that have been made. So they are without excuse."*** (Rom 1:19-20 ESV)

The general revelation of God found in creation is like the

pinpoint meteors that either flash as specks of light or a short streak, lasting only long enough for us to notice, but not enough to observe. However, there are slower-moving fireball meteors that catch and hold our vision. They move spectacularly across the sky, leaving a persistent image in our eyes and minds, and often leaving a visible contrail. These find their counterpart in the messengers of God, the prophets who proclaimed, "Thus saith the Lord."

In talking to the the leaders of Israel during His brief time on Earth, our Lord said of John the Baptist, *"He was a burning and shining lamp, and you were willing to rejoice for a while in his light."* (John 5:35 ESV) John did not write anything, but he proclaimed the gospel of the kingdom. Of John himself, the Scriptures say, *"He came as a witness, to bear witness about the light, that all might believe through him. He was not the light, but came to bear witness about the light."* (John 1:7-8 ESV)He was not the way, but a way point. John blazed across the sky of awareness of his time, and, although he wrote nothing, his testimony persisted beyond his presence. Well into the spread of the gospel in the early church, we find the residue of the testimony of John the Baptist.

Consider this meteor shower. The apostle Paul went to Corinth. So did Aquila and Priscilla. Being of the same trade, the three spent a year and a half working together, and declaring the gospel of the Lord Jesus Christ. Then, Paul set sail for Syria, and took Aquila and Priscilla with him. He left them at Ephesus, intending to rejoin them, as the Lord willed.

The gospel of grace then intersected with the gospel of the kingdom, and supplanted it. *"Now a Jew named Apollos, a native of Alexandria, came to Ephesus. He was an eloquent man, competent in the Scriptures. He had been instructed in the way of the Lord. And being fervent in spirit, he spoke and taught accurately the things concerning Jesus, though he knew only the baptism of John."* (Acts 18:24-25 ESV)

Apollos knew the Jewish Scriptures well. He was aware of the Light, but his knowledge was indirect. He knew the way point, but needed to know the Way.

Returning, Paul found the same residue of John's testimony at Ephesus: *"And it happened that while Apollos was at Corinth, Paul passed through the inland country and came to Ephesus. There he found some disciples. And he said to them, 'Did you receive the Holy Spirit when you believed?' And they said, 'No, we have not even heard that there is a Holy Spirit.' And he said, 'Into what then were you baptized?' They said, 'Into John's baptism.' And Paul said, 'John baptized with the baptism of repentance, telling the people to believe in the one who was to come after him, that is, Jesus.'"* (Acts 19:1-4 ESV)

Our Lord pointed out other way points. In His account of Lazarus and the rich man, we find the rich man pleading that Lazarus return from the grave to warn the brothers of the rich man concerning the suffering that lay beyond death apart from the grace of God. The response is instructive: *"And he said, 'Then I beg you, father, to send him to my father's house-- for I have five brothers--so that he may warn them, lest they also come into this place of torment.' But Abraham said, 'They have Moses and the Prophets; let them hear them.' And he said, 'No, father Abraham, but if someone goes to them from the dead, they will repent.' He said to him, 'If they do not hear Moses and the Prophets, neither will they be convinced if someone should rise from the dead.'"* (Luke 16:27-31 ESV) The way points are already set. "Let them hear" Moses and the prophets. Let them be attentive to the messengers who have already been sent.

We find another way point towering over the others. Peter goes beyond the spoken testimony, and underscores it as vital. *"And we have something more sure, the prophetic word, to which you will do well to pay attention as to a lamp shining in a dark place, until the day dawns and the morning star rises in your hearts, knowing this first of all, that no prophecy of Scripture comes from someone's own interpretation. For no prophecy was ever produced by the will of man, but men spoke from God as they were carried along by the Holy Spirit."* (2Pet 1:19-21 ESV) Peter himself was a meteor, an eyewitness to the majesty of Christ. However, the Word of God provides the more reliable way point.

Recall the pattern of the comet. It comes into view, and, as it loops around the sun in the perihelial portion of its orbit, it is a shining arrow pointing to the sun. So are the lights God has sent for our direction. John the Baptist was not the Light, but pointed to the Light. Moses and the prophets filled the same role. The Scriptures, that Peter terms the *more sure...prophetic word,"* are the consummate pointers.

After His resurrection, our Lord joined two disciples who were trudging toward Emmaus. In the interchange, as they journeyed together, he brought into focus for them that which they had already heard: *"And he said to them, 'O foolish ones, and slow of heart to believe all that the prophets have spoken! Was it not necessary that the Christ should suffer these things and enter into his glory?' And beginning with Moses and all the Prophets, he interpreted to them in all the Scriptures the things concerning himself."* (Luke 24:25-27 ESV) The Scriptures they had were sufficient to point them to Christ. Later, He expanded the reference beyond Moses and the prophets: *"Then he said to them, 'These are my words that I spoke to you while I was still with you, that everything written about me in the Law of Moses and the Prophets and the Psalms must be fulfilled.'"* (Luke 24:44 ESV)

Christ had had the same discussion with the leaders of the Jews. In the same conversation in which he spoke of John the Baptist as a *burning and shining lamp*, we read, *"You search the Scriptures because you think that in them you have eternal life; and it is they that bear witness about me, yet you refuse to come to me that you may have life."* (John 5:39-40 ESV) Their refusal of the testimony of the Scriptures led to their rejection of the One to whom they pointed. They suppressed the Truth in unrighteousness. Jesus told them, *"Do not think that I will accuse you to the Father. There is one who accuses you: Moses, on whom you have set your hope. For if you believed Moses, you would believe me; for he wrote of me. But if you do not believe his writings, how will you believe my words?"* (John 5:45-47 ESV)

To those whose understanding God opened, the result was radically different. At the beginning of our Lord's earthly ministry, we read, *"Philip found Nathanael and said to him, 'We have found him of whom Moses in the Law and also the prophets wrote, Jesus of Nazareth, the son of Joseph.'"* (John 1:45 ESV) At His birth, the magi were guided by the star above, and the Scriptures below. When they asked where Jesus was, the officials consulted the scrolls to find the location prophesied. Shining through the darkness, increasing in brilliance, all the lights, whether prophets, apostles or the Scriptures themselves, point to the Son. However, the testimony lingers.

In each generational orbit, the earth passes through the residue of witness left by those of previous generations. The witness of the Scriptures combines with the witness of saints of earlier times, and all point to the Son of God.

Believers today are continuing lights, bearing witness to the reality of the Son. Jesus prayed for His own: *"I do not ask for these only, but also for those who will believe in me through their word..."* (John 17:20 ESV) After His resurrection, He told them, *"But you will receive power when the Holy Spirit has come upon you, and you will be my witnesses in Jerusalem and in all Judea and Samaria, and to the end of the earth."* (Acts 1:8 ESV) His purpose for His own in this world resonates through the pen of the apostle Paul: *"...that you may be blameless and innocent, children of God without*

blemish in the midst of a crooked and twisted generation, among whom you shine as lights in the world, holding fast to the word of life..." (Php 2:15-16 ESV)

Lights in the darkness, we point to the Light of the world. As we fade from the place of brightness, do we pause to consider the contrail of witness we may leave? Will there be flashes of testimony that linger for other generations?

16

PAY STREAK

California's Klamath River has a gold-producing history. It winds through the Klamath Mountains that straddle the border between Oregon and California, on its way to the Pacific Ocean, and, through rapids and pools, floods and trickles, it trails a plume of placer gold that is constantly refreshed and redistributed, waiting to reward, and perhaps enrich, the diligent seeker. As it roars seaward during the floods of Winter and Spring, the winding river takes shortcuts, straightening bends, gouging hillsides, swallowing whole landslides, and using accumulated bowlders to crush lesser stones to sand, freeing any imprisoned gold they may contain. Sand and soil are sifted and swirled, and gold the weather has freed is mingled with that which the river has pounded free, and the treasure is carried by the rushing water until the river pauses to rest, or slows to deal with obstacles. In its haste to move on, the water leaves a portion of its burden in gravel bars, or under bowlders, or carelessly dropped in crevices. It little notices its diminished hoard. There is always more, waiting to be torn from its source, to be dropped again later.

The placer miner, whether using a shovel and pan, or a sluice box or rocker, highbanker or dredge, follows the same search pattern. A gravel bar may be a hundred feet wide or more, and a quarter of a mile in length. It will be a tangle of bowlders and rocks, gravel and sand, silt and clay, and, yes, perhaps gold. Scattered throughout the deposit may be wood, bones, bottles, and other evidences of human occupation upstream. The experienced miner will survey this debris field, imagining where the rushing flood waters ran their fastest, and where the swirling eddies of slower water might have paused, dropping their burden of gold. The practiced eye can visualize the winter cataract where summer shows only dry stones. The watercourse imagined, the miner begins the labor of discovery.

Either mentally or physically, gold seeker lays out a systematic gridwork that divides the section of the gravel bar into an organized pattern. Wherever grid lines cross, the miner digs a sampling hole. The process is tedious. In most cases, the gravel bar is covered with an unproductive overburden that might vary in depth from a few inches to a several feet. The upper layer can be scraped aside, then, digging will reveal the soil profile. In sampling dry material, a classifier will separate the coarser rock and gravel from the sand, soil, and silt that can then be washed in the gold pan. Layer by layer, the miner notes the quality of the heavier material that remains in the pan. Black sand? A hopeful sign. Colors? Those pinpoints of gold that gleam in the sunlight, but seem to be gossamer promises? Better. A flake of gold? Or two? Better yet.

The sample hole may be four or five feet deep, and a dozen or more gold pans of material excavated and separated from the coarser gravel may take an hour or more to process. Then, fill in the hole, move a few feet away, and start the process again. And again. And again, until a pattern of sampling shows where in the seemingly endless field of rubble, or under it, will give the greatest reward for the labor. Careful sampling will establish the line and depth of the greatest placer concentration. That is the pay streak.

That plume of gold, that treasure trail, will extend upstream beyond the gravel bar, continuing under the river, with its richest pockets in the depths of the stream. The diligent searcher will come, at last, to the source from which the placer gold originated. He may find the seam, the mother lode. The placer gold residue will be but a thread of evidence that has pointed, and eventually led, to the true treasure.

So it is with God. Scattered in the debris field of human thought we find fragments of wisdom that are of far greater worth. Though mingled with pretty pebbles of worthless wit, or colorful chips of intellectual inanity, these hidden treasures of eternal wisdom derive from a source far higher than the human mind. They are the residue of the true knowledge of God, fragmented and deformed by the arrogance of human chaos, and coated with the grime of corrupt minds. Those harboring this residual wisdom are lauded as wise beyond their peers, as though those fragments of divine truth impart worth to the abundant foolishness surrounding them, as scattered flakes of gold cause a gravel bar to be deemed rich.

Those bits of wisdom stand as a testimony of the existence of the Source of wisdom, God Himself. Paul, by the Spirit, notes in Romans 1:20, ***"For his invisible attributes, namely, his eternal power and divine nature, have been clearly perceived, ever since the creation of the world, in the things that have been made. So they are without excuse."*** (ESV) But, with their understanding blinded, people trudge over the gravel bar of life, unaware of the eternal treasure that surrounds them, or else disdaining it. On a more sinister level, there are those ***"... who by their unrighteousness suppress the truth."*** (Rom 1:18 ESV) They labor to invent ***"...another Jesus than the one we proclaimed, or if you receive a different spirit from the one you received, or if you accept a different gospel..."*** (2Cor 11:4 ESV) Indeed, the striving against God is as tedious as the labor of the prospector searching for earthly treasure.

The book of Job, written over four thousand years ago, recounts the extreme measures employed by treasure seekers of his day, and still in use today: ***"Man puts an end to darkness and searches out to the farthest limit the ore in gloom and deep darkness. He opens shafts in a valley away from where anyone lives; they are forgotten by travelers; they hang in the air, far away from mankind; they swing to and fro. Man puts his hand to the flinty rock and overturns mountains by the roots. He cuts out channels in the rocks, and his eye sees every precious thing. He dams up the streams so that they do not trickle, and the thing that is hidden he brings out to light."*** (Job 28:3-4, 9-11 ESV) We have here a portrait of the toil of the treasure seeker, burrowing in the earth, dangling over a precipice, dancing back and forth over the face of cliff or a canyon wall, and then chipping a tunnel through solid rock, or turning aside a river or stream, in order to search its muddy bottom.

To what purpose? The search for riches has an ominous end: ***"Do not toil to acquire wealth; be discerning enough to desist. When your eyes light on it, it is gone, for suddenly it sprouts wings, flying like an eagle toward heaven."*** (Prov 23:4-5 ESV) I read an article recently about a man who found a twelve-pound gold nugget. He spoke of it to very few people, and only granted an interview, showed the nugget, and allowed it to be photographed on condition of absolute anonymity. Why? The joy of finding leads to the pride of having, which quickly changes to the fear of losing. Our Lord cautioned, ***"Do not lay up for yourselves treasures on earth, where moth and rust destroy and where thieves break in and steal, but lay up for yourselves treasures in heaven, where neither moth nor rust destroys and where thieves do not break in and steal."*** (Mat 6:19-20 ESV)

God's desire is that we would be drawn to apply that same striving diligence to the acquisition of true treasure. Note the call to an eager pursuit of His treasure in Proverbs, chapter two: *"...making your ear attentive to wisdom and inclining your heart to understanding; yes, if you call out for insight and raise your voice for understanding, if you seek it like silver and search for it as for hidden treasures, then you will understand the fear of the LORD and find the knowledge of God. For the LORD gives wisdom; from his mouth come knowledge and understanding; he stores up sound wisdom for the upright; he is a shield to those who walk in integrity, guarding the paths of justice and watching over the way of his saints. Then you will understand righteousness and justice and equity, every good path; for wisdom will come into your heart, and knowledge will be pleasant to your soul..."* (Prov 2:2-10 ESV) The residual pay streak of God's wisdom is used by His Spirit to draw the one whose eyes are opened to the true worth of those nuggets of truth to His source of revealed knowledge, the Scriptures, and through them, to Christ Jesus, *"...in whom are hidden all the treasures of wisdom and knowledge."* (Col 2:3 ESV) Listen again to Job: *"But where shall wisdom be found? And where is the place of understanding? Man does not know its worth, and it is not found in the land of the living. It cannot be bought for gold, and silver cannot be weighed as its price."* (Job 28:12-15 ESV) The Spirit uses the pen of James to answer Job's question: *"If any of you lacks wisdom, let him ask God, who gives generously to all without reproach, and it will be given him."* (James 1:5 ESV) Then, in Christ, we are to bring the same diligence to the mining of the deep riches of God's Word: *"Do your best to present yourself to God as one approved, a worker who has no need to be ashamed, rightly handling the word of truth."* (2Tim 2:15 ESV)

My wife and I enjoy the labor and the reward of prospecting. There is a thrill of that flash of gold in a rich pan. But, we keep it in perspective, in the light of the eternal reality that it is only pavement. Far greater and of far greater duration, is the thrill of seeing with deeper understanding a gleaming nugget of truth and grace in His word, as His Spirit guides us into the truth that He has for us.

17

THERE IS A WAY THAT SEEMS RIGHT

Chores were done that sunny morning. I was engaged in the work assignment for the day. Our back hay field was being overrun by bracken fern fronds that towered over the grass and clover, and it was my responsibility to trudge through that ten acres, gathering armloads of the bracken and piling it under the firs that formed the field's back border. A seventh grader's mind is easily turned from its focus, and I had been distracted by bugs, flowers and birds. Along a fence, I had watched a small weasel stalk and slay a field mouse,and in that bit of entertainment, I had easily gained a half-hour rest from my task, hidden from view by the brow of the hill.

Now, as the sun approached zenith, the warmth of the day made me long for a shady respite under the timber, but I had already cleared the lower portion of the field, and was working in plain sight of the kitchen window. Work day or weekend, habit took my dad to his regular coffee break, and I was compelled to keep trudging and gathering until I got high enough on the hill that the hay barn hid me. The cow barn was a low-roofed structure, and the view from the house was unobstructed. Another two acres, and I could dawdle.

I was distracted now by an unusual sight for our location. The flight path to the Portland airport was just north of us. We were used to seeing passenger planes descending toward the runway 20 miles down the Columbia River, most of them four engine propeller-driven craft lumbering earthward. Occasionally, one of the new jet liners roared over. But today, a bug-eyed helicopter clattered into view, scarcely a hundred feet above the treetops. It was off the flight path, low enough for me to see the pilot clearly, and headed due east. I waved at the pilot as the copter, looking very much like a dragonfly with skis, popped overhead, and faded into the distance. It was a good excuse to stand upright, stretch tired muscles, and ignore the bracken.

I had nearly finished the fern gathering when I heard the chatter of the helicopter on its return trip. It surged low over the trees and into view, its rotor pops echoing off the barn as it approached. I looked up to watch its passage, and saw that it had a long basket fastened to one of its skis. I wondered.

I got my wondering answered Monday morning. The desk one row over and three back from mine was empty. Billy's desk. Billy was my best friend.

The story came out in bits and pieces. Billy's family had been to the top of Larch Mountain for a birthday celebration. The mountain had a basalt viewpoint, Sherrard Point, accessible by a trail that led to the promontory that overlooked the caldera far below. For safety, workers had drilled into the stone, placed posts, and strung a fence to keep people back from the edge of a thousand-foot vertical drop-off.

Billy's balsa airplane, caught by a fitful breeze, had blown over the fence, and lodged in the branches of a stunted tree that had a tenuous hold on the cliff's edge. Ignoring the tacit warning of the barrier, and the weathered warning sign, he scrambled over, and, clinging to a dead branch to balance himself, he placed one foot out on a moss-covered rock. As he leaned out to reach for the airplane, his weight shifted over the rounded face of the rock. The moss peeled away, the branch broke off in his hand, and Billy was gone.

I had never been to a funeral. Death had always been a distant concept, abstract and irrelevant. The open casket at the front of the room was concrete, its reality hard and hammering at the core of my being, bringing the first stirrings of dissatisfaction with self-centered littleness, and apprehension of an awareness whose comfortable curtains had been torn away.

Barriers are beneficial. Guard rails, warning signs, prohibitions, and social mores form the waypoints of our daily journey. All are challenged, circumvented, ridiculed or ignored daily, often to the grief of those who fail or refuse to honor them.

Boundaries, restrictions, prohibitions and limitations are, at the same time, challenges against which we rebel. They are viewed as obstacles to be surmounted, to be overcome by whatever means we can invent. If they are too large to get around, our selfish nature sulks, complains, and watches for an opportunity. Listen to the cry of suffering Job, against God: ***"You put my feet in the stocks and watch all my paths; you set a limit for the soles of my feet."***(Job 13:27 ESV) The first part underscores Job's irritation with the working of God in his life. Stocks imprison the feet, so the one shackled cannot walk where he would.

Whether literal or figurative, we find these limitations scattered throughout Scripture. They are rooted in the sovereignty of God, as He works out His good pleasure in those who are His own. *"...for it is God who works in you, both to will and to work for his good pleasure."* Php 2:13 ESV)

It is that sovereignty against which our flesh rebels. *"For the desires of the flesh are against the Spirit, and the desires of the Spirit are against the flesh, for these are opposed to each other, to keep you from doing the things you want to do."* Gal 5:17 ESV) Our flesh, attuned to this world system with its values, craves the temporal, the sensual, the immediate gratification. The orchestrator of this *Cosmos Diabolicus,* the prince of this world, has beset us with a minefield of enticements that appeal to our flesh. Our natural cravings seek *"...the lust of the flesh, and the lust of the eyes, and the pride of life..."* (1John 2:16) These categories, which are pleasure, possessions and prestige, hold all the snares set for our souls. Glittering baubles catch our eye. We want...we reach...we fall.

Protection is built into the prescriptions and the proscriptions of God. Note the second part of Job's lament: *"...you have set a limit for the soles of my feet."* We see the prescriptive "walk here," as well as the proscriptive "don't walk there." David, by the Spirit, put it this way: *"Blessed is the man who walks not in the counsel of the wicked, nor stands in the way of sinners, nor sits in the seat of scoffers; but his delight is in the law of the LORD, and on his law he meditates day and night."* (Psalm 1:1-2 ESV) Here again, we note the boundary imposed by the Lord between verses one and two.

Our problem is our fleshly willfulness. We think we know best. We put confidence in our own wisdom, our own thoughts. We view boundaries as being for others. We trust ourselves, and rely on our own strength. Solomon, in advising his son, cautioned against such foolishness: *"Trust in the LORD with all your heart, and do not lean on your own understanding. In all your ways acknowledge him, and he will make straight your paths. Be not wise in your own eyes; fear the LORD, and turn away from evil."* (Prov 3:5-7 ESV) He underscored the warning in Proverbs 14:12 very pointedly: *"There is a way that seems right to a man, but its end is the way to death."* (ESV)

We find the same dual admonition in a repeated warning in the Old Testament, where God cautions His people to "...turn not to the right or to the left," either of which would lead away from the path He had marked out for them. But, He knew their wandering ways, as He knows ours. *"And your ears shall hear a word behind you, saying, "This is the way, walk in it," when you turn to the right or when you turn to the left."* (Isa 30:21 ESV) We see in this passage the exclusivity of *the way*, and the inevitability of wandering in *when you turn...*

God cites the obedience of creation to His sovereignty to highlight humanity's rebellion. Consider the waters that once inundated the earth: *"He has inscribed a circle on the face of the waters at the boundary between light and darkness."* (Job 26:10 ESV) *"You set a boundary that they may not pass, so that they might not again cover the earth."* (Psalm 104:9 ESV) *"Do you not fear me? declares the LORD. Do you not tremble before me? I placed the sand as the boundary for the sea, a perpetual barrier that it cannot pass; though the waves toss, they cannot prevail; though they roar, they cannot pass over it."* (Jer 26:10 ESV) In contrast, we see God's admonition: *"... beware lest you act corruptly by making a carved image for yourselves, in the form of any figure, the likeness of male or female, the likeness of any animal that is on the earth, the likeness of any winged bird that flies in the air, the likeness of anything that creeps on the ground, the likeness of any fish that is in the water under the earth. And beware lest you raise your eyes to heaven, and when you see the sun and the moon and the stars, all the host of heaven, you be drawn away and bow down to them and serve them, things that the LORD your God has allotted to all the peoples under the whole heaven."* (Deut 4:16-19 ESV) Then, we see the response of humanity: ***"Claiming to be wise, they became fools, and exchanged the glory of the immortal God for images resembling mortal man and birds and animals and creeping things...they exchanged the truth about God for a lie and worshiped and served the creature rather than the Creator, who is blessed forever! Amen. "*** (Rom 1:22-23 ESV)

For the believer in the Lord Jesus Christ, there is an escape from the snares of the devil. Again, it is in the prescription set down by God: ***"But I say, walk by the Spirit, and you will not gratify the desires of the flesh."*** (Gal 5:16 ESV) Responsive to the Spirit of God indwelling us, we are led in paths of righteousness for His name's sake. The path of righteousness is Christ Himself, who said, ***"I am the way, and the truth, and the life. No one comes to the Father except through me."*** (John 14:6 ESV) Note again the exclusivity of **the way.** He is the "narrow way, the way of righteousness. He is our boundary. ***"For we are his workmanship, created in Christ Jesus for good works, which God prepared beforehand, that we should walk in them."*** (Eph 2:10 ESV)

18

Greedy Birds

At various times over the past few decades, for one reason or another, we have kept one kind of fowl or another. We have raised chickens of all sizes and varieties, as well as ducks, peafowl, geese, guineas, doves, pigeons and quail. No matter the variety, we have found them to be greedy. Selfish pigs in feathers, they provide endless entertainment in their mindless drive to get just a little more than the next bird, or to take what another bird has.

Our ducks would bury their bills in the food dish, stuffing their mouths and throats until they had to stand back, gyrate their necks in an effort to swallow, and then run to the water trough to wash it down. Then they would run back to the food dish, and climb over the backs of those gathered around it, forcing others out of their way. They had plenty of food to go around, and when they could hold no more, they would waddle away with sagging crops, leaving some for later. But their stampede to be first and to get the most was a morning ritual.

Chickens were even more entertaining. They relished table scraps. I was naughty. I would select a morsel that was too large to be swallowed whole, and toss it into the chicken yard. Bedlam ensued. Flapping and squawking, hens ran from all quarters to be the first to reach the new food. The first one to reach it seized it in her beak, and ran, dodging and circling, trying to get away from all of the other chickens, who were determined to catch her, and take what she had. She could not run and swallow, so eventually she would stop, drop the morsel, and try to peck it into more manageable pieces. Wrong choice. Another hen would seize the prize, and the race would start afresh, with a new quarry. Depending on the durability of the tidbit, one scrap was good for several minutes of laughter.

Free-range chickens were even funnier. I didn't have to provide anything to get them started. They found their own objects of the chase, providing humor of a darker sort. One time, in a grotesque twist on the "I want whatever you have" quest, it was amusing to see first one chicken, and eventually the whole flock, chasing a hen who ran with a half-swallowed garter snake, still writhing, hanging out of her beak. Another time, it was a mouse, hind legs and tail sticking out of a distended beak, that became the object of pursuit. Those chases didn't last long, as it was difficult, if not impossible, to breathe around half-swallowed prey. Winded and reeling, the hapless hen would struggle to finish her meal, while the others mobbed her, seizing what part they might, and struggling vainly to dislodge the vanishing victim. The poor hen was then dragged staggering about the field, unable either to swallow or disgorge.

Funny? Yes, in a morbid fashion, except when it ended with the death of the poor hen who had captured what turned out to be her last meal. In either case, the episodes are instructive. We have that same greedy streak within ourselves.

Offer a child a cookie from a full plate, and watch as the hand circles, pauses, and then takes the biggest one. We have a built-in more-for-me, king-on-the-mountain bent that reveals itself in the most awkward, most frustrating ways, when we pride ourselves that we have outgrown selfishness.

Consider the disciples of Jesus, gathered with Him in the upper room for the Passover meal, before His betrayal and crucifixion. Two significant, but contrasting scenes stand before us in Scripture. Their order of occurrence is not clear, but their juxtaposition is startling.

Luke gives us the first vignette. Jesus opened the time together by telling them, *"I have earnestly desired to eat this Passover with you before I suffer."* (Luke 22:15 ESV) Leading up to this feast day that foreshadowed the offering of the Lamb of God, He had told them several times that he would be betrayed and killed. The mention of His suffering should have resonated with His earlier words. It did not. Next, He said, *"But behold, the hand of him who betrays me is with me on the table."* (Luke 22:21 ESV) Imagine them looking at each other, each denying culpability. *"And they began to question one another, which of them it could be who was going to do this."* (Luke 22-23 ESV) But look at the impact of the "Not I!" attitude. Their focus is on self and innocence, rather than centering on the looming suffering of the Savior. That self-focus led directly to the incongruous part that followed: *"A dispute also arose among them, as to which of them was to be regarded as the greatest. And he said to them, 'The kings of the Gentiles exercise lordship over them, and those in authority over them are called benefactors. But not so with you. Rather, let the greatest among you become as the youngest, and the leader as one who serves.'"* (Luke 22:24-26 ESV) Betrayal and suffering fade into insignificance as the disciples embark on a campaign of self-importance.

Self-promotion seems to be thematic in the circle of disciples closest to Jesus. Earlier in Luke's gospel, we read, *"An argument arose among them as to which of them was the greatest. But Jesus, knowing the reasoning of their hearts, took a child and put him by his side and said to them, 'Whoever receives this child in my name receives me, and whoever receives me receives him who sent me. For he who is least among you all is the one who is great.'"* (Luke 9:46-48 ESV) When James and John desired the most important positions for themselves in Christs kingdom, the positions of highest honor, the other ten disciples were indignant. Why? Might it be they wanted those positions for themselves?

Notice how Jesus responds in each of these disputes. In each case, He lays out before them the way of humility. Be as the youngest. Be as the lowliest. Be as a child. *"Whoever humbles himself like this child is the greatest in the kingdom of heaven."* (Mat 18:4 ESV) *"If anyone would be first, he must be last of all and servant of all."* (Mark 9:35 ESV)

Jesus uses object lessons to convey spiritual realities. The upper room image He presents to reprimand the disciples' selfish ambition is a particularly sharp one. Non-Jews, which in Scripture are called Gentiles, were held in contempt by Jews of Jesus' day. The disciples are not to emulate the rulers of the Gentiles, but rather seek the position of least significance. Christ's message to his followers is simple: Do not use foreign authorities as role models. There were plenty in Israel in those days who illustrated what not to be. Roman authorities strutted everywhere.

Jesus uses Himself as the contrasting image. Earlier in the day, the disciples had asked where they would eat the Passover. Jesus gave interesting instructions. *"And he sent two of his disciples and said to them, 'Go into the city, and a man carrying a jar of water will meet you. Follow him, and wherever he enters, say to the master of the house, "The Teacher says, Where is my guest room, where I may eat the Passover with my disciples?" And he will show you a large upper room furnished and ready; there prepare for us.'"* (Mark 14:13-15 ESV)

Embedded in this instruction is an image of humility. It was not the task of a male servant to carry water. In a male-superior society such as theirs, it was the duty of a female to take the water jars or pitchers to the water source. Even in this mundane chore, we find an image of the humility of Christ, Who took on Himself the form of a servant.

The description of the upper room is equally important. It was ample for their needs. But, most significant to our meditation are the words *furnished and ready*. It would not be a stretch of credulity to follow the servant up to the upper room, and watch him set the pitcher of water in the basin, and lay out the towels, ready for the necessary cleansing of the guests.

When Jesus and the disciples were gathered later, the meal having been prepared, we see the contrasting vignette. Jesus takes the image of the man carrying water even further. It was the duty of the lowest-ranking servant to wash the feet of the guests at a feast. The servants of the house in which Jesus and His disciples were gathered did not come with the room. The disciples, as we have seen, were too bound up in self-importance to think of dirty feet.

"Jesus, knowing that the Father had given all things into his hands, and that he had come from God and was going back to God, rose from supper. He laid aside his outer garments, and taking a towel, tied it around his waist. Then he poured water into a basin and began to wash the disciples' feet and to wipe them with the towel that was wrapped around him." (John 13:3-5 ESV) No disciple was willing to stoop to serve. But, in the ultimate demonstration of humility, the Lord of Glory laid aside the teacher's robe, and donned the servants towel. The Creator served the creature.

This modeling of servanthood pictured a greater laying aside revealed through the pen of the apostle Paul. **"Have this mind among yourselves, which is yours in Christ Jesus, who,** *though he was in the form of God, did not count equality with God a thing to be grasped, but made himself nothing, taking the form of a servant..."* (Php 2:5-7 ESV) He washed their feet. The scene was not without controversy or pathos. Peter, unwilling to wash anyone's feet himself, resisted having his own feet washed. What must have run through Judas's mind as Jesus washed his feet, knowing Judas had already bargained to betray Him?

Jesus next resumed the teacher's position. *"When he had washed their feet and put on his outer garments and resumed his place, he said to them, 'Do you understand what I have done to you? You call me Teacher and Lord, and you are right, for so I am. If I then, your Lord and Teacher, have washed your feet, you also ought to wash one another's feet. For I have given you an example, that you also should do just as I have done to you.'"* (John 13:12-15 ESV) Their thoughts were still wrapped up in the towel. Their focus was on the object, not on the spiritual lesson underlying it. Their thoughts were on the literal, not the symbolic.

Indeed, before Jesus asked them whether they had understood what He had done, He told them that they would not. When Peter resisted having his feet washed, *"Jesus answered him, 'What I am doing you do not understand now, but afterward you will understand.'"* (John 13:7 ESV) It would be weeks later when they, indwelt by God's Holy Spirit, would see beyond basin and the towel to the life of service to which they, and we, are called, as the Spirit opened their understanding of spiritual truths. It is only through the washing Christ provides that we enter into the fellowship with God that is the foundation of fellowship with one another, the fellowship of the love of God. It is that superhuman, sacrificial love that consistently and actively seeks the best interest of the object of that love. It does not have its source in us, but *"...God's love has been poured into our hearts through the Holy Spirit who has been given to us."* (Rom 5:5 ESV) That love of God, flowing through us, is the testimony of the body of believers. Jesus, speaking to His disciples, underscores that reality: *"By this all people will know that you are my disciples, if you have love for one another."* (John 13:35 ESV)

Remember He had said they were not to pattern themselves after the authority figures of the nations. Instead, He had given them, and us, another model to follow. Paul was part of the fulfillment of the statement, *"but afterward you will understand."* He writes *"Do not be conformed to this world, but be transformed by the renewal of your mind, that by testing you may discern what is the will of God, what is good and acceptable and perfect. For by the grace given to me I say to everyone among you not to think of himself more highly than he ought to think, but to think with sober judgment, each according to the measure of faith that God has assigned."* (Rom 12:2-3 ESV) Do not be like the world, he says. Apart from God's Holy Spirit within us, applying God's Word by God's grace to the hearts of God's own, he might as well ask the chickens not to act like chickens. Our natural drive is to be like, not to be different.

To the believers at Ephesus, *"I do not cease to give thanks for you, remembering you in my prayers, that the God of our Lord Jesus Christ, the Father of glory, may give you a spirit of wisdom and of revelation in the knowledge of him, having the eyes of your hearts enlightened, that you may know what is the hope to which he has called you, what are the riches of his glorious inheritance in the saints..."* (Eph 1:16-18 ESV) His prayer for those believers trickles down to us, and holds the key to standing out as different from the world, with its focus on self. It is the Spirit, through the Word, who opens our ability to understand the whole concept of humility, of servanthood, pictured in the washing of the disciples' feet. Only through His ministry in us, the ministry of making us like Christ, can we be emptied of self, and have the beseechings of grace become our reality: *"Do nothing from rivalry or conceit, but in humility count others more significant than yourselves. Let each of you look not only to his own interests, but also to the interests of others. Have this mind among yourselves, which is yours in Christ Jesus..."* (Php 2:3-5 ESV) What an opposite image we see here, in contrast to the attitude prevailing in the world.

Can we fall under the influence of the mindset of the chickens? John writes of one who did: *"I have written something to the church, but Diotrephes, who likes to put himself first, does not acknowledge our authority. So if I come, I will bring up what he is doing, talking wicked nonsense against us. And not content with that, he refuses to welcome the brothers, and also stops those who want to and puts them out of the church."* (1John 1:9-10 ESV) The drive for more prestige, more applause, more authority, more power can send us scrambling to keep what we have seized, and can choke us. Solomon warns us that *"When pride comes, then comes disgrace, but with the humble is wisdom."* (Pro 11:2 ESV)

Should there be competition within the body of Christ? Paul thinks so. He encourages it, but in a focused fashion: *"Love one another with brotherly affection. Outdo one another in showing honor."* (Rom 12:10 ESV) Imagine the impact of a love-driven, Spirit-controlled, Christ-honoring contest to out-serve one another. How could that be possible? Peter tells us what is needed: *"Finally, all of you, have unity of mind, sympathy, brotherly love, a tender heart, and a humble mind."* (1Pet 3:8 ESV) He also tells us the source: *"His divine power has granted to us all things that pertain to life and godliness, through the knowledge of him who called us to his own glory and excellence, by which he has granted to us his precious and very great promises, so that through them you may become partakers of the divine nature, having escaped from the corruption that is in the world because of sinful desire."* (2Pet 1:3-4 ESV) Paul gives us the key to avoiding a fowl existence of selfishness: *"But I say, walk by the Spirit, and you will not gratify*

the desires of the flesh." (Gal 5:16 ESV) Walk responsive to the Spirit of God within, as He leads us in paths of righteousness. Pattern our behavior, our relationships and our aspirations after His leading. It spares us many a featherbrained kerfuffle.

19

SALT WATER

During World War II, the crew of a B-17 Flying Fortress ferrying Captain Eddie Rickenbacker to an undisclosed location survived a wet landing in the South Pacific, and drifted in life rafts for weeks under the oppressive tropical sun. They saved little from the aircraft beyond a few oranges. When the plane sank, they were left with no food supply, and worse, no drinking water. During their twenty-three days adrift, the only drinking water they had came from the few rain squalls that pelted them. They were lost at sea, wave-tossed somewhere in the 68 million square miles of the biggest ocean on earth. Tormented by deeply burned skin that blistered and ulcerated, tortured by hunger, driven mad by thirst, and surrounded by sharks, eight men strained their eyes for signs of land, for search planes, or for ships that might bring rescue.

Some days, they spotted clouds in the distance, and watched as rain squalls passed them by. Their water ration, when they had any, was limited to the capacity of a flare shell. It was just enough to keep them on the borderline of insanity. It fanned the flames of thirst, but did not quench it.

One man of the crew scooped a handful of sea water and drank it. It was warm and salty, but it was wet. Captain Rickenbacker, the dominant member of the castaways, reprimanded all of them, warning of the dangers of salt water. The engineer, though, merely hid his sea water consumption. The effect of his desperate efforts to assuage his thirst was his doom. Salt water hastened his dehydration. He drank, but was never satisfied. He was left with a deeper craving instead. The more he drank, the more he wanted. It killed him. Of the eight, he alone was buried at sea.

Many things in this world stir up insatiable cravings in us. A little kindles an appetite for more, and more does not satisfy. The very act of trying something is the spark that flares into a raging inferno that engulfs us, and has the capacity to destroy us, and others. The ever-widening categories of dependency and addiction are modern words for what Scripture terms slavery and bondage. Paul, in the seventh of Romans, terms these things the law of sin that dwells within our flesh.

God's call to those trapped in futile pursuits resonates to us today: *"Ho, everyone who thirsts, come to the water; and he who has no silver, come buy grain and eat. Yes, come buy grain, wine and milk without silver and with no price. Why do you weigh out silver for that which is not bread, and your labor for what never satisfies? Listen carefully to Me and eat the good; and let your soul delight itself in fatness."* (Isa 55:1-2) What do we exchange for that which does not satisfy? In truth, all of our resources are at risk, and, apart from the wisdom of God, they will be consumed completely. Our finances, our energy, our minds, our relationships and our very lives can be spent in futile pursuits. What is it that does not, and indeed cannot satisfy?

John, in his first epistle, gives us three categories of empty pursuit that take, and never give: **"Do not love the world nor the things in the world. If anyone loves the world, the love of the Father is not in him, because all that which is in the world: the lust of the flesh, and the lust of the eyes, and the pride of life, is not of the Father, but is of the world."** (1John 2:15-16) These three, *the lust of the flesh, and the lust of the eyes, and the pride of life,* shimmer before us, gossamer mirages, rainbow's ends that flee before us, yet linger oh, so near. Empty bubbles that dance around us, we chase them, and should we catch one, we hold it for a moment, and then its emptiness strikes us. Pleasure, possessions and prestige all fail to satisfy.

John's admonition rings down through the centuries to us today. "Love not...the things that are in the world," the *Cosmos Diabolicus*. To love the things of the world is to devote everything to getting as much as possible, no matter the cost. Initially, a little seems enough. But, all three have the capacity to enslave. The one taken captive by any or all three of the lusts John mentions finds the reality of Isaiah 44:20: **"Feeding on ashes, a deceived heart turns him aside, and he does not deliver his soul, nor say, Is there not a lie in my right hand?"**

"How much money is enough?"

"A little bit more than I have!"

That exchange expands to embrace all of the lusts John mentioned. It is always, "A little bit more than I have." A little more pleasure. A little more treasure. A little more applause. That which seemed satisfactory is now inadequate. Solomon, in writing his book of wisdom, gave a stark comparison: **"Sheol and destruction are never satisfied, so the eyes of man are never satisfied."** (Pro 27:20) In Proverbs chapter 30, Agur speaks of four things that are never satisfied, that never have said, "Enough!" The fourth one is fire. In the same way, the fire of desire for any of the things in the world system is never satisfied.

We are born with that fire smoldering deep within us. It was kindled by our first parents in the Garden of Eden: *"And the woman saw that the tree was good for food, and that it was pleasant to the eyes, and the tree was desirable to make one wise. And she took of its fruit and ate; and she also gave to her husband with her, and he ate."* (Gen 3:6) In one enticement, all three categories of desire burst into flame. Satan's underlying temptation was, "Declare your independence. Be your own god." Adam and Eve responded to anti-God counsel, and the result has engulfed all generations in a tormenting thirst that God alone can satisfy. *"For My people have done two evils: they have forsaken Me, the Fountain of living waters, to hew out cisterns for themselves, broken cisterns that can hold no water."* (Jer 2:13) God had provided fellowship of relationship with each other and with Himself for pleasure, His own garden for possession, and His own glory in which to glory. They were satisfied with none of them. Notice that in the response to the temptation, the three categories of desire were focused not on God, but on the fruit. Intertwined in the temptation, they continue intertwined in the fruitless quest for satisfaction apart from God Himself.

Pursuit of possessions, the feeding of the appetites that they afford, and their accumulation leads to pride. Moses warned the children of Israel, *"...that when you have eaten and are satisfied, and have built goodly houses, and have lived in them; and when your herds and your flocks multiply, and your silver and your gold have multiplied, and all that you have is multiplied, then it rises up into your heart, and you forget Jehovah your God who brought you out of the land of Egypt, out of the house of slaves."* (Deut 8:13-14) That very pursuit of possessions becomes an all-consuming focus, and yet, it is futile.

Consider the personal account of Solomon, in his pursuits: *"I sought in my heart how to drag my flesh with wine...and to lay hold on folly...I made my works great; I built houses for myself; I planted vineyards for myself; I made gardens and parks for myself; I made pools of water for myself; I bought slaves and slave girls...Also livestock, a herd and a great flock were mine...I also gathered to me silver and gold, I made ready male singers and female singers for myself; and... concubines. And I became great...And all that my eyes desired, I did not set aside from them."* (Eccl 2:3-10) This brief passage, filled with his quest for pleasure, possessions and prestige, is entirely self-focused. Note the repeated use of first person pronouns, I and myself. He was able to indulge the desires of his flesh, eyes and ego on a grand scale. The fires of cravings consumed it all, and demanded more. He was left unsatisfied: *"Then I faced on all my works that my hands had done, and on the labor that I had labored to do. And, lo, all is vanity and striving after wind, and there is no profit under the sun."* (Eccl 2:11)

Why was he left so empty, so thirsting, when his indulgence should have quenched the fires within? Like the rest of us, he had an inherent dissatisfaction at his core. He confesses, *"He who loves silver will not be satisfied with silver; and he who loves abundance does not gain. This is also vanity. When the good thing increases, those who devour it increase; then what profit is it to its owners, except to see it with his eyes?"* (Eccl 5:10-11) Possessions deteriorate. Pleasure is transient. Prestige is momentary. Like the children's game of "king on the mountain," prestige ushers in a constant battle to stay on top. Pleasure grows routine and stale. Possessions are subject to moth, rust and theft. In each case, the drive to obtain brings the thrill of having, which gives way to the fear of loss. Satisfaction eludes us.

Our fleshly nature is driven to increasingly competitive and destructive efforts to attain that which can never sate our desires. *"For where jealousy and contention are, there is confusion and every foul deed."* (James 3:16) Indeed, the

Scriptures broaden the scope of this indictment to encompass all of the global unrest seething around us: ***"From where do wars and fightings among you come? Is it not from this, from your lusts warring in your members? You desire and do not have. You murder, and are jealous, and are not able to obtain. You fight and you war, and you do not have, because you do not ask. You ask, and do not receive, because you ask wrongly, in order that you may spend on your lusts."*** (James 4:1-3) The struggle to feed the monster of lust turns deadly, in one way or another destroying us, and those around us. Consider the discontent we see in Numbers 11:4, when some grew weary of God's provision: ***"And the mixed multitude among them lusted with a great lust; and the sons of Israel also turned back and wept, and said, Who shall cause us to eat flesh?"*** The disease of discontent spread throughout the camp. They rejected God's supply that was fresh every morning in favor of that which decays. The result? ***"And one called the name of that place, The Graves of Lust; for there they buried the people who lusted."*** (Num 11:34)

Solomon gives us an admonition that is true of all of the substitutes we pursue to fill the place of God. ***"Do not toil to acquire wealth; be discerning enough to desist. When your eyes light on it, it is gone, for suddenly it sprouts wings, flying like an eagle toward heaven."*** (Pro 23:4-5) Fun, fortune and fame all fly away, and chasing them is, as Solomon concluded, striving after wind.

The discernment to desist comes only from God. David writes, ***"Turn my eyes from seeing vanity; in Your way give me life."*** (Psa 119:37) It is only God Himself who can turn us from broken cisterns to the Fountain of Living Water, from that which is not bread to the Bread of Life. It was only by the working of the Holy Spirit of God, and by his response to His leading, that ***"By faith Moses, when he was grown up, refused to be called the son of Pharaoh's daughter, choosing rather to be mistreated with the people of God than to enjoy the fleeting pleasures of sin."*** (Heb 11:24-25) God alone gives us the grace, the discernment, the strength to respond to His beseechings of grace. The invitation issued through the pen of the prophet Isaiah is repeated by our Lord Jesus Christ: ***"And in the last day of the great feast, Jesus stood and cried out, saying, 'If anyone thirsts, let him come to Me and drink.'"*** (John 7:37) Even the capacity to respond to Him is of God, and not of ourselves. Drawn to Him by the Spirit of God and the Word of God, our eyes are indeed turned from seeing vanity. Beholding Him, our desires are refocused, our energies redirected, as He lifts us from imbibing sea water to partake of the water of life.

Initially, His seems to be such a simple invitation. However, it demands a radical change. Hear our Lord's plea: ***"Come to Me, all those laboring and being burdened, and I will give you rest. Take My yoke upon you and learn from Me, because I am meek and lowly in heart, and you will find rest to your souls."*** (Mat 11:28-29) Concealed within this plea is the call to newness of life, springing from a complete change. Apart from Jesus Christ, I am arrogant and prideful at heart. It is only in being recreated in Him that I can learn gentleness and humility and selflessness. It is only in a Christ-life of gentleness of humility that I can desist from pointless pursuit of the desires of the flesh.

Pride versus humility. We find the tale of two kings instructive. Remember Nebuchadnezzar, king of Babylon? ***"At the end of twelve months, he walked in the palace of the kingdom of Babylon. The king spoke and said, 'Is this not great Babylon that I have built for the house of the kingdom, by the might of my power, and for the honor of my majesty?' The word was still in the king's mouth when a voice fell from the heavens, saying, 'O King Nebuchadnezzar, to you it is declared: The kingdom has been taken from you!'"*** (Dan 4:29-31) Arrogant of mind and proud of heart, as soon as he looked upon all that he had accumulated, it sprouted wings and flew away to heaven.

What a contrast we see in the words of David, king of Israel: *"To you, O Jehovah, be the greatness, and the power, and the glory, and the victory, and the majesty; for all in the heavens and in the earth belongs to You, O Jehovah; Yours is the kingdom, and You lift up Yourself to all as Head; and the riches, and the honor come from before You, and You rule over all; and in Your hand is power and might; and it is in Your hand to make great, and to give strength to all. And now, our God, we are giving thanks to You, and giving praise to Your glorious name; yea, for who am I, and who are my people, that we should be able to offer willingly in this way? For all is of You, and we have given to You out of Your hand..."* (1Chr 29:11-14) Focus and perception changes everything.

For believers in Christ Jesus, new creations in Him, that focus change is a lifestyle. *"If, then, you were raised with Christ, seek the things above, where Christ is sitting at the right of God; mind the things above, not the things on the earth."* (Col 3:1-2) Look to the Fountain of living waters, and be satisfied in Him.

20

LIFE OR DEATH

Science has always intrigued me. True science, based on observation rather than speculation, reveals the wonders of God's creative wisdom. False science, which the Bible classifies as "science so-called," promotes ideas and speculations that omit the Creator's involvement and intent. Human philosophies replace the oracles of God.

Such speculative ideas influence even the most basic areas of life. Special sections of the grocery store promote what is touted as organic food, which, of course, sells for a much higher price than its counterpart. In scientific terms, the opposite of organic is inorganic. Therefore, the food sold in the section not labeled as organic must be inorganic. That which is inorganic is not and has never been living. It is that which is not living, life-promoting, or life sustaining.

The dirt and rocks of the earth are lifeless in themselves. Collectively, they contain all the nutrient components required for our dietary needs. However, should we consume nothing but dirt and rocks, we would die of malnutrition, or poisoning. The inorganic elements in their pure form will kill us.

We need potassium as a nutrient. Pure potassium is a soft, highly-reactive, silvery metal you can cut with a pocket knife. A sliver of it, dropped into cold water, will react with the water, forming bubbles of hydrogen that adhere to the sliver, causing it to float. The heat of the rapid reaction will ignite the hydrogen, causing the reacting potassium to putter around the surface of the water in a series of mini explosions as the hydrogen bubbles and burns.

The warmer the water, the more rapid the reaction between the potassium metal and the water. Dropped in hot water, the sliver of metal will start to sink, and suddenly explode, sending spiraling streamers of smoke and steam radiating outward, tipped by orange-flamed fragments.

Potassium exists in the earth in a variety of inorganic compounds. It combines with other elements to form a variety of inorganic salts, such as potassium nitrate or potassium chlorate. These salts are useful in a variety of applications, but must be used with caution. They are hazardous and toxic. Both salts, in combination with other substances, form incendiary or explosive mixtures.

In order to provide the needed nutrient, and avoid injuring those around us with flying teeth, God packaged the potassium, in organic compound form, in bananas, which promote equanimity and quietness. A bit of potassium metal in the mouth would cause quite the opposite.

In establishing the environment in which living creatures could thrive, the Creator first formed a life-sustaining buffer between the mineral and animal realms. The producers in the food chain are the plants. They take inorganic elements, and convert them into organic compounds. The plants themselves make food out of non-food, organic substances from inorganic, living from dead, all by the natural laws set in motion at their creation. That which is unusable becomes useful by means of the buffer so purposed and established by God. Thus we find the plants are producers, and all the rest of creation is composed of consumers, either consuming the vegetation, or consuming those who consume the vegetation. Either way, life is sustained by that buffer between that which has life, and that which does not.

In the spiritual condition of humanity, we find a similar dynamic. Only in this case, the Living Bread is available, and it is the consumer that must be made alive. Paul writes to believers in Ephesus, **"And you were dead in the trespasses and sins in which you once walked, following the course of this world, following the prince of the power of the air, the spirit that is now at work in the sons of disobedience-- among whom we all once lived in the passions of our flesh, carrying out the desires of the body and the mind, and were by nature children of wrath, like the rest of mankind."** (Eph 2:1-3 ESV) That is all-inclusive. There are no exceptions. Descended from Adam, we all fell heir to his fallen nature, his inclination to sin, and the consequences he drew upon himself and his posterity. We were akin to the rocks of the earth in their lifelessness. We were spiritually dead, alienated from God, and destined for an eternal separation from all that God is in His character and nature. Paul's description is bleak: **"...remember that you were at that time separated from Christ...having no hope and without God in the world."** (Eph 2:12 ESV)

God Himself is the buffer, the only One who can bring life from death. He places that work in His own hands. That labor of love is the on-going work of the Godhead – the Father, the Son and the Holy Spirit. Paul encapsulates that work in two verses: **"But God, being rich in mercy, because of the great love with which he loved us, even when we were dead in our trespasses, made us alive together with Christ--by grace**

you have been saved..." (Eph 2:4-5 ESV) God's labor of love made us alive in Christ Jesus, gave us a new heritage and relationship, and instilled within us a hunger for the Word of Life, the living food he had prepared for us.

That food, termed the milk and the meat of the Word, through the ministry of the Holy Spirit within the believer, nourishes us, strengthens us, and causes us to grow in grace and in the knowledge of our Lord and Savior. It has no such impact in the lives of those without Christ, those still dead in trespasses and sins. It holds no appeal for them, apart from the intervention by God's Spirit. They prefer to consume lifeless dirt.

Consider the conversation between our Lord Jesus Christ and the religious leaders of His time on Earth. The conversation, on the surface, revolves around eating and washing and dirt. More subtly it involves those who were dead in sin, and He who was Life itself. It was a contrast between the Word of Life and dead traditions.

The religious leaders begin the conversation: ***"Then Pharisees and scribes came to Jesus from Jerusalem and said, 'Why do your disciples break the tradition of the elders? For they do not wash their hands when they eat.'"*** (Mat 15:1-2 ESV) To understand the significance of the confrontation, we must understand what is behind the term *tradition of the elders*. To the Jews it looks back to what they call the oral law, affirmed by them to have been handed down from generation to generation, through centuries, a successive paraphrase of what Moses taught. This message, re-couched for each new generation, was finally pulled together, edited and recorded into what is known as the Mishneh. The Jerusalem Talmud and the Babylonish Talmud were composed to explain the Mishneh. The rule of life for the Jews had become the teachings of the Talmud, the ideas of man. They had the Books of Moses, the poetry of David and Solomon, and the books of the prophets. They had the Scriptures. But to their minds, *"The words of the Scribes are lovely beyond the words of the law, for the words of the law* *are weighty and light, but the words of the Scribes are all weighty."* And so, their question: **"Why do your disciples break the tradition of the elders?"**

Now, we see the contrast in our Lord's question: **"He answered them, "And why do you break the commandment of God for the sake of your tradition?"** (Mat 15:3 ESV) Both our Lord and the Pharisees and scribes referred to violations. The contrast, though, is obvious. The higher Authority overrules the lesser. Our Lord points out one commandment and the consequences for violating it: **"For God commanded, 'Honor your father and your mother,' and, 'Whoever reviles father or mother must surely die.'"** (Mat 15:4 ESV) We have a clear statement of action and consequence. However, the traditions of the elders created space to maneuver around the commandment. Tradition created a concept and a deceitful term, transliterated as *corban,* to indicate that something was dedicated to God, although God was not going to get it directly. The thought was, "I am dedicated to God, therefore whatever I have, though used for my benefit, is also dedicated to God." Jesus said, **"But you say, 'If anyone tells his father or his mother, "What you would have gained from me is given to God," he need not honor his father.' So for the sake of your tradition you have made void the word of God."** (Mat 15:5-6 ESV)

The word of God was set aside by those who were supposed to lead in the worship of God. Our Lord now changes from the Book of the Law to the Book of the Prophets in His rebuke of their presumption: **"You hypocrites! Well did Isaiah prophesy of you, when he said: 'This people honors me with their lips, but their heart is far from me; in vain do they worship me, teaching as doctrines the commandments of men.'"** (Mat 15:7-9 ESV) They were feeding the spiritually-starved people artificial food. This confrontation focuses on the Jews, who, as Paul described them, **"They are Israelites, and to them belong the adoption, the glory, the covenants, the giving of the law, the worship, and the promises. To** *them belong the patriarchs, and from their race, according to the flesh, is the Christ who is God over all, blessed forever. Amen."* (Rom 9:4-5 ESV) They had the Scriptures. Jesus said to them, *"You search the Scriptures because you think that in them you have eternal life; and it is they that bear witness about me, yet you refuse to come to me that you may have life."* (John 5:39-40 ESV) What was their response? To those same religious leaders, Peter said, *"...let it be known to all of you and to all the people of Israel that by the name of Jesus Christ of Nazareth, whom you crucified, whom God raised from the dead--by him this man is standing before you well. This Jesus is the stone that was rejected by you, the builders, which has become the cornerstone. And there is salvation in no one else, for there is no other name under heaven given among men by which we must be saved."* (Act 4:10-12 ESV)

The Jews, then, had the witness of the Word of God, the recorded revelation of His will. The nations around them did not. However, Paul records that there is yet a general revelation that points to the reality and the wisdom of God. He writes, *"For what can be known about God is plain to them, because God has shown it to them. For his invisible attributes, namely, his eternal power and divine nature, have been clearly perceived, ever since the creation of the world, in the things that have been made. So they are without excuse."* (Rom 1:19-20 ESV) The rest of humanity is indicted with the same sin of substitution, not for the Word of God, but for God Himself: *"Claiming to be wise, they became fools, and exchanged the glory of the immortal God for images resembling mortal man and birds and animals and creeping things."* (Rom 1:22-23 ESV)

When the people at Lystra concluded that Barnabas and Paul were gods, and prepared to sacrifice to them in worship, Paul, in his effort to dissuade them, referred to the general revelation of God, saying, *"Men, why are you doing these things? We also are men, of like nature with you, and we bring you good news, that you should turn from these vain things to a living God, who made the heaven and the earth and the sea and all that is in them. In past generations he allowed all the nations to walk in their own ways. Yet he did not leave himself without witness, for he did good by giving you rains from heaven and fruitful seasons, satisfying your hearts with food and gladness."* (Act 14:15-17 ESV) In declaring the reality of the Living God, and His testimony to Himself, they denied any assumed godhood concerning themselves. The people were blind to the truth of God, however. Scripture tells us that *"Even with these words they scarcely restrained the people from offering sacrifice to them."* (Act 14:18 ESV)

Those without the direct revelation of God had the same reaction to the message of Life. They decided to kill the messenger. *"But Jews came from Antioch and Iconium, and having persuaded the crowds, they stoned Paul and dragged him out of the city, supposing that he was dead."* (Act 14:19 ESV)

Believers in the Lord Jesus Christ have a ministry to those who do not know the Savior, to the ones who are dead in trespasses and sins, who are enemies of God. As ambassadors for our Lord Jesus Christ, we function in hostile territory, among those who may well be as opposed to our message as they were to that of Paul and Barnabas, and as they were to that of Jesus Christ Himself. The dead do not want the nourishment of life. And yet, that is what we offer. We constitute the channel through which God has chosen to work in this age. Our Lord said, *"Truly, truly, I say to you, whoever hears my word and believes him who sent me has eternal life. He does not come into judgment, but has passed from death to life."* (John 5:24 ESV) That is the power of the message. The light of the gospel of Jesus Christ alone has the power to impart spiritual life to those who are spiritually dead.

We are not authorized to change the message, to diminish it in any of its aspects, or to substitute an imitation. No matter the response, we are to ***"Do all things without murmurings and disputings, that you may be blameless and harmless, children of God, without fault in the midst of a crooked generation, even having been perverted, among whom you shine as luminaries in the world, holding up the Word of Life..."*** (Php 2:14-16) As the hymn says, we are 'channels only,' for His use. We serve as lamp stands, upon which He rests His glorious Lamp. We serve as implements in His skilled hands, that He may work, using us for His purposes, for His pleasure, for His own glory. Our Lord Jesus Christ summarizes it this way: ***"It is the Spirit who gives life; the flesh is no help at all. The words that I have spoken to you are spirit and life."*** (John 6:63 ESV) May the Living Bread satisfy our deepest hunger! May all true believers, with one voice, join in the prayer of the Son, when He prayed, "Father, glorify Thy Name!"

21

BEE STINGS

Helping our neighbor, my nephew picked up a piece of firewood, and quickly dropped it as pain knifed through his hand. In picking it up, he had inadvertently disturbed an estivating yellow jacket. The wasp took exception to having its rest interrupted, and took what it deemed appropriate action against the intruder: it delivered a subcutaneous injection of irritating venom. Asked if he was all right, my nephew responded stoically, "It'll hurt until it quits."

He happened to encounter an over-wintered queen caught in the fluctuating temperatures of April. Pushed back into a cool-weather torpor, she stung once in reaction to the disturbance, but because the temperature was cool, she was not moving about. In warmer weather, she would have stung and bitten repeatedly.

The injected venom is a lasting memento of the encounter.

The burning pain of a sting is prolonged by the body's response to the toxin. The area is flooded with histamine, and the swelling stretches the surrounding tissues, adding to the pain.

Had the encounter occurred during late summer, the attack would have been much more serious. These wasps are aggressive, attacking seemingly without provocation in hot weather. As the colony grows, the caste charged with protecting the nest increases. An attack by one incites others to join in, and also marks the victim with a chemical, a pheromone, that alerts other wasps in the vicinity to the danger of an intruder. Running from the gathering swarm, the target of the attack trails the smell of bananas, the scent used by yellow jackets to identify their attacker. They will continue to pursue and sting for surprising distances.

Less aggressive, but no less potent, is the honey bee. I once picked up a floral spray, not noticing that a honey bee was busy in one of the blossoms. My thumb trapped the bee in the flower, and I was reminded to be more cautious. I got stung.

A honey bee's sting is different from other stinging insects. The act is fatal for the honey bee. The stinger is barbed, and once it pierces the skin, the stinging assembly tears away from the body of the bee. That structure includes two venom glands, a muscle system that continues to contract in pulses, pumping more venom through the stinger into the wound, a continuing reminder to be more attentive in the future. Flicking the stinger out with a fingernail, from underneath, avoids crushing more venom into the already-irritated member.

The tearing away of the stinger, or the crushing of the honey bee causes it to emit a pheromone that causes other bees in the area of the hive to attack. Farther from the hive, the sting of a single bee does not seem to incite others to attack, but the pain of even one sting is a lingering reminder of the encounter.

The knowledgeable recipient of such a memento from a wasp, a hornet, a bumblebee or a honey bee will immediately start looking for a lowly weed, the plantain. Chewing the leaves to make a poultice activates the venom-neutralizing juices that, when applied to the sting, eases the pain, but the consequences of the encounter continue long after the assailant is gone. For some, the suffering is short-lived. For some, the encounter can be fatal.

Consequences. Over the years, one of the things I have emphasized to my students is that every action, every choice and every decision comes with its own package of consequences, some good, some bad. Discernment recognizes and anticipates those consequences that will follow, and wisdom governs our behavior in the light of that recognition. We choose courses of action on a daily basis. We choose on the basis of knowledge, or of ignorance. We choose prudently, or rashly. Even failing to choose is a choice, and it brings its own consequences.

We ignore safety precautions, arrogantly concluding the warnings are for those less capable than we deem ourselves, and suffer. We rely on past experience, on "it's never happened before," and harm ourselves or others. We are quick to label events as accidents. In truth, there are no accidents. There are only incidents that reveal a lack of forethought, of foresight, of wisdom. Chainsaw chaps and caution would have spared my knee.

If choices and consequences are interrelated in our daily lives, how much more in the spiritual aspect of our existence. The inevitability of consequences is encapsulated in a pair of rhetorical questions in the book of Proverbs. **"Can a man take fire into his bosom and his clothes not be burned? Or can a man walk on hot coals and his feet not be burned?"** (Pro 6:27-28) The implied reality is negative, yet, on a daily basis, we try to prove we are exempt from the logical outcome.

In every dispensation, God has given man a revealed aspect of His will, and the consequences for failure to meet that will. In every case, man has failed. It started in the Garden of Eden. **"And Jehovah God commanded the man, saying, Eating you may eat of every tree in the garden; but of the Tree of the Knowledge of Good and Evil you may not eat, for in** *the day that you eat of it, dying you shall die."* (Gen 2:16-17) They ate. The scope of the consequences is bound up in that last portion, *dying you shall die*. It includes immediate spiritual death in the breaking of fellowship with God. It extends to physical death that would befall them eventually. It culminates with their pending eternal death, separation from God forever, absent intervention by God Himself. Spiritual death, the separation from God caused by sin, had an immediate impact. Their relationship with God became one of alienation, based on fear on the part of our first parents. They hid themselves.

Physical death was an unknown concept to them. Nothing had ever died. They had a theoretical knowledge of death, but its reality did not penetrate their comfort zone until that first substitutionary sacrifice, when God clothed them with the skins of animals. Animals that they had known, perhaps cared for, perhaps loved, died to provide a covering for their nakedness, and a blood covering for their sin.

In choosing disobedience, yielding himself as a servant of sin, Adam acted as the federal head of humanity. His choice and its consequences resonate through the ages. *"Because of this, even as sin entered the world through one man, and death through sin, so also death passed to all men, inasmuch as all sinned."* (Rom 5:12) Adam, in yielding, sold himself into slavery to sin. The offspring of slaves are themselves counted as slaves. Thus, that one act had far-reaching results. *"For if by the deviation of the one death reigned through the one..."* (Rom 5:17a) *"So then, as through one deviation it was toward all men to condemnation..."* (Rom 5:18a) *"For as through the one man's disobedience the many were constituted sinners..."* (Rom 5:19a)

Sinners. Death. Condemnation. A bleak prospect stood before all humanity. *"And as it is reserved to men once to die, and after this, Judgment..."* (Heb 9:27) The plight of every generation since that ancient rebellion has been a painful, despairing trudge toward the grave. From the human perspective, the desperate quest for a self-contrived deliverance only leads to further sin.

The impact of that first rebellion had a broader impact. It destroyed our first parents' fellowship with God, condemned their progeny, and polluted their context. Creation itself was altered by sin. In expelling them from the Garden of Eden, God told Adam, ***"...cursed is the ground because of you; in pain you shall eat of it all the days of your life; thorns and thistles it shall bring forth for you; and you shall eat the plants of the field. By the sweat of your face you shall eat bread, till you return to the ground, for out of it you were taken; for you are dust, and to dust you shall return."*** (Gen 3:17b-19 ESV) We are not told how long they had enjoyed the joys of the Garden, the sweet communion with God, and the abundant fruit that satisfied their needs. However long or short that time, their choice altered their context, and ours. Paul writes of that change, many centuries later: ***"For the creation was subjected to futility, not willingly, but because of him who subjected it, in hope that the creation itself will be set free from its bondage to corruption and obtain the freedom of the glory of the children of God. For we know that the whole creation has been groaning together in the pains of childbirth until now."*** (Rom 8:20-22 ESV)

Hopelessness and that despairing trudge toward the grave and eternal separation from God would be the lot of all humanity, without intervention by God Himself. He imposed the penalty: ***"Behold, all souls are mine; the soul of the father as well as the soul of the son is mine: the soul who sins shall die."*** (Eze 18:4 ESV) He alone could intervene.

He did. ***"And we have seen and testify that the Father has sent his Son to be the Savior of the world."*** (1John 4:14 ESV) God, in concluding all humanity under sin, eliminated any possibility that we might somehow deliver ourselves, but opened the door of grace. God is a God of active mercy, and His mercy withholds from us what we deserve, what He has decreed as the penalty for sin. He is a God of active grace, and His grace freely gives us what we do not deserve. ***"But where sin abounded, grace much more abounded, that as sin ruled in death, so also grace might rule through righteousness to everlasting life, through Jesus Christ our Lord."*** (Rom 5:20b-21)

Christ Jesus our Lord is the new and living way of reconciliation to God, to restored communion and fellowship with Him, to confidence in our acceptance in His presence. Ours is a fellowship of faith in this earthly existence, as we await the consummation of His purpose for us who are His cherished love gift to His Son. ***"For if by the deviation of the one death reigned through the one, much more those who are receiving the abundance of grace and the gift of righteousness shall rule in life by the One, Jesus Christ. So then, as through one deviation it was toward all men to condemnation, so also through one righteous act toward all men to justification of life. For as through the one man's disobedience the many were constituted sinners, so also through the obedience of the One the many shall be constituted righteous."*** (Rom 5:17-19)

The consequences of that original rebellion continue to hedge us in as we live out our brief stay on Earth. We still contend with thorns and thistles. We still labor for our food. We still pursue our journey to the end of physical life. But, for those who believe, the journey is not a hopeless one. ***"For as by a man came death, by a man has come also the resurrection of the dead. For as in Adam all die, so also in Christ shall all be made alive."*** (1Cor 15:21-22 ESV) We have a confident anticipation that reaches beyond physical death, an expectation of standing before Him without spot or blemish, perfectly pure within and without, accepted in the Beloved One. As Paul assures us, ***"There is therefore now no condemnation for those who are in Christ Jesus."*** (Rom 8:1 ESV)

There is no terror of what Scripture terms the second death for the one who is in Christ Jesus. That eternal separation from God, away from His presence, apart from all that He is, cannot touch the one whose confidence is in the finished work of salvation on the cross of Calvary, wrought by God Himself in human flesh. Death could not hold Him. Though we die, death will not be able to hold us. *"The last enemy to be destroyed is death."* (1Cor 15:26 ESV)

The Thessalonian believers were being told that their loved ones who had died would not see the glory of the Lord Jesus Christ, that they had missed His coming for His own. Paul assured them that the grave could not keep them, and that death was not their final destiny. *"But we do not want you to be uninformed, brothers, about those who are asleep, that you may not grieve as others do who have no hope. For since we believe that Jesus died and rose again, even so, through Jesus, God will bring with him those who have fallen asleep. For this we declare to you by a word from the Lord, that we who are alive, who are left until the coming of the Lord, will not precede those who have fallen asleep. For the Lord himself will descend from heaven with a cry of command, with the voice of an archangel, and with the sound of the trumpet of God. And the dead in Christ will rise first. Then we who are alive, who are left, will be caught up together with them in the clouds to meet the Lord in the air, and so we will always be with the Lord. Therefore encourage one another with these words."* (1Thes 4:13-18 ESV)

Paul penned a soaring doxology of assurance to the believers at Corinth that reassures believers of the heavenly foundation on which our confidence rests. His messages, penned by the instruction of God's Holy Spirit, combine to encourage believers today. *"Behold! I tell you a mystery. We shall not all sleep, but we shall all be changed, in a moment, in the twinkling of an eye, at the last trumpet. For the trumpet will sound, and the dead will be raised imperishable, and we shall be changed. For this perishable body must put on the imperishable, and this mortal body must put on immortality. When the perishable puts on the imperishable, and the mortal puts on immortality, then shall come to pass the saying that is written: "Death is swallowed up in victory." "O death, where is your victory? O death, where is your sting?" The sting of death is sin, and the power of sin is the law. But thanks be to God, who gives us the victory through our Lord Jesus Christ."* (1Cor 15:51-57 ESV)

22

CHAMELEONS

Artist Bev Doolittle paints a variety of western-themed scenes, including hidden-image pictures. Pinto horses stand among or in front of snow-covered bowlders, hidden in plain view. Other hidden-in-plain-sight pictures include tribal people, wildlife, and birds. These are some of her favorite works among collectors.

Camouflage in nature is a fascinating study. In most cases, the Creator has designed animals in a pattern that blends in not only with the hues that color their environment, but vanish in a pattern of light and shadows as well, in most cases regardless of color. Most species instinctively seek out the setting where they will be inconspicuous when danger threatens. The bittern stands motionless, chin up, in the reeds or sedges of the shoreline. A mottled moth flattens itself against similarly colored bark.

Unusual among those in nature who seek to vanish into their surroundings is the chameleon. These lizards range in size as adults from just over half an inch in length, the smallest of the reptiles, to about 30 inches, depending on the variety. Some have heads ornamented with spikes or horns. Most are mottled, with dark patches or random stripes over a background color. This wallpaper, if we can call it that, varies in color from species to species, in shades of pink, blue, red, orange, turquoise, yellow, and green. With such gaudy colors, they might blend into a flower garden, but hardly anywhere else, except for one creative characteristic. Chameleons, or at least some varieties, are endowed by the Creator with the ability to change color. Instead of seeking a setting that matches their appearance, these chameleons change themselves to match their surroundings.

Like other reptiles, chameleons have a transparent outer skin. Underneath, they have three layers with specialized cells. In the upper layer, cells contain red or yellow pigments. Below that, in the next layer, are cells with white or blue, and a third layer below that contain cells with dark melanin. Signals from the chameleon's brain control whether the pigment bits in each cell is concentrated or scattered. If the fragments of color are scattered, the cell shows the intense color. If the color chips are concentrated in the center of the cell, the cell becomes almost transparent, allowing the color below to show through. Thus, the lizard can almost vanish in plain view, by changing to appear like its surroundings.

The adaptation is entirely subconscious. The eyes of the chameleon focus on its immediate surroundings. The signals from the brain to the cells to gather or scatter the pigment are automatic, not calculated. Blending in is a natural response.

People imitate the chameleon. We have an internal urge to blend in, to be like those around us. Despite our much-acclaimed individualism, we are driven to belong, to be identified with a group. It is our nature. How early in childhood did we cry, "But everyone else is," as our justification of the demand for gratification of the urge to conform? Even our vaunted rebellious individualism is nothing more than "I want to be different, like everyone else!"

Scripture brings to light the chameleon reality in us, the reality that we are shaped by our context, either apart from, or because of our cognitive inclinations. God's purpose for each believer in our Lord Jesus Christ is that we be made like Him. **"For those whom he foreknew he also predestined to be conformed to the image of his Son..."** (Rom 8:29 ESV) This spiritual work of changing us in our very character is being done to us by an agency other than ourselves. We are not, and indeed, we cannot change ourselves to be like Christ. It is a work God has laid upon Himself, **"...for it is God who works in you, both to will and to work for his good pleasure."** (Php 2:13 ESV) The *"will"* is God's blueprint, His purpose for the believer. Christ-likeness is our positional reality. It is expressed by our Lord Jesus Christ in His high-priestly prayer for His own: **"They are not of the world, just as I am not of the world."** (John 17:16 ESV) The blueprint is God's plan. Christ Jesus is the Pattern, the Form to which we will be conformed. Our standing before a holy God is one based on imputation. **"For our sake he made him to be sin who knew no sin, so that in him we might become the righteousness of God."** (2Cor 5:21 ESV) Our sin was imputed to the Lamb of God. The righteousness of Christ was imputed to those *"in Him."* This imputation is true, in the mind and purpose of God, the instant we are brought to faith in Christ, the moment we are placed in Him by the Holy Spirit. At that instant, among other positional realities, God sees us as already seated in the heavenlies in Christ Jesus. That is our place, our home. **"But our citizenship is in heaven, and from it we await a Savior, the Lord Jesus Christ, who will transform our lowly body to be like his glorious body, by the power that enables him even to subject all things to himself."** (Php 3:21-22 ESV)

The perfections of all that is ours positionally await us. There is another reality interposed between our salvation and our glorification. That reality is wrapped up in the last part of Philippians 2:13, that assures us that God, who has purposed Christ-likeness for us, **"...works in you...to work for His**

good pleasure. *"* What He has planned, He works to accomplish. He works in each believer, in this world, to reveal the reality of the Savior in His own to the ones enslaved in this world's system of values and behaviors, this *kosmos diabolikos*, who so desperately need the Redeemer. Our Lord prayed, ***"I do not ask that you take them out of the world, but that you keep them from the evil one."*** (John 17:15 ESV) The on-going work of God to make us holy, to make us like His Son, to sanctify us, is indeed the process of revealing His Son in each of us. As He continues this transforming work, faith leads us to respond to His Spirit within us, to yield to His leading, to rest in His working. With Paul, we can say confidently, ***"And I am sure of this, that He who began a good work in you will bring it to completion at the day of Jesus Christ."*** (Php 1:6)

Our responsibility, then, is response. He, by His Spirit, prompts, leads, inclines and urges. We, in the wisdom and strength and understanding He provides, speak, or act, or move by His grace, and as we are yielded to Him and His purpose, He glorifies Himself.

There is a counter-spiritual aspect to being conformed. Rather than yielding to His Spirit within us, we have the inclination in our natures to yield to forces around us. Paul warns, ***"Do not be conformed to this world, but be transformed by the renewal of your mind, that by testing you may discern what is the will of God, what is good and acceptable and perfect."*** (Rom 12:2 ESV) Again we see the outside agency at work, implied by the admonition ***"do not be conformed..."*** We might think that we are freely choosing, but, in reality, we are merely yielding to shaping forces around us. We are not conforming ourselves. We are being conformed to a pattern, a standard imposed by an agent other than ourselves. Again, Paul's warning is incisive: ***"Do not be deceived: 'Bad company ruins good morals.'"*** (1Cor 15:33 ESV) Or, as David wrote in his songbook, The Psalms, ***"Blessed is the man who walks not in the counsel of the wicked, nor stands in the way of sinners, nor sits in the seat of scoffers..."*** (Psa 1:1 ESV) David used the word *blessed* in an exclamatory meaning "Oh, the many happinesses." In this case, the plural happinesses is tied to a negative, the word *not*. David traces the progress of conformation from listening to the advice of those with the values base of this world's system, to fellowship in the behaviors of those who act according to those values, to participation in the mockery of holiness. The opposite side of "Oh, the many happinesses" is "Oh, the many sorrows." That is the experiential reality that awaits the believer who yields to the conforming forces of this world. ***"For the Lord disciplines the one he loves, and chastises every son whom he receives." It is for discipline that you have to endure. God is treating you as sons. For what son is there whom his father does not discipline?"*** (Heb 12:6-7 ESV) God's purpose for His own is sure. His working is inexorable. He will complete that good work He began.

His call is for separation. ***"Therefore do not become partners with them; for at one time you were darkness, but now you are light in the Lord. Walk as children of light."*** (Eph 5:7-8 ESV) ***Do not be unequally yoked with unbelievers. For what partnership has righteousness with lawlessness? Or what fellowship has light with darkness?*** (2Cor 6:14 ESV) Separation is not the same as isolation. We are in the world for God's purpose. Notice above Paul said, "You were darkness." That spoke of our nature, not our context. In that nature, we blended in with those of like nature. We were darkness. Now we have been made light in the Lord, who is Light. We are now in contrast to our context in this world. We have been made light, ***"that you may be blameless and innocent, children of God without blemish in the midst of a crooked and twisted generation, among whom you shine as lights in the world..."*** (Php 2:15 ESV) There is the purpose God has for believers in this world, while we wait for the appearing of our Lord.

His Spirit can override the commands from the flesh to scatter the color chips of self in our camouflage response to blend in to the world around us, as we walk responsive to Him. ***"But I say,*** *walk by the Spirit, and you will not gratify the desires of the flesh. For the desires of the flesh are against the Spirit, and the desires of the Spirit are against the flesh, for these are opposed to each other, to keep you from doing the things you want to do."* (Gal 5:16-17 ESV) Abiding in Him; living with our affections set on things above, where Christ is; feasting on His nourishing truth; gazing into the glory – these things make up the walk of faith. It is a daily way of life, an on-going mindset. *"And we all, with unveiled face, beholding the glory of the Lord, are being transformed into the same image from one degree of glory to another. For this comes from the Lord who is the Spirit."* (2Cor 3:18 ESV)

23

RIP CURRENTS

There is a mesmerizing allurement in the rolling swell of the ocean, and in the waves that break along the shore. Foam-laced wavelets surge up the beach, pause, and flow seaward once again. Their cool gentleness calls to bare feet on a hot day. Sea bathers are tantalized into unwariness. If the ankles are cooled, why not the knees? The cool water tickles the feet as its current scours away the sand on which we stand. Waist deep, the ocean dares us with its larger waves that break beyond us, and then roll toward us in a swell that says, "Jump!"

We jump the waves, then stagger out a bit, unbalanced by the shifting sand. Chest deep, we watch the next incoming swell, our focus on what lies before us, ignoring what is happening behind. The summer idyll is shattered all too often by cries of helplessness as the joy of jumping waves is snuffed out by a seaward rush of water. With relentless force, it sweeps its victim ever farther from the shore. The shouts for help are mingled with the cries of anguish from the watchers on the beach, only to dissolve into desperate silence, leaving only the murmur of the surf, and the mocking laughter of the gulls that circle overhead.

Rip currents are the product of a variety of factors. The shape of the shore can circle the waves, collide them, and pile the water in a heap that collapses in a rush to its own level. The frequency of waves can have a similar effect. But, the most common contributor to the powerful seaward current is concealed beneath the surf.

The constant currents present within the ocean waters redistribute the sand in the tidal zone. The waves that roll in have within themselves a rolling current, so that they roll up the underwater slope that leads to the beach like a huge water rolling pin, picking up sand, shells and pebbles as it approaches. The backwash of the spent waves pulls sand back toward the ocean. Where the two collide, they drop their load of sand, forming an underwater sandbar. The Coriolis current sweeps parallel to the shore, gently moving the sand, scouring away at the face of the hidden sandbar. This has a riffle effect, creating a low pressure zone on the shoreward side, which hastens the building of the sandbar, which acts as a dam, trapping the water of the spent waves. The weight of this impounded water will eventually cause part of the sandbar to collapse, creating a gap, forming a hidden channel through which the returning water rushes. It is this channelized water that forms the rip current.

Water in most areas returns seaward at a foot or two per second. We feel its force, but our ability to walk through it toward the shore is stronger than its its ability to carry us away. At water speeds of three to four feet per second, we are overwhelmed. Rip currents may reach velocities of up to eight feet per second. Captured by the current, the victim is swept down the hidden channel, perhaps hundreds of feet offshore, in a matter of seconds.

A rip current has characteristics that are at once destroying and limiting. The rip is sudden. The water shoreward will display a temporary calm as the flood pauses with latent energy, and then rush through the channel in an abrupt collapse. The rip is narrow and focused. The rip current may be only a few yards wide, seldom more than forty or fifty. It is the tapered gathering of the water through the narrow passage that accelerates it. The rip is fast. Its power is in its speed. But it is brief. Once the flow has passed through the channel, it loses speed and force, flaring and dissipating. It will release its victim, but that release may come too late.

The initial response to being caught in a rip current is to fight it, to try to swim against it. This is often a fatal error. The speed of the rip current exceeds that of the strongest Olympic sprint swimmer. Its force is relentless, and fighting it will lead to exhaustion and death. The only escape possible is to swim across the rip, parallel to the shore. Since it is narrow, escape may be only a few strokes away. Recognizing the signs and the nature of the rip current is the only avenue of deliverance. Flee, don't fight. Water with breaking waves, whether the ocean or a lake, is an attractive menace. The best way to avoid danger is to stay out of the water. Whether we like it or not, we are not creatures of the sea.

We find a parallel reality in our spiritual existence. Waves of alluring pleasures of the world lap at our feet. Our flesh wants to wade out, to indulge, perhaps just a little. The gentle swells promise greater thrills, if we will just wade out a little deeper. The satisfying sigh of having, of possessing, breeds a drive for more. The heady wine of prestige dulls our perception of reality, and draws us even farther into the rolling surf of desire, jumping the waves in the excitement of danger. We toy with temptation, until it seizes us in the teeth of the powerful forces of destruction. Nowhere in Scripture are we admonished to fight temptation. The warning is to flee. Just as the juxtaposition of position, fascination, daring and inattentiveness is the recipe for disaster in the surf, so the confluence of opportunity, inclination, fascination and self-focus lead to the abrupt juggernaut of sinful disaster.

This world's value system and ways are full of rolling waves of opportunity to indulge fleshly cravings. Our flesh is saturated with the inclination of desire. Our theater of the mind plays out vignettes of possibility that fascinate and entice us ever deeper. The attitude of Brer Rabbit in the movie *Song of the South*, "I does what I pleases, and I pleases *me!*" is the heartbeat of our fleshly nature. Apart from the restraining ministry of God's indwelling Holy Spirit in the believer in Christ Jesus, that mixture plunges headlong into ruin.

We find three general categories of enticement attributed to the value system of this world in Scripture. The Apostle John, writing in his first corrective epistle, writes, **"Do not love the world nor the things in the world. If anyone loves the world, the love of the Father is not in him, because all that which is in the world: the lust of the flesh, and the lust of the eyes, and the pride of life, is not of the Father, but is of the world."** (1John 2:15-16) The drive for pleasure, for possessions, and for prestige subdivide what the Scriptures term the *lusts of the flesh*. These three forces pulse within the fallen nature we have inherited from our first parents, and were the very three that plunged them into sin: **"And the woman saw that the tree was good for food, and that it was pleasant to the eyes, and the tree was desirable to make one wise. And she took of its fruit and ate; and she also gave to her husband with her, and he ate."** (Gen 3:6) The lifestyles of hedonism, materialism and egotism reveal themselves in the unrestrained indulgence of these cravings. These rip currents will sweep the unwary to destruction.

Scripture gives the believer four specific warnings to flee these flesh-focused forces of ruin. The first is from the pen of the Apostle Paul, and targets the most personal and intimate quest for pleasure: **"Flee fornication. Every sin which a man may do is outside the body, but he doing fornication sins against his own body."** (1Cor 6:18) The term *fornication* covers all avenues of indulgence of the sexual aspect of our being outside of the God-ordained confines of marriage between a man and a woman. God affirms His boundaries for sexual fulfillment, again through Paul's pen: **"Marriage is honorable in all, and** *the bed undefiled; but God will judge fornicators and adulterers."* (Heb 13:4)

Paul's words, *"but he doing fornication sins against his own body,"* are instructive. The crushing force of sexual sin is reflexive. Though adultery may cause the heart and soul of a spouse to writhe in the agony of betrayal, the grinding weight of consequence falls on the sinner. Its indictment echoes in the silence of sleep, whispers behind the back, and shouts from the housetop. It corrupts from the core outward. ***"Fornication...take[s] away the heart."*** (Hos 4:11) Core values are deteriorated through excuses and self-justification. The next impact corrupts the mind, will and emotions, that set the course of defilement in the first place: ***"He who commits adultery with a woman lacks heart; he who does it is a destroyer of his own soul."*** (Pro 6:32) Although the Scriptures are couched in masculine terms, the consequences of sin are universal, and do not discriminate between male and female.

Ultimately, the blot of sin corrupts the reputation: ***"He shall find a wound and dishonor, and his shame shall not be wiped away."*** (Pro 6:33) The stain persists. Consider David's sin of lust with Bathsheba. The consequences of his behavior were fixed. God's message to David was, ***"And now the sword shall not turn aside from your house continually, because you have despised Me, and have taken the wife of Uriah the Hittite to be a wife to you."*** (2Sam 12:10) His sin filled his own home with violence and sorrow. The stain still clung to him in death, corrupting his memory. ***"For David did that which is right in the eyes of Jehovah, and did not turn aside from all that He commanded him all the days of his life, except in the matter of Uriah the Hittite."*** (1Kings 15:5) Centuries later, his shame shows in the genealogy of our Savior, and his: ***"...and Jesse fathered David the king. And David the king fathered Solomon out of her who had been the wife of Uriah..."*** (Mat 1:6) Thus we find the admonition to *"flee fornication."* The consequences are dire and sure, as Paul notes, *but he doing fornication sins against his own body...and receiving back within themselves the reward which was fitting for their error.* " (1Cor 6:18, Rom 1:27) Indeed, sexual sin leads the list of the obvious fleshly behaviors over which the wrath of God broods: **"Now the works of the flesh are clearly revealed, which are: adultery, fornication, uncleanness, lustfulness, idolatry, sorcery, enmities, fightings, jealousies, angers, rivalries, divisions, heresies, envyings, murders, drunkenness, revelings, and things like these; of which I tell you beforehand, as I also said before, that the ones practicing such things will not inherit the kingdom of God."** (Gal 5:19-21) A pattern of repeated indulgence in these makes any claim to a saving relationship with our Lord and Savior Jesus Christ an empty lie. **"For this is God's will, your sanctification, for you to abstain from fornication..."** (1Thes 4:3) **"For be knowing this, that every fornicator, or unclean one, or covetous one, who is an idolater, has no inheritance in the kingdom of Christ and of God."** (Eph 5:5)

The second admonition to flee follows the thought in this somber warning Paul wrote to those in Ephesus. To those in Corinth, he wrote, **"On account of this, flee from idolatry, my beloved."** (1Cor 10:14) The lust of the eyes John mentioned as part of the world's value system is termed by God to be covetousness. It is rooted in the fleshly nature of all humanity, and has no place in the life of a believer. Paul writes, **"Then put to death your members which are on the earth: fornication, uncleanness, passion, evil lust, and covetousness, which is idolatry..."** (Col 3:5) Covetousness is just as self-focused as fornication, both in its wounding impact on others, and in its powerful sweep that carries the greedy one ever deeper into churning chaos. **"But those purposing to be rich fall into temptation, and a snare, and many foolish and hurtful lusts, which plunge men into ruin and destruction. For the love of money is a root of all evils,**

by means of which some having lusted after it were seduced from the faith, and they themselves pierced through by many pains." (1Tim 6:9-10)

Here again, it is the confluence of opportunity and inclination that entices the ignorant and the scoffers into the place of danger, and washes them relentlessly into self-indulgence. Consider the lot of Achan in the aftermath of the collapse of the walls of Jericho. In his words, when he was cornered and compelled to confess: ***"When I saw among the spoil a goodly robe of Shinar, and two hundred shekels of silver, and a wedge of gold, one of fifty shekels in weight, then I lusted after them, and took them. And behold, they are hidden in the earth, in the middle of my tent, and the silver under it."*** (Josh 7:21) The rip current of greed swept him to judgment. Solomon pinpoints the eye problem of idolatry: ***"A man with an evil eye hastens after wealth, but he does not know that poverty will come on him."*** (Pro 28:22) The evil eye is the one that looks with confidence to wealth, to possessions, rather than looking with thankfulness to God. It is impossible to trust in both. In the words of our Savior, ***"No one is able to serve two lords; for either he will hate the one, and he will love the other; or he will cleave to the one, and he will despise the other. You are not able to serve God and wealth."*** (Mat 6:24)

The third warning to flee comes in the middle of a passage rife with contention. The pointless disputing over words that spirals into profane chatter and ungodliness, that spreads like a gangrene, shows the impact of smug arrogance. The warning attaches the impulsive selfishness of youth: ***"But flee youthful lusts and pursue righteousness, faith, love, peace, with the ones calling on the Lord out of a pure heart."*** (2Tim 2:22) Rebellion and unteachability blossom in the young, springing from the fleshly nature inherited from the parents. Pride demands recognition, craves applause, and asserts superiority. The Spirit of God, through the pen of the Apostle Paul, warned against putting the immature into places of leadership, for this very reason: ***"He*** *should not be a novice, lest being puffed up he may fall into the devil's judgment."* (1Tim 3:6) The pride of position and the prestige of office inflate the ego, releasing a destructive force that defiles both the proud one, and those around him. *"Argument only comes by pride, but wisdom is with those who take advice."* (Pro 13:10)

Peter picks up that thread of thought: *"Likewise, younger ones be subject to older ones; and all being subject to one another. Put on humility, because God sets Himself against proud ones, but He gives grace to humble ones."* (1Pet 5:5) God opposes the proud ones, sets Himself against them. That is a military term of battle array. The rip current of pride sweeps the prideful relentlessly into the teeth of breaking waves of judgment.

Interestingly, Scripture uses a military term for what pride does, as well: *"Pride goes before destruction, and a haughty spirit before a fall."* (Pro 16:18) Pride leads destruction in its wake, and a haughty spirit brings a fall behind it, as a king led, or went before an army in Solomon's day. What does pride's army look like? Why does God set Himself against it? He tells us: *"These six things Jehovah hates; yea, seven are hateful to his soul; a proud look, a lying tongue, and hands that shed innocent blood, a heart that plots evil plans, feet hurrying to run to mischief, a false witness who breathes lies, and he who causes strife among brothers."* (Pro 6:16-19) Pride leads the way, and the others follow, all of them hard on the heels of pride. Individually and collectively, they are the character of destruction.

In rebuking the pride of the Babylonian king Belshazzar, Daniel encapsulated that which befell Nebuchadnezzar for his continued arrogance, despite God's warning: *"But when his heart was lifted up, and his mind hardened in pride, he was deposed from his kingly throne, and they took his glory from him..."* (Dan 5:20) Two kings with the same sin issue suffered the same consequences: *"Before shattering, a man's heart is haughty, but humility goes before honor."* (Pro 18:12) That which is hardened, shatters.

Paul warned the Ephesian elders of an immanent danger lurking in their midst: *"...and out of you yourselves will rise up men speaking perverted things, in order to draw away the disciples after themselves."* (Acts 20:30) Self-importance would lead into false teaching, and lead those becoming aware of Christ to a false christ and a false gospel, the false teachers making disciples for themselves rather than for Christ Jesus. John, writing a few years later, noted the fulfillment of Paul's warning, naming one offender: *"I wrote to the assembly, but he loving to be first of them, Diotrephes, does not receive us. Because of this, if I come, I will recall his works which he does, ranting against us with evil words. And not being satisfied with these, neither does he receive the brothers; and those intending it he prevents, and thrusts them out from the assembly."* (3John 1:9-10) We are not told the age of Diotrephes, but his immature behavior and his craving for prideful prestige mark him as personifying that which God hates, as He says, *"The fear of Jehovah is to hate evil; I hate pride and loftiness, and the evil way, and the perverse mouth."* (Pro 8:13)

Each of these warnings, focused on each of the elements of the world John warned us not to love. The lust of the flesh, the lust of the eyes and the boastful pride of life each bring with them a multitude of associated evils. The fourth warning to flee is an all-inclusive caution: *"But you, O man of God, flee these things and pursue righteousness, godliness, faith, love, patience, and meekness."* (1Tim 6:11) Indeed, for God's own, Scripture calls for separation from the scoffers. Note the clear warning from the mouth of God, when Korah and company disdained the ordained authority established by the Lord: *"And Jehovah spoke to Moses, saying, Speak to the congregation, saying, You get away from around the tent of Korah, Dathan, and Abiram. And Moses rose up and went to Dathan and Abiram, and the elders of*

Israel went after him. And he spoke to the congregation, saying, Please turn away from the tents of these wicked men, and do not touch anything that they have, lest you be consumed in all their sins." (Num 16:23-26) The final part of the warning is the most solemn part of the warning. God's own are not immune from being contaminated by the sin of others. Paul mirrored the warning when he cautioned the believers at Corinth: *"But now I wrote to you not to associate intimately; if anyone is called a brother and is either a fornicator, or a covetous one, or an idolater, or a reviler, or a drunkard, or a plunderer, with such a one not to eat."* (1Cor 5:11) The so-called brother, living out a false profession of faith, had then, and has today, the potential to lead the unwary into wave-jumping.

Is there hope for the one carried away? Yes. For the careless believer caught in the current of sin through failure to watch and pray, there is restoration in repentance and confession. Consequences continue, scars remain, usefulness to God is forever diminished, but the believer's fellowship with God is restored. For the would-be rescuer, there is a sobering warning: *"Brothers, if a man is overtaken in some deviation, you, the spiritual ones, restore such a one in the spirit of meekness, considering yourself, that you not also be tempted."* (Gal 6:1) For the unsaved, there is hope in the regenerating work of God's Holy Spirit. Salvation is entirely of God. *"For by grace you are saved, through faith, and this not of yourselves; it is the gift of God; not of works, that not anyone should boast..."* (Eph 2:8-9)

The one drawn staggering ashore, freed by God's grace from the destroying forces of sin can find refuge and cleansing only in our Savior. The place of safety is the Rock, Christ Jesus. He is the Rock that is higher, the Foundation, the Cornerstone. Falling on Him in brokenness, in humility, we are above the reach of the destructive currents. Speaking of Himself, our Lord said, *"And he who falls on this Stone will be broken; but on whomever It falls, It will pulverize him."* (Mat 21:44) Flee to Him.

24

SOUNDWAVES

A century ago, that Wee Scotsman, Sir Harry Lauder, recorded a gramophone record of "Roamin' in the Gloamin'." My wife and I, sharing his heritage, can identify with the sentiment of that auld Scots ditty: "When the sun has gone to rest, that's the time that we love best. Oh, it's lovely roamin' in the gloamin'!" We were out strolling in the twilight on a warm evening last August, watching as the stars appeared, one by one. My wife asked if I could hear the crickets. I had to laugh. "Crickets? That's all I ever hear, is crickets!"

I earned money for my college education working in the shipyards as a pipefitter. It was an interesting time. With a conflict in progress, ships from World War II and the Korean conflict were brought out of the Mothball Fleet to be refitted for new service. On the Portland waterfront, workers swarmed over the old ship, stripped it of its pipes, wiring and fixtures, installed bulkheads, and cut the ship in half. While that work was in progress, workers in Louisiana built a new middle section, floated it through the Panama Canal, brought it up the coast to the Columbia River, and towed it upriver to Portland. The three pieces were then connected to make a larger ship. It was noisy work, and earplugs were not issued. The constant resonating impacts of pneumatic chippers on steel hammered my eardrums. As a result, now in my later years, I have the continual sound of crickets in my ears, a ringing that keeps me from hearing the real chirping of crickets on a summer evening.

Our ears are a marvel of creation. We have two of them, which gives us the capacity to estimate the direction and distance of the sounds we hear, much the same as our two eyes give us depth perception. They are tuned to detect sounds within a limited frequency range, from about 31 hertz, or 31 cycles per second, to 18 kilohertz, or 18,000 cycles per second. Musically speaking, that is a range of about nine octaves. The other limitation is the measurement of loudness, or intensity. Advancing years diminish the sensitivity of our ears' ability to detect portions of the hearing range.

A whispered endearment, a shout of rejoicing, or the snap of a twig will send vibrations through the air, compression waves that impact our eardrums. Those vibrations are transferred by to the inner ear by three tiny bones that act as shock absorbers. The mallus, or hammer, connects to the incus, or anvil, which in turn connects to the stapes, or stirrup. The plate at the end of the stirrup inserts into the window of the cochlea, and acts as a diaphragm pump, changing the vibrations to compression waves in the fluid that fills the cochlea.

The snail shaped cochlea is like a rolled up piano keyboard, with hair-like nerve endings corresponding to the keys. Each nerve ending senses its own pitch. The keyboard is backwards, with the highest pitch sensors nearest the window, and it is these that are the first to be damaged. It is these high pitch sensors that are associated with the detection of the hard consonant sounds of speech, the sounds that give shape and distinction to the words we hear.

When the shock absorber system is overwhelmed, those tiny sensors can be snapped off. If that occurs, either that range of sound cannot be detected any longer, or the sensors short-circuit in their detection mode, and give a continuous signal that the brain detects as the constant high-pitched ringing or hissing of auditory static that cancels out the real crickets, or the chirp of a hummingbird, and makes other people seem to mumble.

Scripture has much to say regarding our ears, both physically, and symbolically. Ecclesiastes chapter 12harmonizes with the old hymn, "Give of Your Best to the Master." Its version is give thought and attention to your Creator while you are young, before things fall apart. ***"Remember also your Creator in the days of your youth, before the evil days come and the years draw near of which you will say, 'I have no pleasure in them'... and the doors on the street are shut--when the sound of the grinding is low, and one rises up at the sound of a bird, and all the daughters of song are brought low..."*** (Ecc 12:1, 4 ESV) Indeed, we find two aspects to hearing addressed in the Word of God, ability and willingness.

Jesus miraculously gave the ability to hear to those who were deaf. There were those who affirmed that wondrous work of our Lord: ***"And they were astonished beyond measure, saying, 'He has done all things well. He even makes the deaf hear and the mute speak.'"*** (Mark 7:37 ESV) But more important to Him was the willingness to hear. Again and again He said, ***"He who has ears to hear, let him hear."*** (Mat 11:15 ESV) If we could see the people around Him as he spoke those words, we would see they were equipped to hear. But His meaning went beyond the physical perception of sound. The willingness to hear included the mind to understand and the heart to respond. Where the things of God are concerned, the capacity to understand and to respond comes only from God Himself, through the working of His Holy Spirit within.

We find an instructive statement from Moses in the relationship between God and the people of Israel, the ones He had chosen for His own glory. After forty years of seeing the blessing and the wrath of God, he told them, *"But to this day the LORD has not given you a heart to understand or eyes to see or ears to hear."* (Deut 29:4 ESV) It is the reality of that statement that shaped the course of Israel through the ensuing centuries. What Elihu told Job was true for Israel as well: *"Surely you have spoken in my ears, and I have heard the sound of your words."* (Job 33:8 ESV) The same thing would be true for me in Russia, or China, or any other country whose language I cannot speak or understand. A person there could speak to me, and I would hear the sound of the words. However, I would not know the meaning. Elihu knew the key. *"But it is the spirit in man, the breath of the Almighty, that makes him understand."* (Job 32:8 ESV) Without God's Holy Spirit opening our understanding, we cannot comprehend God's Word to us, or His purpose. As Paul wrote, *"Now we have received not the spirit of the world, but the Spirit who is from God, that we might understand the things freely given us by God. And we impart this in words not taught by human wisdom but taught by the Spirit, interpreting spiritual truths to those who are spiritual. The natural person does not accept the things of the Spirit of God, for they are folly to him, and he is not able to understand them because they are spiritually discerned."* (1Cor 2:12-14 ESV)

Israel was unable to understand. They would reject God's evaluation of them, just as we, in our unregenerate state, deny our inability to comprehend. But, in our denial, we, like they, condemn ourselves. After healing the man blind from birth, we find a pointed conversation: *"Jesus said, 'For judgment I came into this world, that those who do not see may see, and those who see may become blind.' Some of the Pharisees near him heard these things, and said to him, 'Are we also blind?' Jesus said to them, 'If you were blind, you would have no guilt; but now that you say, "We see," your guilt remains."* (John 9:39-41 ESV) They gloried in their shame.

Israel's persistence in rebellion against God led to an ominous commission. Of Pharaoh in the days of Israel's bondage in Egypt we read again and again that he hardened his heart. Then, we read that God hardened his heart. In sending the prophet Isaiah, God implied a parallel: *"And he said, 'Go, and say to this people: "Keep on hearing, but do not understand; keep on seeing, but do not perceive."' Make the heart of this people dull, and their ears heavy, and blind their eyes; lest they see with their eyes, and hear with their ears, and understand with their hearts, and turn and be healed."* (Isa 6:9-10 ESV) We find the same thread of commitment to judgment in Romans, where humanity is concluded in willful opposition to God, suppressing the Truth in unrighteousness. The repeated words are a condemning knell: *"Therefore God gave them up...For this reason God gave them up...And since they did not see fit to acknowledge God, God gave them up..."* (Rom 1:24, 26, 28 ESV) In His permissive sovereignty, God released them from restraint to pursue to its bitter conclusion the course they had chosen.

Jesus referred to Isaiah's message when He told His disciples, *"This is why I speak to them in parables, because seeing they do not see, and hearing they do not hear, nor do they understand. Indeed, in their case the prophecy of Isaiah is fulfilled that says: 'You will indeed hear but never understand, and you will indeed see but never perceive. For this people's heart has grown dull, and with their ears they can barely hear, and their eyes they have closed, lest they should see with their eyes and hear with their ears and understand with their heart and turn, and I would heal them.'"* (Mat 13:13-15 ESV)

In the days when the judgment foretold was being fulfilled, Jeremiah's message from God to the wayward people was direct:

"Hear this, O foolish and senseless people, who have eyes, but see not, who have ears, but hear not." (Jer 5:21 ESV) Hear what? For twenty-three years, Jeremiah pleaded with the people, with tears, giving them the admonitions of God. Yet, after all those years, he told them, *"You have neither listened nor inclined your ears to hear, although the LORD persistently sent to you all his servants the prophets..."* (Jer 25:4 ESV)

To the prophet Ezekiel God gave the heart of the problem in Israel, which was a problem of the heart: *"Son of man, you dwell in the midst of a rebellious house, who have eyes to see, but see not, who have ears to hear, but hear not, for they are a rebellious house."* (Eze 12:2 ESV) That overt rebelliousness is pictured by the prophet Zechariah: *"But they refused to pay attention and turned a stubborn shoulder and stopped their ears that they might not hear."* (Zec 7:11 ESV)

Selective hearing is a skill we all develop early in life. To my shame, I confess I cultivated the ability to generalize my parents into background noise when I did not want to listen to what they had to say. It was an inward rebellion, not the outward turning of the stubborn shoulder or the physical covering of the ears. We can brush aside the obvious admonition of Scripture, saying, "That was Israel. It does not apply to me!" But, Scripture precludes such an avenue of escape of guilt. Paul wrote to the believers at Rome, *"For whatever was written in former days was written for our instruction, that through endurance and through the encouragement of the Scriptures we might have hope."* (Rom 15:4 ESV) He recalls the chastening of the Lord that came as a result of failing to pay attention to the words of the Lord. The opposite side of the warning against rebellion is the encouragement and hope found in willing submission. To the believers at Corinth, he wrote, *"Now these things happened to them as an example, but they were written down for our instruction, on whom the end of the ages has come."* (1Cor 10:11 ESV)

We, unlike those in previous ages, are indwelt by God's Holy Spirit. His ministry within us is to open our understanding, to guide us in the Truth, and to apply God's Word to the core of our being, that the Word of God might be the controller of our lives. Jesus told His disciples, ***"But the Helper, the Holy Spirit, whom the Father will send in my name, he will teach you all things and bring to your remembrance all that I have said to you."*** (John 14:26 ESV) We have good forgetters. How desperately we need Him to remind us of God's wonderful truth, and how faithful He is in that ministry, if only we would listen.

But, His ministry reaches beyond our minds, to our very lives. He guides our steps in our walk of obedience. It is God's purpose in and through us that our Lord Jesus Christ be revealed in this world. ***"When the Spirit of truth comes, he will guide you into all the truth, for he will not speak on his own authority, but whatever he hears he will speak, and he will declare to you the things that are to come. He will glorify me, for he will take what is mine and declare it to you."*** (John 14:13-14 ESV) As He has declared the Word to us, we, as witness bearers, are by His grace to treasure it and live it: ***"Let the word of Christ dwell in you richly, teaching and admonishing one another in all wisdom, singing psalms and hymns and spiritual songs, with thankfulness in your hearts to God. And whatever you do, in word or deed, do everything in the name of the Lord Jesus, giving thanks to God the Father through him."*** (Col 3:16-17 ESV) Like the prophets of old, we are to proclaim it: ***"Do all things without grumbling or questioning, that you may be blameless and innocent, children of God without blemish in the midst of a crooked and twisted generation, among whom you shine as lights in the world, holding fast to the word of life..."*** (Php 2:14-16a ESV) It may not be comfortable, shining in a dark world, but the hiding of the Light will be less comfortable. The admonition to be witness bearers is not optional for us, even as it was not optional for them.

Consider Ezekiel's marching orders: *"And the man said to me, 'Son of man, look with your eyes, and hear with your ears, and set your heart upon all that I shall show you, for you were brought here in order that I might show it to you. Declare all that you see to the house of Israel.'"* (Eze 40:4 ESV)

Our declaration is to a lost and dying world. Our marching orders are just as urgent: *"And Jesus came and said to them, 'All authority in heaven and on earth has been given to me. Go therefore and make disciples of all nations, baptizing them in the name of the Father and of the Son and of the Holy Spirit, teaching them to observe all that I have commanded you. And behold, I am with you always, to the end of the age.'"* (Mat 28:18-20 ESV) Our message does not come from visions. Peter assures us, *"And we have something more sure, the prophetic word, to which you will do well to pay attention as to a lamp shining in a dark place, until the day dawns and the morning star rises in your hearts, knowing this first of all, that no prophecy of Scripture comes from someone's own interpretation. For no prophecy was ever produced by the will of man, but men spoke from God as they were carried along by the Holy Spirit."* (2Pet 1:19-21 ESV) Note the urgent **pay attention** in that passage. We can. Our minds are renewed, our understanding is no longer darkened, our ears are opened, and our new, clean hearts are inclined by the indwelling Spirit to respond. Therefore, in His letters to the seven churches in Asia, representing church ages in the Book of Revelation, we find our Lord repeating, *"He who has an ear, let him hear what the Spirit says to the churches..."* (ESV)

25

MOLES

Rarely do they come out in the open. They work unseen, under the surface, undermining in their hidden pursuits, and damaging in their aftermath, heaping dirt randomly, and revisiting their scenes of harm with a disheartening regularity. Strong, persistent, these destroyers systematically gouge away in their subterranean network, strewing the surface above them with mounds of dirt and stones, heedless of the impact of their industry.

Moles are the bane of of both the landscape and those who work to maintain it. Fields, gardens and lawns are all at risk. Overnight, a sidewalk or driveway adds a border of dirty pom poms. The newly-sprouted garden has its miniature forest overturned or buried by erupting dirt volcanoes. The manicured lawn displays a labyrinth of buckled sod, sometimes including one or more hulking minotaur mounds.

Moles are relentless in their subsurface excavations. They construct an underground network of intersecting tunnels, shafts, nests and storehouses, then routinely patrol, maintain and expand them. A single mole will dig and occupy a tunnel web extending for hundreds of feet, and can be solely responsible for a system that covers an acre or more. The mounds of dirt are multifunctional. They serve as tailing disposals for the tunneling operations, filters for the ventilation system, barriers to the entrances to the network, and emergency exits, should the mole have to relocate.

Eliminating a single mole can quiet a large area of damage, but the connections remain unseen beneath the surface. Eventually, another mole will stumble upon the ready-made tunnel system, and take up residency. Depending on the length of the vacancy and the surface activity, there will be repairs to be accomplished, which will be revealed in the sudden reappearance of mole hills in an area that had shown no on-going damage. The network was there, complete with ready outlets, and the new resident could simply pursue the same pattern of destruction.

We find the same pattern in the fields of life. In the discovery process, potential witnesses in court cases must be disclosed. Once their names are revealed, another kind of moles goes to work, digging into their past, searching for anything that will diminish their credibility. In politics, as soon as a candidate files for an office, or is considered a potential candidate, opponents and their operatives begin the destructive work of mud slinging, seeking out or inventing issues that might discredit the one who dares to run against them. Damage to the viability of the opponent is primary. Truth is secondary. Since the candidate becomes a public figure upon announcing for the office, libel laws do not apply. The politics of slander has become the norm. Working unseen, operatives dig out bits of information that, edited and recast, can be pushed to the surface at strategic points in a hidden network. By truth, lies or innuendo, the smear campaign has become the accepted political process.

Ingrained in the depths of fallen nature of humanity, gossip and slander are woven into the fabric of society. As accepted and expected as character assassination is in the value system of the world, God's view is unequivocal. ***"There are six things that the LORD hates, seven that are an abomination to him...a false witness who breathes out lies, and one who sows discord among brothers."*** (Pro 6:16, 19 ESV) Discord. Disharmony. Disunity. Division. These are the destructive molehills of the behind-the-scenes destroyer with the slashing tongue. By the Spirit, David's portrayal of the slanderer is revealing: ***"Hide me from the secret plots of the wicked, from the throng of evildoers, who whet their tongues like swords, who aim bitter words like arrows, shooting from ambush at the blameless, shooting at him suddenly and without fear."*** (Psa 64:2-4 ESV)

Scripture employs several terms to describe these divisive mischief workers. They are called slanderers, talebearers, gossips, busybodies, meddlers, whisperers and simple babblers. Society tends to trivialize the terms, and the ones they describe are accepted as a necessary thread in the fabric of life. Indeed, they find a ready ear nearly anywhere. ***"The words of a whisperer are like delicious morsels; they go down into the inner parts of the body."*** (Pro 18:8 ESV) The delicious bits of gossip, though, whispered by talebearers, are a time-release pill of poison. ***"They make their tongue sharp as a serpent's, and under their lips is the venom of asps. Selah"*** (Psa 140:3 ESV) Pause and ponder. That is the meaning of that word, *selah*. Stop and think. In the view of God, these whisperers are not trivial, or acceptable. God hates them, and their deeds. They are an abomination to Him. Consider His perspective: ***"A worthless person, a wicked man, goes about with crooked speech, winks with his eyes, signals with his feet, points with his finger, with perverted heart devises evil, continually sowing discord..."*** (Pro 6:12-14 ESV) The body language we see includes more: the wiggled eyebrow, the smirk, the rolled eyes, and in this modern technology age, the thinly-veiled post, the suggestive question or the draw-your-own-conclusions half-statement carry the gestures by implication or icon. A good name is sullied. More mole hills. There is nothing trivial about the terms God uses: worthless, wicked, crooked and perverted. These are condemning terms in Scripture. They underscore the nature of the wickedness in the eyes of God, who places His own holy character as the plumb line: *"You shall not go around as a slanderer among your people, and you shall not stand up against the life of your neighbor: I am the LORD."* (Lev 19:16 ESV) In His instructions to His chosen people, Israel, God repeatedly placed that phrase, *I am the LORD*, after a commandment, emphasizing His holiness as the standard upon which the commandment stood. The divisiveness of discord was thus juxtaposed with the unity of the Godhead as its opposite.

Our Lord Jesus Christ, in His high priestly prayer for His own, for those the Father had given Him out of the world, includes the eternal purpose of unity in the body of Christ, the church. *"I do not ask for these only, but also for those who will believe in me through their word, that they may all be one, just as you, Father, are in me, and I in you, that they also may be in us, so that the world may believe that you have sent me. The glory that you have given me I have given to them, that they may be one even as we are one..."* (John 17:20-22 ESV) The analogy of the body Scripture presents emphasizes God's purpose of unity: *"...so we, though many, are one body in Christ, and individually members one of another."* (Rom 12:5 ESV) Even as with our physical bodies that suffer pain with the piercing of thorns, the bumps and bruises, and the cuts and scrapes of our daily journey, so the body of Christ suffers pain. *"If one member suffers, all suffer together; if one member is honored, all rejoice together."* (1Cor 12:26 ESV)

The world, without God, without Christ and without hope, operates by its own standards, its own values. Those lost in the world's system, the *Cosmos Diabolicus*, exude the fruit of selfishness that is intrinsic to the depraved nature of fallen humanity. The deeds of the flesh, in all of their diabolical variety, characterize the lifestyle of the lost. Believers, born of God, created anew in Christ Jesus, and indwelt by God's Holy Spirit, are called to a higher lifestyle of humility and service: ***"Do nothing from rivalry or conceit, but in humility count others more significant than yourselves."*** (Phil 2:3 ESV) The wording in the first part of this beseeching of grace emphasizes that believers must still contend with the residue of Adam. Lurking within our outward man, our flesh, we find the conceit, the malice, the envy and jealousy that, unchecked, will bear its poison fruit that damages relationships, and destroys unity. Indeed, in the church at Corinth, Paul warned, ***"For I fear that perhaps when I come I may find you not as I wish, and that you may find me not as you wish--that perhaps there may be quarreling, jealousy, anger, hostility, slander, gossip, conceit, and disorder."*** (2Cor 12:20 ESV) Whisperers abounded in the assembly in Paul's day. Tongues were wagging, egos clashing, and sin in the assembly dividing. Paul's *perhaps* was an understatement.

The impact within the body of believers is devastating. Solomon writes, ***"A dishonest man spreads strife, and a whisperer separates close friends."*** (Pro 16:28 ESV) The personal impact of the slanderer's whispers is visceral. ***"The words of a talebearer are as wounds, and they go down into the innermost parts of the belly."*** (Pro 18:8 KJV) Slander is a body blow that staggers us, debilitates us. It pierces to our emotional core, and, the flesh unchecked, draws retribution, that further divides the body of believers. Scripture cites factions and party spirit as the result, as fleshly believers take sides, expanding the rift.

Consider what subsurface forces are at work to produce these dirt mounds of divisiveness. God's Spirit uses James to give us a glimpse of the root. ***"But if you have bitter jealousy and selfish ambition in your hearts, do not boast and be false to the truth. This is not the wisdom that comes down from above, but is earthly, unspiritual, demonic.***

For where jealousy and selfish ambition exist, there will be disorder and every vile practice. But the wisdom from above is first pure, then peaceable, gentle, open to reason, full of mercy and good fruits, impartial and sincere. And a harvest of righteousness is sown in peace by those who make peace." (James 3:14-18 ESV)

The word *unchecked* is pivotal in our considerations. Believers are indwelt by the Holy Spirit of God. Our Lord Jesus Christ said of the ministry of the Spirit, *"But the Helper, the Holy Spirit, whom the Father will send in my name, he will teach you all things and bring to your remembrance all that I have said to you. When the Spirit of truth comes, he will guide you into all the truth, for he will not speak on his own authority, but whatever he hears he will speak, and he will declare to you the things that are to come."* (John 14:26, 16:13 ESV) God's Spirit in the believer actively guides the walk, the actions and attitudes, the thoughts, words and relationships of the one in Christ, in and through the Word of God.

Often, though, the believer does not respond to the Spirit within. Note Paul's beseeching of grace to the Galatian believers: *"But I say, walk by the Spirit, and you will not gratify the desires of the flesh. For the desires of the flesh are against the Spirit, and the desires of the Spirit are against the flesh, for these are opposed to each other, to keep you from doing the things you want to do."* (Gal 5:16-17 ESV) Our flesh delights to whisper, to slander, to gossip. We hear a shocking bit of news, and our tongues are wagging before we find an ear to listen. The Spirit urges love, and the flesh plots hate. We face a moment of decision. We can respond to the Spirit's guidance, or we can resist the Spirit, and choose our own fleshly way. *"Whoever goes about slandering reveals secrets, but he who is trustworthy in spirit keeps a thing covered."* (Pro 11:13 ESV)

Responsiveness to the Spirit and to the Word are vital. James sets a stark reality before us: *"...but no human being can tame the tongue. It is a restless evil, full of deadly poison."* (James 3:8 ESV) Control, then, is only possible through the ministry of God's Spirit within us, and our response to His prompting. Indeed, self-control is not, and cannot be, self in control, but rather self under control, yielded to the direction of the Holy Spirit.

Solomon knew the power of slander and malicious gossip from his childhood days, seeing the chaos in the household and reign of his father, David. *"A worthless man plots evil, and his speech is like a scorching fire."* (Pro 16:27 ESV) He was a witness to the incendiary nature of talebearers. James agrees: *"So also the tongue is a small member, yet it boasts of great things. How great a forest is set ablaze by such a small fire! And the tongue is a fire, a world of unrighteousness. The tongue is set among our members, staining the whole body, setting on fire the entire course of life, and set on fire by hell."* (James 3:5-6 ESV)

Again, Solomon gives God's remedy: *"Whoever goes about slandering reveals secrets; therefore do not associate with a simple babbler."* (Pro 20:19 ESV) Paul endorses the solution: *"And we enjoin you, brothers, in the name of our Lord Jesus Christ, to draw yourselves back from every brother walking in a disorderly way, and not according to the teaching which you received from us."* (2Thes 3:6 ESV) We are to admonish the unruly one. If there is no responsiveness to the Word of God, no repentance, no change, no confession of sin, then there can be no fellowship. We are not to listen to slander, and certainly not to repeat it. *"For lack of wood the fire goes out, and where there is no whisperer, quarreling ceases."* (Pro 26:20 ESV) Deprived of a listening ear, the flaming tongue is quenched. Remember the words of James, earlier? *"But the wisdom from above is first pure, then peaceable, gentle, open to reason, full of mercy and good fruits, impartial and sincere. And a harvest of righteousness is sown in peace by those who make peace."* (James 3:17-18 ESV) Making peace may involve rebuke, and it may involve turning away. But quashing gossip is an act of love. *"Whoever covers an offense seeks love, but he who repeats a matter separates close friends."* (Pro 17:9 ESV) Paul's caution is the other side of Solomon's: *"But if you bite and devour one another, watch out that you are not consumed by one another."* (Gal 5:15 ESV) Again, through Solomon, God gives the solution to a multitude of evils that spring from the same seed: *"The beginning of strife is like letting out water, so quit before the quarrel breaks out. He who justifies the wicked and he who condemns the righteous are both alike an abomination to the LORD."* (Pro 17:14-15 ESV)

26

REFRESHING

Summers on the farm where I grew up brought endless work that had to be done under a sky that was often cloudless. The sun trudged across the sky, and, unable to contain its burden of heat, it spilled it endlessly on the fields where we labored. The hottest time of the year was the time for putting up the hay supply for the cows' winter feeding, for cutting and splitting eight to ten cords of firewood for our winter comfort, and for endlessly trying to stay ahead of the weeds in over an acre of garden, so it would supply winter food for our family that included four growing farm boys who were never full, or so it seemed. The wood and hay were the most challenging, since they were farthest from the house. Thirst was our constant companion.

In the canyon below the house and the hay field flowed a creek that ran cold throughout the year. It increased in volume along its half-mile course through our farm, due to the many springs that flowed from the hillsides on both sides of the creek. Water ran cold and refreshing from the heart of the hill, in some cases over five gallons per minute. Scooped from the very mouth of the spring, clean and pure, that water brought relief to the dry throat and the sweaty brow. However, the walk to the spring was long, and the trudge back up the slope was longer. Besides, in its frequency, it robbed too much valuable work time from the work window in the weather patterns.

We took a jug of water with us, but when the temperature is over a hundred degrees in the shade, a jug of water warms quickly. There is nothing refreshing or satisfying about tepid water to a worker who has been parched by a relentless sun. It is wet, and meets an inner need, but it is only the need to rehydrate that keeps us from spitting it out. The solution turned out to be simple. When we wrapped the jug in a thick towel soaked in water, and tucked it under a thick layer of hay on the shady side of a haystack, there was an interesting effect that proved delightful. The towel dried slowly, and the evaporating water cooled the water in the jug. Hot as the sun was, the temperature of the water in the jug actually dropped. It is the same as the chilling effect we feel when we step out of a hot bath or shower.

This phenomenon has been used around the world throughout human history. In many cultures, the household water needs are supplied using an unglazed earthenware vessel. Whatever its size, this cistern serves as the in-home water cooler. It is filled from whatever outside water source is available, and, throughout the day, water seeps through the porous walls of the vessel, evaporates, and thus cools the contents. A canvas water bag or a blanket-wrapped canteen are equally effective. No matter how hot the day, the thirsty one is refreshed by the cold water, whether it is consumed, or used to bathe sun-scorched skin.

A cup of cold water has been the desire of those who labor since God told Adam that it would be by the sweat of his face that he would earn his meals. Fresh-water springs and wells have been the focus of many feuds through the centuries. Clean, fresh water is vital to our survival, second only to air in its power to sustain life. Without water, we perish within about one hundred hours.

In its early stages, thirst is irritating, prompting abrasive behavior. When God used Moses to lead the Israelites out of Egypt, where they had been enslaved for four hundred years, their journey led through a desert region. Such regions receive less than nine inches of rainfall annually, and what surface water sources available are scattered, and are varied in their quality. Some are refreshing. Some are polluted. Some, due to their dissolved mineral content, are deadly.

An estimated two million people, with their livestock, would require a tremendous amount of water. In the early stage of thirst, they grew irritable. ***"But the people thirsted there for water, and the people grumbled against Moses and said, 'Why did you bring us up out of Egypt, to kill us and our children and our livestock with thirst?'"*** (Exo 17:3 ESV) How narrow our focus, and faulty our memories when our cravings press us but a little! God's message to them said nothing of perishing of thirst. His word was that He would take them to the land He had promised to the patriarchs. Instead of resting in the certainty of His word, they grew strident in their complaining against the visible presence, Moses.

God's answer was to give them His miraculous supply. Where human perception failed, God Himself provided for their desperate need from His perfect abundance. He told Moses, ***"'Behold, I will stand before you there on the rock at Horeb, and you shall strike the rock, and water shall come out of it, and the people will drink.' And Moses did so, in the sight of the elders of Israel."*** (Exo 17:6 ESV) Our focus, when we read that portion, naturally focuses on the water, desperately needed, that flowed from the rock. We tend to overlook the prophetic picture that introduces the provision. "Behold," God said, "I will stand before you there on the rock at Horeb." When Moses struck, he struck more than a protruding portion of the lithosphere, so much more than an outcropping of stone. That we might fully comprehend the prophecy in the type, Paul, writing to the believers at Corinth, said of the Israelites, ***"...and all drank the same spiritual drink. For they drank from the spiritual Rock that followed them, and the Rock was Christ."*** (1Cor 10:4 ESV)

The channel of God's supply of their great need was Jesus Christ. That adds clearer significance to the sin of Moses, the act that barred him from entering the land God had promises, that disqualified him from the final honor of leadership. Thirst again confronted the Israelites. Grumbling was again the result. God again supplied their need in their extremity. However, His instructions to Moses were different, this time: ***"Take the staff, and assemble the congregation, you and Aaron your brother, and tell the rock before their eyes to yield its water. So you shall bring water out of the rock for them and give drink to the congregation and their cattle."*** (Num 20:8 ESV) His staff was the symbol of his authority, extended to him by God. This time, before the assembled Israelites, he was to speak to the rock. He was, in short, to pray. Through the already smitten rock, the Rock, Christ Jesus, their need would be supplied, and God would be glorified. Therein lies the enormity of Moses' sin.

"Then Moses and Aaron gathered the assembly together before the rock, and he said to them, 'Hear now, you rebels: shall we bring water for you out of this rock?' And Moses lifted up his hand and struck the rock with his staff twice, and water came out abundantly, and the congregation drank, and their livestock." (Num 20:10-11 ESV) Moses claimed God's rightful glory for himself. Worse, in anger, he berated the people in the supplying of God's blessing. But the most grievous violation of God's instructions to him centered in his action of striking the rock, not once, but twice. The Smitten Savior was smitten again; in type, He was crucified afresh.

God gave them abundant, refreshing water from the rock, in

spite of the disobedience of Moses. The craving of the people for that which God supplied was satisfied. But, tracing their journey from that day through the ensuing centuries confirms that they craved the blessings, not the Giver of the blessings. Their focus was on the temporal, not on the eternal. Their cravings were physical, not spiritual. They drank the water from the rock, and were satisfied, but thirsted again.

God gives a gracious invitation through the pen of the psalmist, David: *"Oh, taste and see that the LORD is good!"* (Psa 34:8 ESV) In transitioning from the temporal to the eternal, David uses physical needs to portray our deep need for God Himself. The psalmist, in a personal cry that resonates in our own hearts, voices our deepest need that transcends our narrow existence: *"As a deer pants for flowing streams, so pants my soul for you, O God. My soul thirsts for God, for the living God..."* (Psa 42:1-2 ESV) For the one who has indeed tasted, and found that the Lord is good, His temporal supply is no longer enough. Our longing hearts join David's plea: *"O God, you are my God; earnestly I seek you; my soul thirsts for you; my flesh faints for you, as in a dry and weary land where there is no water."* (Psa 63:1 ESV) *"I stretch out my hands to you; my soul thirsts for you like a parched land."* (Psa 143:6 ESV)

Remember that Rock in the desert? Jesus Christ is God's answer to our deepest needs. To our cry of thirst to God, He gives a gracious answer. *"Come, everyone who thirsts, come to the waters; and he who has no money, come, buy and eat! Come, buy wine and milk without money and without price."* (Isa 55:1 ESV) The Savior Himself repeated the invitation centuries later. *"On the last day of the feast, the great day, Jesus stood up and cried out, 'If anyone thirsts, let him come to me and drink. Whoever believes in me, as the Scripture has said, "Out of his heart will flow rivers of living water."'"* (John 7:37-38 ESV) Christ Himself, the Giver of life, the Living Word, takes the satisfaction of deepest thirst to a higher level. Filled with Himself, filled with His word, we will not have our own craving assuaged, but will be the channel through which He will bless others with that cup of cold water, both physically and spiritually. The giving of a cup of cold water brings a blessing. Jesus said, **"And whoever gives one of these little ones even a cup of cold water because he is a disciple, truly, I say to you, he will by no means lose his reward."** (Mat 10:42 ESV) But, in His conversation with the Samaritan woman of Sychar, He drew a distinction between the physical water and the spiritual. Speaking of the water from Jacob's well, **"...Jesus said to her, 'Everyone who drinks of this water will be thirsty again, but whoever drinks of the water that I will give him will never be thirsty again. The water that I will give him will become in him a spring of water welling up to eternal life.'"** (John 4:13-14 ESV)

Notice the imagery, and the reality it implies. Within the one who has imbibed our Lord Jesus Christ Himself, the water of His word, will be "...a spring of water welling up." Water welling up, bubbling out, becomes "...rivers of living water," flowing out from our innermost being, from our very core, to nourish, to nurture, to bless those around us. The body-life blessings of believers giving those cups of cold water, living water given in the name of the Savior, will be a testimony to those who still have that spiritual thirst unsatisfied, who have never experienced the heart-deep filling of the water of life. Our Lord's voice resounds through time from the threshold of eternity: **"It is done! I am the Alpha and the Omega, the beginning and the end. To the thirsty I will give from the spring of the water of life without payment."** (Rev 21:6 ESV) Every believer, as a channel of blessing, joins in the eternal invitation: **"The Spirit and the Bride say, 'Come.' And let the one who hears say, 'Come.' And let the one who is thirsty come; let the one who desires take the water of life without price."** (Rev 22:17 ESV)

27

CORMORANTS

The Young's Bay Enhancement program was designed as a fall-back opportunity for local commercial fishermen. The concept behind the program was sound, but the implementation of the ideas proved to be flawed.

Hatchery salmon smolts were fin-clipped for identification, then raised in net pens in the bay. During the rearing time, workers would broadcast food pellets, sized appropriately for the growth stage of the baby fish, scattering the food over the surface of the water. The salmon smolts were thus programmed to swarm to the top in response to the disturbance of the surface.

To discourage predation, vertical plastic pipes surrounded the pens, pipes that flexed with the slightest breeze, the gentle rocking of the ripples on the water, or any attempt to use the pipe as a perch. The growing fish had their inherent fear of deadly threats dulled by exposure without consequence. Caspian terns circled above the pens, fluttered overhead, but did not dive. Cormorants flew by, circled, and perched on near-by pilings, but did not attack.

These two conditioned responses, one active, the other passive, would combine to undermine the whole enhancement program.

My living room window overlooks Young's Bay. I have never needed to ask when the salmon smolts were released from the net pens. That was announced by frustrated predators who descended with a vengeance.

Screaming terns circled randomly, scanning the waters of the bay. The cormorants, however, employed a tactic that took advantage of the conditioned response ingrained in the smolts. Hundreds, at first, then more than a thousand, marshaled into successive ranks, flew low over the water's surface with their wingtips tapping the bay. Theirs was a systematic search for the schools of young salmon. The fish, reared and fed in the restrictive quarters of the net pens, stayed in a relatively small cloud that peregrinated throughout the several square miles of the bay as a unit. This pattern set up the disastrous encounter that undermined the economic program.

The tapping searchers eventually passed above the swirling smolts, drawing them to the surface, sometimes in front of the second line of searchers, or the third. The resulting tumult of squawking and splashing drew the leading ranks swarming back, no longer orderly, but each hurrying to plunge into the maelstrom of the feeding frenzy, diving, seizing, and surfacing, to gulp down the captured smolt, and dive again. The following ranks joined the boiling chaos, as did the terns, drawn by the noise. They hovered, wheeled and plunged, to capture the scattering refugees that ventured too near the top of the water.

Within minutes, a thousand predators would consume perhaps ten thousand young fish. The smolts that dived and scattered would swirl through the area, regrouping, trading the safety of isolation for the vulnerability of companionship, and the sated hunters would withdraw, to rest and preen, only to return, guaranteed another orgy of destruction, day after day, until the scattered survivors stayed scattered. Only those who learned to flee survived to make the seaward journey, to return a few years later to face another predator – man. But that is another story.

How very like those salmon smolts we can be. We harbor within our natures the vulnerability to become desensitized to dangers that surround us. Repeated stimulus-response patterns become ingrained habits, instinctive behavior or speech that bypass cognitive thought. Habits weave the fabric of lifestyle. We do things because we've always done them that way. We say things because that's just the way we speak. In our habits, we find ourselves products of our society, our culture and our heritage. We are shaped by our value programmers. At the same time, we are the product of our choices. We are responsible for what we are.

The Bible acknowledges both of these realities. By the Spirit, Peter attests to the heritage aspect of life patterns: ***"And if you call on him as Father who judges impartially according to each one's deeds, conduct yourselves with fear throughout the time of your exile, knowing that you were ransomed from the futile ways inherited from your forefathers, not with perishable things such as silver or gold, but with the precious blood of Christ, like that of a lamb without blemish or spot."*** (1Pet 1:17-19 ESV) Those futile inherited ways were our context when we were value programming. We learned. We observed. We complied. We emulated. In so doing, we transitioned into the realm of choice.

That pattern of choice personalized the inheritance. Paul wrote, ***"And you were dead in the trespasses and sins in which you once walked, following the course of this world, following the prince of the power of the air, the spirit that is now at work in the sons of disobedience-- among whom we all once lived in the passions of our***

flesh, carrying out the desires of the body and the mind, and were by nature children of wrath, like the rest of mankind." (Eph 2:1-3 ESV) We find a distinction of terms in this passage. The use of the word ***sons*** denotes those with the capacity to choose. The sons of disobedience chose disobedience willfully and willingly. That usage asserts responsibility. The course (values) of this world, this age, established by Satan himself, resonated with the fallen desires lodged in our flesh. We chose the self-focused, self-pleasing, self-serving lifestyle common to mankind. The common nature of the ***children*** of wrath fell heir to the consequences of the ancestral choices, all the way back to Adam, who, in his rebellion, chose independence from God on behalf of all of his descendents.

Such, then, was the plight of all of mankind. Dead in trespasses and sins, enemies of God, hostile toward God, we were helpless. We were powerless to change, and did not desire anything different than what we knew. ***"But God, being rich in mercy, because of the great love with which he loved us, even when we were dead in our trespasses, made us alive together with Christ--by grace you have been saved-- and raised us up with him and seated us with him in the heavenly places in Christ Jesus, so that in the coming ages he might show the immeasurable riches of his grace in kindness toward us in Christ Jesus."*** (Eph 2:4-7 ESV)

Praise God for that little contrastive word, *but*. "But God..." God, who, rich in mercy, reached down into that quagmire, that cesspool of humanity, and drew out a remnant for His glorious purpose. In His high-priestly prayer in John chapter 17, our Lord spoke repeatedly of believers as those the Father had given Him ***"out of the world."*** It is they who ***were ransomed from the futile ways inherited from*** [their] ***forefathers,*** and ***and raised...up with him.***

On the basis of God's working, believers are called to a new lifestyle, a new manner of conducting ourselves. The King James

Version refers to this as our conversation, and our walk. In either case, Scripture has our daily conduct and habits, not just our words, in view. Paul wrote, ***"Now this I say and testify in the Lord, that you must no longer walk as the Gentiles do, in the futility of their minds. They are darkened in their understanding, alienated from the life of God because of the ignorance that is in them, due to their hardness of heart."*** (Eph 4: 17-18 ESV) In Christ, we have a new existence. We were born into a living death, but born again into life eternal. We were children of wrath, but now are sons of God. We were slaves to passions of the mind and body, to sin, and to Satan, but now are servants of the living God, and of righteousness. We are, at the same time, in hostile territory, surrounded by enemies of God, who are out to destroy the testimony of the Lord in us. ***"Look carefully then how you walk, not as unwise but as wise, making the best use of the time, because the days are evil."*** (Eph 5:15-16)

We are commissioned to carry a message with us wherever we go. The message is first written in our lives by the indwelling Spirit of God, as He applies the Scriptures, the written Word of God to our center of core values, our hearts. We are then called to live in conformity to the message of life, the message of grace that we have received, and proclaim. ***"Only let your manner of life be worthy of the gospel of Christ..."*** (Php 1:27 ESV)

The values of the Christlife are programmed into our hearts. We learn them, as we learn Christ. As Paul said to the believers at Ephesus, ***"But that is not the way you learned Christ!-- assuming that you have heard about him and were taught in him, as the truth is in Jesus, to put off your old self, which belongs to your former manner of life and is corrupt through deceitful desires, and to be renewed in the spirit of your minds, and to put on the new self, created after the likeness of God in true righteousness and holiness."*** (Eph 4:20-24 ESV) The purpose of our new value programming is related to our commission, ***"...so as to walk in a manner worthy of the Lord, fully pleasing to him,*** *bearing fruit in every good work and increasing in the knowledge of God."* (Col 1:10 ESV)

Just as the salmon smolts had to abandon shallow habits of mere surface existence, and go deeper, exercising new patterns of behavior, so does the believer. *"Therefore, as you received Christ Jesus the Lord, so walk in him, rooted and built up in him and established in the faith, just as you were taught, abounding in thanksgiving."* (Col 2:6-7 ESV) It is not optional for the believer. John tells us, *"whoever says he abides in him ought to walk in the same way in which he walked."* (1John 2:6 ESV)

Just as the young salmon found themselves trained in habits, and then retrained through trial and testing, so it is for us. But, our destiny is higher than theirs. Theirs is to grace a dinner plate. Ours is the full realization of God's grace, and all that it intends for us. *"For the grace of God has appeared, bringing salvation for all people, training us to renounce ungodliness and worldly passions, and to live self-controlled, upright, and godly lives in the present age, waiting for our blessed hope, the appearing of the glory of our great God and Savior Jesus Christ, who gave himself for us to redeem us from all lawlessness and to purify for himself a people for his own possession who are zealous for good works."* (Titus 2:11-14 ESV) The work is His. The way is His. The glory is His. He alone is able. He alone is worthy.

28

THE FUNGUS AMONG US

In Oregon's Blue Mountains, motorists can drive to the highest viewpoint accessible by automobile in the state. While several Cascade peaks tower over it, Vinegar Hill, in Eastern Oregon's gold-producing region, has a terrain that will allow drivers to drive to an elevation of over 8,000 feet. Beneath their tires, an enormous network of seams and veins of mineral-rich ore interlaces the mountain, an unseen web that connects numerous mine tunnels, prospects, dreams and disappointments.

The Blues are also home to the largest single organism on Earth discovered to date. Covering nearly four square miles beneath the forest floor is a pathogenic fungus, whose unseen mycelium, a network of root-like fibers, spreads along tree roots, secreting digestive juices that eventually kill the tree. The fungus is able to send out flat shoestring-like fibers, probing from tree to tree, from grove to grove, and, using current growth rates, may have been doing so for thousands of years. Some scientific estimates establish this particular Oregon fungus as perhaps the oldest organism on the planet, perhaps more than 5,000 years old. It is pervasive over more than 2,300 acres, and yet has been identified as a single living organism, a destructive menace whose only visible evidence shows in clusters of fruiting bodies known as honey mushrooms. This massive parasite works its hidden mayhem inexorably, leaving destruction in its wake.

Although not all fungi are pathogenic, all share this same structure. The organism itself is the hidden mycelium network that creeps unseen, invading, spreading, secreting, breaking down and destroying. Some are pathogenic, killing their hosts, and some are saprophytic, breaking down those already dead.

In December, 2007, a series of Pacific storms converged into one massive blast that slammed into the coastal region of Oregon and Washington with wind gusts of up to 150 miles per hour. The sustained pounding uprooted or snapped off wide swaths of timber, leaving thousands of acres strewn with downed trees, some still connected to their upturned root disks, some lying at the foot of their own broken snags. Large areas were salvaged, with broken trees turned to paper and boards. Other large tracts lay untouched, and within a year, showed the first stages of decay. Tiny fungal bodies showed along the creases and cracks in the bark of downed hemlocks, like strings of flat beads. The next year, the fungus had spread up the broken snags, and even showed along the damaged trunks of leaning trees that were still clinging to life.

I have been watching the progress of deterioration over the last few years as I cut downed trees into firewood. The wood has changed from sound and solid to porous and punky. Logs have sagged and finally snapped under their own weight as their structure became unsound under the decaying effects of the fungus that spread through them.

The pervasiveness of the destroyer was underscored this year as I worked my way into a tangle of uprooted trees. I had sliced one hemlock, two and a half feet in diameter, into stove lengths, back to where it touched the ground. To keep from having to stop to sharpen my chainsaw, I turned to other trees in the tangle, intending to finish the last thirty feet of the big hemlock once I had it uncovered.

It was a little over two weeks before I could get back to the wood cutting. When I did, I was surprised to see that fresh cut on the hemlock ringed with white fungus bubbles. It had a circle where the bark met the outside of the log, another between the sapwood and the heartwood, and still another partial circle where the heartwood had fractured when the tree fell. The root, if we might call it that, that filled the heart of that log bore fruit of destruction, even as the mycelium spread to other logs it touched, to continue the damage.

What a picture of the pervasiveness of sin. Scripture speaks of it as an entity that dwells within the fabric of our being, a nature, a law, a driving force within us. In his letter to believers in Rome, Paul wrote: *"For I delight in the law of God, in my inner being, but I see in my members another law waging war against the law of my mind and making me captive to the law of sin that dwells in my members."* (Rom 7:22-23 ESV) That sin nature, that law of sin, works seemingly not only against our mind and will, but independent of it. Paul says, *"For I do not understand my own actions. For I do not do what I want, but I do the very thing I hate. Now if I do what I do not want, I agree with the law, that it is good. So now it is no longer I who do it, but sin that dwells within me."* (Rom 7: 15-17 ESV) This is the view apart from Christ Jesus. Paul has in view the struggle to do good in our own strength, in fleshly power and understanding. We are indeed new creatures in Christ, but we dwell in the residue of Adam. He *"... fathered a son in his own* [fallen] *likeness, after his* [fallen] *image..."* (Gen 5:3 ESV) Thus Paul concludes: *"For I know that nothing good dwells in me, that is, in my flesh. For I have the desire to do what is right, but not the ability to carry it out."* (Rom 7:22 ESV) Here, the Spirit is underscoring and personalizing the words of our Lord, when He told His disciples, *"...for apart from me you can do nothing."* (John 15:5) Our Lord stated the principle of our absolute dependence on Him. But we, with Paul, have to arrive at the personal realization of that reality.

The mycelium of fungus thrives in darkness, hidden from view, yet its influence is pervasive. So it is with the principle of sin. God's warning to Israel was pointed: *"Beware lest there be among you a man or woman or clan or tribe whose heart is turning away today from the LORD our God to go and serve the gods of those nations. Beware lest there be among you a root bearing poisonous and bitter fruit..."* (Deut 29:18 ESV) The first part of the warning emphasizes the spreading nature of sin. It starts with the individual, and spreads to ensnare successively larger groups. Then, like the fungus, the destructive fruit appears. Through the pen of Paul, the Holy Spirit gives the same warning, *"...that no 'root of bitterness' springs up and causes trouble, and by it many become defiled..."* (Heb 12:15 ESV) The root of bitterness that bears poisonous and bitter fruit is what Paul called the "law of sin" within our members. It remains in us, in our flesh, in our self-will, and is held in check only by the indwelling Holy Spirit. If not yielded to His control, the damage spreads, and quickly. Many become defiled. Both Isaiah and James use the analogy of fire to depict the chaos. *"And the tongue is a fire, a world of unrighteousness. The tongue is set among our members, staining the whole body, setting on fire the entire course of life, and set on fire by hell."* (James 3:6 ESV) *"Therefore, as the tongue of fire devours the stubble, and as dry grass sinks down in the flame, so their root will be as rottenness, and their blossom go up like dust; for they have rejected the law of the LORD of hosts, and have despised the word of the Holy One of Israel."* (Isa 5:24 ESV)

Isaiah records the chief reason for the spread of damage, and the springing up of the root to bear its bitter fruit: the rejection of the Word of God. Remember that the damaging agent thrives in darkness. *"The unfolding of your words gives light; it imparts understanding to the simple."* (Psa 119:130 ESV) Neglect of God's Word, or its outright rejection, deprives the inner workings of our nature of the Light of the Lord, and thereby cultivates the principle of sin. David wrote, *"I have stored up your word in my heart, that I might not sin against you."* (Psa 119:11 ESV) God's Word, then is the beginning point of deliverance, and the means of maintenance. Diminish the storing up of the Word, and the principle of sin bears its fruit in the resulting darkness. That is the gleeful goal of the enemy of all that God is doing. The Lord has spoken. The Gospel is proclaimed. The Word of Life is held forth in the darkness of this world. *"And even if our gospel is veiled, it is veiled only to those who are perishing. In their case the god of this world has blinded the minds of the unbelievers, to keep them from seeing the light of the gospel of the glory of Christ, who is the image of God."* (2Cor 4:3-4 ESV) David asked, *"Open my eyes, that I may behold wondrous things out of your law."* (Psa 119:18 ESV)

By His grace and by His Spirit's effectual working in salvation, He does exactly that: He opens the eyes of our understanding. He alone can accomplish that work, and it is vital that He do so. Our Lord Jesus explained, *"The eye is the lamp of the body. So, if your eye is healthy, your whole body will be full of light, but if your eye is bad, your whole body will be full of darkness. If then the light in you is darkness, how great is the darkness!"* (Mat 6:22-23 ESV) In our great need, God's grace is sufficient. *"For God, who said, "Let light shine out of darkness," has shone in our hearts to give the light of the knowledge of the glory of God in the face of Jesus Christ."* (2Cor 4:6 ESV) That is the way of deliverance from the bondage of darkness, from the slavery to sin. The philosophies of men are of no value. As Isaiah cried, *"To the teaching and to the testimony! If they will not speak according to this word, it is because they have no dawn."* (Isa 8:20 ESV) No dawn. No light. How great is their darkness! Paul writes of our glorious standing before God, when he assures us, *"for at one time you were darkness, but now you are light in the Lord. Walk as children of light..."* (Eph 5:8 ESV) We are to live commensurate with our new reality in Christ, who is our light and life. There is a positive and a negative aspect to that admonition. The negative involves separation: *"Take no part in the unfruitful works of darkness, but instead expose them."* (Eph 5:11 ESV) We are no longer part of the world system, with its values. *"He has delivered us from the domain of darkness and transferred us to the kingdom of his beloved Son..."* (Col 1:13 ESV)

There is a positive side to the admonition to walk as children of light, as well: *"But if we walk in the light, as he is in the light, we have fellowship with one another, and the blood of Jesus his Son cleanses us from all sin."* (1John 1:7 ESV) There is a purifying influence of light. Fungus cannot thrive in the light of the sun. Neither can sin thrive in the light of the Son. There is a bonding, a unity that holds us together in Christ. Even that is of the Lord's doing. His Spirit within us works His perfecting will to the praise of the glory of His grace.

29

LED ASTRAY

From the hillside above our home, I can look westward to the shore of the Pacific Ocean. Viewed from our property, the bit of ocean that I can see seems small, insignificant in proportion to the undulating hills between me and the rim of the water. Half an hour's drive, and I can stand on the sand that is relentlessly caressed or pounded by the waves that ebb and flow with the changing tide. Portuguese explorer Ferdinand Magellan was pleased and relieved to encounter favorable winds and seas after being lashed around the south extremity of South America. He named it the "Peaceful Sea," or *Mar Pacifico*.

Sometimes it is. It can be calm, almost glassy, with gentle swells barely stirring its serenity. In a raging storm, it can crash ashore in wind-lashed breakers that exceed forty feet in height. Even at its quietest, it writhes with restless, explosive energy. Standing beside it, I can sense its power, whether it is softly growling, or roaring with a voice that can be heard miles inland. Although I can see only a sliver of its edge, I can sense its vastness.

That vastness defies imagination. It encompasses nearly half of the Earth's water area. It makes up around a third of Earth's total surface area. Add up the area of all seven continents and all the islands – the world's total land area – and the Pacific eclipses that area by almost six million square miles. On land, the traveler is able to be guided by landmarks of various kinds. Landmarks rarely change. Mountains are distinct and unmoving. Lakes and streams usually stay in place.

The roughly sixty-four million square miles of the Pacific is, apart from its scattered islands, trackless. The sea traveler who hugs the coast can spot shoreline landmarks. But, due to the curvature of the Earth, some thirteen miles out to sea, the shore, indeed even the mountains, are lost to sight. Navigation is now dependent on instruments, and on heavenly way points. Those instruments are as reliable as their calibration.

We are now in a digital age, with electronic instruments and satellites for guidance. But, let us journey back to World War II, in the adolescence of radar and radio communications. Navigation was using the modern developments, but was, at the same time, dependent on methods and instruments that had been in use for centuries: the sextant, and its cousin, the octant. Think of the compass rose as a pie. The sextant divided it into six equal slices, and the octant, eight. The navigator found his position on earth relative to the position of the sun, using carefully measured angles, and calculations, and maps. Accuracy in each was critical.

In October of 1942, a B-17 crew returning to the mainland United States from action in the Pacific Theater of WWII, was reassigned to take WWI flying ace Captain Eddie Rickenbacker on an inspection tour of bases in the South Pacific. They narrowly avoided a crash on take-off, when one of the wheels on their airplane locked up, throwing them off course. In the spin to a stop, equipment was thrown about the interior of the craft. In the nose bubble, the navigator reported that his octant had suffered quite a blow, but that it looked OK. The men transferred to another plane and took off, uneventfully this time, and, once airborne, wheeled about, and headed southwestward over the open ocean.

Fourteen hours later, running out of fuel, they were forced to ditch the plane in the ocean, beginning what would be an agonizing 24 days lost at sea.

The crew followed proper protocol. The pilot followed the course he was given by the navigator. The navigator plotted the course by celestial way points, using his instruments and training. But...

Remember that initial takeoff attempt? The octant suffered an impact in the spin, and it **looked okay.** It was transferred to the new plane for use, without being re-calibrated. In 14 hours the plane would travel about 2800 miles. If the octant was only one degree off, they would miss their island by about 65 miles. They missed their first island stop by hundreds of miles. However far out of adjustment the octant was, it gave a false reading, sending the plane on a false course, and though they pursued that course faithfully, they landed where they did not want to be.

Testing is vital. Examination, cross-checking and resetting to a standard is a must, in marine navigation, in flight, in orienteering, and in life. In the spiritual realm, the Word of God underscores the need and the means of such recalibration: *"Examine yourselves, whether you are in the faith; test yourselves."* (2Cor 13:5) *"All scripture is God-breathed and profitable for doctrine, for reproof, for correction, for instruction in righteousness, so that the man of God may be perfected, being fully furnished for every good work."* (2Tim 3:16-17)

Consider Paul's admonition directed to the church at Corinth. In 2Cor 11:3-4, the apostle writes, *"But I am afraid that as the serpent deceived Eve by his cunning, your thoughts will be led astray from the sincere and pure devotion to*

Christ. For if someone comes and proclaims another Jesus than the one we proclaimed, or if you receive a different spirit from the one you received, or if you accept a different gospel from the one you accepted, you put up with it readily enough." (ESV)

False teaching is in view here. Gathered from elsewhere due to its fleshly attractiveness and introduced in the assembly, a false gospel, false doctrine, false Christ, or false spirit can take root, spread, and explode into dominance, crowding out the Truth. The scattered seeds of falsehood can lie dormant, ready to sprout and flourish anew, whenever conditions afford an opportunity. Paul warned against tolerance. His statement, *"...you put up with it readily enough,"* points out to us our propensity to accept what we deem reasonable, even though they are facsimiles. A false teacher uses familiar terms, but with different meanings. Individuals in Scripture are exalted or diminished, truths are modified, and teachings are recombined to fit a flesh-pleasing purpose. Peter spoke of this tendency of false teachers to mingle parts of God's word with their own ideas in 2 Pet 3:16: *"...which they that are unlearned and unstable wrest, as they do also the other scriptures, unto their own destruction."* (KJV) They wrest the scriptures, twist them, and distort them. Some, in fleshly enthusiasm, relying on their own understanding, stray from the clear teaching of scripture. Others, **unlearned** (not led into all truth by God's Holy Spirit), and **unstable** (without foundation, unregenerate), are more insidious, being **wolves in sheep's clothing,** intent on scattering and destroying the flock. They present **another Jesus...a different spirit...a different gospel.** These are another of a different kind, from a different origin, but tailored to be deceptively like the true Jesus, Spirit and gospel.

Even in the first century, the Apostle John wrote of the proliferating facsimiles of Christ. In 1John 2:18, his warning is clear: *"Little children, it is the last time: and as ye have heard that antichrist shall come, even now there are many antichrists; whereby we know that it is the last*

time." (KJV) The prefix, anti-, can signify that which is opposed to something or someone, or, as in this case, in the place of something or someone. So, John warned against substitute christs, inferior copies of Jesus, man-crafted saviors. Notice he indicated their increasing number: ***"...even now there are many."*** Now, there are many more.

Notice also, the false christs are closely identified with their proclaimers. John continues in verse 19 of chapter two: ***"They went out from us, but they were not of us. For if they were of us, they would have remained with us; but they left so that it might be revealed that they all are not of us."*** (1John 2:19) That little word, ***of***, implies ***of the same kind, of the same origin***. The false teachers, with their false christs, were not of God. Though they claimed association with the apostles, with the church, and with God, they were spurious.

In 1 John 4:1-3, John addresses the issue of ***a different spirit***. Again, the different spirit is closely associated with the false christ and the false teacher: ***"Beloved, do not believe every spirit, but test the spirits, whether they are from God; for many false prophets have gone forth into the world. By this know the Spirit of God: every spirit which confesses that Jesus Christ has come in the flesh is from God. And every spirit which does not confess that Jesus Christ has come in the flesh is not from God; and this is the antichrist which you heard is coming, and now is already in the world. "*** The false teacher in some way diminishes the Person of Christ, or the Work of Christ. He is presented as a mere caricature of Who He truly is. His deity is denied, or His humanity, or His ministry of redemption. His sufficiency is denied, and human merit is added to the basis of salvation. John tells us that any and all such contortions of scripture are not of God, and he tells us that they are wide spread.

In his letter to the Galatian believers, Paul address the issue of a ***different gospel***. In Gal 1:6-9, the apostle writes: ***"I marvel that ye are so soon removed from Him that*** *called you into the grace of Christ unto another gospel: Which is not another [of the same kind]; but there be some that trouble you, and would pervert the gospel of Christ. But though we, or an angel from heaven, preach any other gospel unto you that that which we have preached unto you, let him be accursed. As we said before, so say I now again, If any man preach any other gospel unto you that that ye have received, let him be accursed."* (KJV) False gospels abounded then, and still do. In this portion, Paul includes an ominous warning. The false teachers who present a false gospel of a false christ are under God's unrevoked anathema. In this portion, Paul uses the term *accursed*. In 1 Cor 16:22, the term is transliterated rather than translated: *"...let him be Anathema Maranatha."* It was the strongest condemnation Paul could use. To proclaim another gospel was to nullify the Death of Christ, which was the only way of salvation. God's declaration through the pen of the Apostle: "Let him be cut off at the coming of the Lord." *"For such ones are false apostles, deceitful workers, transforming themselves into apostles of Christ. And did not Satan marvelously transform himself into an angel of light?"* (2Cor 11:13-14)

We need frequent recalibration. We must be like those in Berea. Paul wrote concerning them: *"And these were more noble than those in Thessalonica, for they received the Word with all readiness, daily examining the Scriptures if these things are so."* (Acts 17:11) Heed Jude's admonition: *"Having made all haste to write to you about the common salvation, beloved, I had need to write to you to exhort you to contend earnestly for the faith once delivered to the saints."* (Jude 1:3)The Word of God provides us with solid way points, accurate charts for the journey, and a sure standard. Anything else, anything less, and we will be led astray.

30

FLASH FLOOD

La madrugada. This is part of the Hispanic way of dividing the twenty-four hour day. The dawning. Those darkest, somnolescent hours from midnight to sunrise. It is the time of deepest sleep, of lonely watches, of dreams and of nightmares. It is the time of least awareness, and of greatest vulnerability.

The deserts of the American Southwest are gouged and slashed by miles of steep-walled canyons and arroyos that invite exploration, offer breathtaking vistas, and, by their very nature and origin, conceal within their depths both treasure and tragedy. Carved out by turbulent waters, these deepening scars in the land have, with their twists and turns, flares and narrows, served as riffled sluice boxes during run-off times, trapping pockets of gold here and there to tempt prospectors, offering an easy trail for hikers and an occasional even floor for campers. Therein lurks the tragedy.

The desert is subject to thunderstorms accompanied by torrential rains. These come with little or no warning where they pour out their fury, and none at all in the areas miles removed from the storm itself. With sparse vegetation to slow the runoff, and the propensity of the desert soil to seal itself with dampness, the rain flows in sheets and rivulets off of the slopes, gathering force and volume, to become a turbulent torrent that roars down the dry stream beds, sweeping everything before it. Churning walls of water converge in merging gulches, and rush in a thunderous, boulder-rolling rampage, frothing, roiling, sometimes filling the arroyos brim full with yellow-foamed undulating waves, until, reaching a wide canyon, the flash flood spreads out, thins, slows, and unburdens itself of the burden it has collected, littering the canyon floor with flotsam, camping gear, boulders and silt-shrouded bodies of the unwary, both animal and human. The greatest carnage happens in the *madrugada*.

Indeed, the very existence of arroyos speaks of the power of the rampaging waters. The washes themselves serve as warnings that the area has been washed, and will be again. The name, *arroyo*, means intermittent creek. Intermittent means from time to time, emphasizing a repeated occurrence. Where mayhem has passed, it will pass again. The size of the boulders where the arroyo debouches into the canyon, and the paucity of any but the fastest-growing vegetation proclaim the power and frequency of the floods. Trails and footprints in the bottom of an arroyo give a false sense of security. The fact that others have walked that way with impunity only masks the hazardous nature of the passage. Yet, the meandering network of spidery scars on the land are intriguing and enticing. The broad entrance with its gently sloping sides leads onward, winding into an ever narrower, ever steeper trap with no escape route, until grave-like, it is the way of death.

Areas with frequent flash floods may have warnings posted at access points. The degree of disdain and contempt poured on these cautions can be calibrated by counting the bullet holes they have accumulated. How many who laughed at the warnings, whether physical, written or verbal, have run howling before the onrushing wall of devastation, to become another mournful statistic?

Some venture into the ways of brooding danger out of ignorance, some out of daring, and some out of necessity. When catastrophe strikes, there are those who must risk the same fate to search for survivors or victims. When tragedy is looming, they rush in to attempt evacuation of the ones in danger. Sometimes, they succeed. Sometimes, they die.

Scripture presents a reality that mirrors, in the spiritual reality of humanity, the seductive scarred landscape labyrinth of the physical world. The Lord had a message for His people, a message that resonates through the centuries: **"And you shall say to this people, 'So says Jehovah, Behold, I set before you the way of life and the way of death.'"** (Jer 21:8) That would certainly be an attention-grabbing message, stark and unambiguous. If that were the call for the division of the house, politically speaking, we would expect a stampede for the side designated *the way of life*. But, imagine the consternation the follow-up statement would stir: **"He who remains in this city shall die by the sword, and by the famine, and by the plague. But he who goes out and falls to the Chaldeans who are besieging you, he shall live, and his life shall be for a prize to him."** (Jer 21:9) The stampede for the way of life would come to an abrupt halt. The messenger and the message do not align with the intentions of the hearers. Human reason asks, "Why leave the secure walls of the fortified city, and walk out to surrender to a multitude of soldiers with swords, spears, and a blood lust in their eyes? Safety lies behind the walls, and danger lurks outside." Forgotten are the words of Solomon: **"There is a way that seems right to a man, but the end of it is the ways of death."** (Pro 14:12)

God, through His prophet, posted the warning. Many chose what seemed right to the mind that rebelled against God's will, God's way, and God's Word. As with many who ventured into the arroyo, there came a moment of realization that they had made the wrong choice. Solomon used personification to portray Wisdom in Proverbs. An extended portion applies to those who chose the way of death: **"Because I called, and you refused; I stretch out a hand, and none inclines, but you have ignored all my** *counsel, and you did not desire my warning. I also will laugh in your calamity, I will mock when your dread comes; when your dread comes like a storm; and your calamity arrives like a tempest, when distress and anguish come on you. Then they shall call on me, and I will not answer; they shall seek me early, but they shall not find me. Instead they hated knowledge and chose not the fear of Jehovah. They did not desire my counsel; they despised all my reproof, and they shall eat of the fruit of their own way and be filled with their own lusts. For the going astray of the simple kills them, and the ease of fools destroys them."* (Pro 1:24-32)

Indeed, the Wisdom that calls, that pleads, is God Himself. But He calls to those who refuse to hear, and pleads with those whose rebellious hearts will not respond. His messengers and His message are as contemned as the bullet-riddled warning signs. *"For they have not listened to My Words, says Jehovah, which I sent to them by My servants the prophets, rising up early and sending; but you would not hear, says Jehovah."* (Jer 29:19) Did this lack of response to His warnings surprise God? No.

Notice what He told Jeremiah when He sent him with messages of pending judgment, with warnings of danger, with proclamations of coming disaster. *"But they did not listen nor bow their ear. But they walked in their own plans, in the stubbornness of their evil heart, and went backward and not forward. Since the day that your fathers came out of the land of Egypt until this day, I have even sent to you all My servants, the prophets, daily rising up early and sending. Yet they did not listen to Me nor bow their ear, but they stiffened their neck. They did more evil than their fathers. And you shall speak all these Words to them, but they will not listen to you. And you will call to them, but they will not answer you."* (Jer 7:24-27) After recounting the rebellious history of His chosen people, God tells Jeremiah to go anyway. Both Jeremiah and the message he proclaimed would be rejected, but he was to proclaim it. His responsibility was the delivery of the message, not its reception. The prophets were sent into the *ways of death* with the message of life: **"Say to them, As I live, declares the Lord Jehovah, I do not have delight in the death of the wicked, except in the wicked turning from his way, and so to live. Turn! Turn from your evil ways! For why will you die, O house of Israel?"** (Eze 33:11)

Then came the greatest Messenger of all. **"And the Word became flesh and tabernacled among us. And we beheld His glory, glory as of an only begotten from the Father, full of grace and of truth."** (John 1:14) God donned human flesh, and sojourned among the rebels who refused to hear His message and scorned His messengers. In love and kindness and wisdom, Jesus demonstrated the loving heart of God. John tells us, **"And we have beheld and bear witness that the Father has sent the Son as Savior of the world. By this the love of God was revealed in us, because His Son, the Only begotten, God has sent into the world that we might live through Him. In this is love, not that we loved God, but that He loved us, and sent His Son to be a propitiation relating to our sins."** (1John 4:14, 9-10) In fulfillment of prophecy, Jesus came **"...through the tender heart of mercy of our God, in which the Dayspring from on high will visit us, to appear to those sitting in darkness and in shadow of death, to direct our feet into the way of peace."** (Luke 1:78-79) Jesus Himself presented a message that echoed the one sent through the prophet Jeremiah: **"Go in through the narrow gate; for wide is the gate and broad is the way that leads to destruction, and many are the ones entering in through it. For narrow is the gate, and constricted is the way that leads away into life, and few are the ones finding it."** (Mat 7:13-14) How narrow? He proclaimed, **"...I am the Way, and the Truth, and the Life. No one comes to the Father except through Me."** (John 14:6) How was His gracious message received? What was the attitude regarding the Messenger Himself?

Hear the grieving words of the humble Messenger:

"Jerusalem! Jerusalem! The one killing the prophets, and stoning those having been sent to her, how often I desired to gather your children in the way a hen gathers her brood under the wings, and you did not desire it." (Luke 13:34) John summary was succinct: *"He came to His own, and His own did not receive Him."* (John 1:11) Isaiah the prophet foretold that which was fulfilled in Jesus: *"He is despised and abandoned of men, a Man of pains, and acquainted with sickness. And as it were hiding our faces from Him, He being despised, and we did not value Him."* (Isa 53:3) In the person of Jesus Christ, God posted a warning. Arrogant and rebellious, many mocked the message. They did not have bullets to pierce it. They had spears and nails.

The Father sent the Son, Jesus Christ, into the ways of death. He gave His beloved Messenger the Words of life, but with the same knowledge He gave Jeremiah: *"...they will not listen to you."* The message of life did not die at Calvary. Starting with the first eleven who were with Jesus the night before the crucifixion, a growing army of ambassadors has been sent with the message of the gospel of grace. Praying there on the road to Gethsemane, Jesus said to His Father, *"As You have sent Me into the world, I also have sent them into the world..."* (John 17:18) We are sent, as He was, into the ways of death with the message of life. As we traverse the canyons and arroyos of temptation, proclaiming freedom in Christ to the slaves of sin, what reception can we anticipate? Jesus told those with him, *"If the world hates you, you know that it has hated Me before it has hated you. If you were of the world, the world would love its own. But because you are not of the world, but I chose you out of the world, because of this the world hates you."* (John 15:18-19) Paul wrote to Timothy, *"And, indeed, all desiring to live godly in Christ Jesus will be persecuted."* (2Tim 3:12) Why?

We bring the gospel of grace to those who scoff at the warnings. *"Through pride of his face, the wicked will not seek; there is no God in all of his schemes. His ways are perverted at all times. Your judgments are high from his sight; as for all distressing him, he puffs at them."* (Psa 10:4-5) Solomon noted the reality that guides the wicked. *"Where sentence on an evil work is not executed speedily, on account of this the heart of the sons of men is fully set in them to do evil."* (Ecc 8:11) Paul addresses the attitude of the ones without Christ in this world: *"Or do you despise the riches of His kindness, and the forbearance and the long-suffering, not knowing that the kindness of God leads you to repentance? But according to your hardness and your impenitent heart, do you treasure up to yourself wrath in a day of wrath, and revelation of a righteous judgment of God?"* (Rom 2:4-5) As the time of warning and pleading stretches out over the centuries, we see more and more the derisive response Peter predicted: *"...first, knowing this, that during the last days scoffers will come walking according to their own lusts, and saying, Where is the promise of His coming? For from which time the fathers fell asleep, all things remain so from the beginning of creation."* (2Pet 3:3-4) The perishing laugh at the concept of a coming judgment. They ridicule the messengers of life. In some cases, they blast holes in the ones posted as a caution sign. Paul explains: *"But also if our gospel is being hidden, it has been hidden in those being lost, in whom the god of this age has blinded the thoughts of the unbelieving, so that the brightness of the gospel of the glory of Christ who is the image of God, should not dawn on them."* (2Cor 4:3-4)

And so, believers in the Lord Jesus Christ, ambassadors for Him, are commissioned to go into the very ways of death. It will not do to stand on the edge of the canyon and shout to those in peril below. We must go into the ways of temptation, yet, by His grace, without sin. We must go into the places of danger, yet, by His grace, without fear. As David wrote, *"Yea, though I walk through the valley of the shadow of death I will fear no evil; for You are with me; Your rod and Your staff, they comfort me."* (Psa 23:4) His abundant grace enables us, grace appropriate to the challenge we face. We do not go in our own strength, nor do we formulate our own message. It is all of Him. As our Lord told His disciples centuries ago, **"...you will receive power, the Holy Spirit coming upon you, and you will be witnesses of Me both in Jerusalem, and in all Judea, and Samaria, and to the end of the earth."** (Acts 1:8)

This commission applies to every believer in the Lord Jesus Christ. Each is an ambassador, a messenger. Each is not of the world, that is, holding the same values, the same nature, the same lifestyle as the unsaved. But, each is sent into the world, to be yielded to God for His use in His way and His time for His own glory. Our commission is to proclaim. God's purpose is to save. The perishing ones are blind to the reality of their peril. We, aware of our own danger, walk circumspectly, alert for both opportunities and hazards. The peril of those without Christ is eternal. Ours is temporal, and can only press us closer to His loving heart, depending only on His strength, or usher us into His glorious presence. As Paul wrote to Timothy, **"Then I solemnly witness before God and the Lord Jesus Christ, He being about to judge the living and dead at His appearance and His kingdom: preach the Word, be urgent in season, out of season, convict, warn, encourage with all long-suffering and teaching."** (2Tim 4:1-2) Some, hearing, will be drawn by the Father to the Son, through the ministry of the Holy Spirit sensitizing the heart to receive the Word and the gift of faith. Paul writes, **"Then faith is of hearing, and hearing through the Word of God."** (Rom 10:17) Others, arrogantly encamped in the ways of death, will stop their ears. Trusting in their seeming safety, they will disdain pleading. But, **"...when they say, Peace and safety! Then suddenly destruction comes upon them, like the travail to the one having babe in womb, and not at all shall they escape."** (1Thes 5:3)

31

TICKLING TROUT

Patience. Stealth. Caution. A tolerance for water temperatures in the not-really-that-far-above-freezing range. Combine these with slow, steady motion and a light touch, and dinner may rest just beneath that cut-bank, that submerged log or rock. In a craft as old as dining on trout, tickling them lurks between the status of folk practice and folklore, between fact and fiction, depending on the experience of the classifier. Those hearing of the idea for the first time dismiss it as incredible. Some are able to be convinced, and some remain dubious until they observe a successful demonstration. My success has been minimal, limited to one tiny capture, and one that managed to flop back into the water and escape.

The practice shows up in an ancient Greek book on angling, and in Greek writings of nearly two thousand years ago. Shakespeare used it in his plays to set up the artful manipulation of the naive, the pompous or the gullible. Tickling trout has been a means of survival in dire economic times, and a standby method of poaching, where possession of fishing gear would have been an obvious point of conviction. The practice has been outlawed in the United Kingdom.

Details vary slightly, but the practice follows a basic pattern. The tickler wades upstream, scanning for resting trout behind boulders, underneath undercut banks, or under partially submerged logs in backwater eddies. Remember, trout like water to be about 50 degrees Fahrenheit. Ticklers like it to be slightly colder, because the trout are more sluggish in colder water.

Since the trout rest facing upstream, an agonizingly slow approach (Cold water, remember?) from behind may not frighten them into a hasty dash to another pool or hiding place. An approach that keeps the rock, log or some other obstacle between the tickler and the fish's eyes is best.

The would-be captor then kneels in the water, on one knee, and slips his hand to the bottom, where he can slide it, inch by inch, to where his index finger can just touch the trout's tail. The idea is to make the trout believe that the vegetation or debris at the bottom of the water is brushing his tail, and then his belly. That very light, very slow tickling action induces a trance-like state after about a minute. Wariness is suspended. The trout is now vulnerable, its alarm system temporarily disabled.

It is at this point that variety of method occurs. Some ticklers, when their hand reaches the pectoral fins, abruptly scoop and throw the trout out onto dry land, hopefully far enough that its frantic flopping will not end in a splash. Others use the two-hand method, bringing the second hand to the tail as the first approaches the lower jaw. Then, with a simultaneous grasping motion, one hand comes up to grasp the snout, as the other seizes the tail. Ticklers who consider themselves purists claim to be able to gently lift the hypnotized fish out of the water.

Whatever the landing method, the result is the same. The

deceived trout either thrashes out his life on dry land, or is bonked and bagged. His destiny is hot oil, a touch of salt and pepper, a sprinkling of toasted almonds, and a sprig of parsley. He has fallen victim to pretense that so resembles the familiar, and his own innate propensity to trust pleasant sensations, to be groomed into submission.

People are not immune to manipulation. The massage may be physiological, or it may be psychological. Whether it stimulates the pleasure receptors of the body or the ego, the grooming process lulls us into that same trance-like state of diminished resistance, disables our built-in alarm system, short-circuits our discernment, and leaves us willingly vulnerable. The root of the word captivated is captive. Wealth and power utilize this potent tool. Advertising and politics follow the same hidden maxim: "Discover what they want, and promise to deliver it." Often, the corollary to the rule gains traction: "Create a need. Convince them they want it, then promise to give it to them." The ability to deliver is unimportant. The promise is everything. Tidbits whet desire, but satisfaction is always dangled just out of reach.

The process crosses over from the natural realm to the spiritual. The stakes, however, are eternal. The temporal motivations for spiritual deception are the same. Wealth and power fuel a burgeoning religious market. This is not a modern phenomenon. In his letter to believers at Corinth, Paul wrote, ***"For we are not, like so many, peddlers of God's word, but as men of sincerity, as commissioned by God, in the sight of God we speak in Christ."*** (2Cor 2:17 ESV) These peddlers subtly tailor the message for marketability, with an eye for profit. Peter speaks of those merchandisers of God's Word, concerning Paul's letters: ***"There are some things in them that are hard to understand, which the ignorant and unstable twist to their own destruction, as they do the other Scriptures."*** (2Pet 3:16 ESV)

Writing to Timothy, Paul touches the root, stem and fruit of deception: ***"If anyone teaches a different doctrine and*** *does not agree with the sound words of our Lord Jesus Christ and the teaching that accords with godliness, he is puffed up with conceit and understands nothing. He has an unhealthy craving for controversy and for quarrels about words, which produce envy, dissension, slander, evil suspicions, and constant friction among people who are depraved in mind and deprived of the truth, imagining that godliness is a means of gain."* (1Tim 6:3-5 ESV) Some may appear pious, quoting scriptures, even occupying places of church leadership. They may write religious books that fill the shelves in stores catering to believers. They may write or perform religious songs that fill the airwaves. They may occupy pulpits, lead Bible studies, and still be tares amid the wheat. Consider what Paul told the elders from Ephesus: *"For I know this, that after my departure grievous wolves will come in among you, not sparing the flock; and out of you yourselves will rise up men speaking perverted things, in order to draw away the disciples after themselves."* (Acts 20:29-30)

False teachers would arise from among the very ones Paul had instructed, who had been ordained as leaders in the local assembly. It is not only the wolves outside the assembly that are the danger. The greater danger is the wolves in sheep's clothing within the body, who pipe a pleasant tune, and draw the gullible dancing and skipping to destruction. Paul's warning is clear: *"For such men are false apostles, deceitful workmen, disguising themselves as apostles of Christ. And no wonder, for even Satan disguises himself as an angel of light. So it is no surprise if his servants, also, disguise themselves as servants of righteousness. Their end will correspond to their deeds."* (2Cor 11:13-15)

If their appearance is deceptive, their message is more so. Like counterfeiters of currency, these deceivers tailor their facsimiles to approximate the authentic. The message is as diabolical as the messengers. Paul writes to those at Corinth, *"But I am afraid that as the serpent deceived Eve by his cunning, your thoughts will be led astray from a sincere and pure devotion to Christ. For if someone comes and proclaims another Jesus than the one we proclaimed, or if you receive a different spirit from the one you received, or if you accept a different gospel from the one you accepted, you put up with it readily enough."* (2Cor 11:3-4 ESV) Another Jesus, a different spirit, or a different gospel are different in nature and origin, but are so cleverly devised as to be embraced as authentic. To those in Galatia, Paul writes, *"I am astonished that you are so quickly deserting him who called you in the grace of Christ and are turning to a different gospel-- not that there is another one, but there are some who trouble you and want to distort the gospel of Christ. But even if we or an angel from heaven should preach to you a gospel contrary to the one we preached to you, let him be accursed."* (Gal 1:6-8 ESV) Paul uses the strongest condemnation available for those who deceive. Accursed. Anathema. Cut off at the coming of the Lord.

Deceitful messengers present a divergent message, and massage it in by diverse methods. False doctrine, set to a catchy melody lodges in the mind, and becomes a steppingstone into greater deception. In this case, the music is the carrier that can pass through the barrier of discernment. Years ago, when we had dairy goats and poultry, we treated them with a systemic medication against parasites. The toxin was blended into a transdermal carrier capable of transporting the poison through the skin, and into the life blood of the goats and chickens. That was beneficial. It is also instructive when we consider the methods of the false teachers of Paul's day, and of today.

Consider the tools of the ticklers. In writing to the believers at Colossae, Paul focused his warning on flesh-focused implements: *"I say this in order that no one may delude you with plausible arguments."* (Col 2:4 ESV) He uses an interesting choice of word structure. Others deceive us. We delude ourselves. Plausible arguments find a beachhead in our thoughts. We consider them, entertain them, weigh their pleasantness, and embrace them. That was the process in effect in the Garden of Eden. Reading between the lines, we see Eve moving step by step down that thought path.

Paul digs deeper into the toolbox of the deceivers: ***"See to it that no one takes you captive by* philosophy *and* empty deceit, *according to* human tradition, *according to the* elemental spirits of the world, *and not according to* Christ."*** (Col 2:8 ESV) The concrete logic of plausible arguments transitions to the abstract emotion of philosophical manipulation, a nebulous, Earth-bound reasoning that plays on feelings. Human tradition is historical, the "this is our heritage" approach. The appeal is to earlier generations, or even an ancestor. Again, it appeals to the emotional core and fleshly response. The elemental spirits of the world invokes social mores, appeals to culture and community values. Any and all of these can be blended into a salve and massaged into consciousness, the meditative processes of an individual, shaping the journey. Think of it as a religious spa, with the pleasant blend of music, aroma therapy and sensual massage combining to induce a relaxed susceptibility to embrace a lie.

In writing to the believers at Thessalonica, Paul targets forgeries as the method of deceit. ***"Now concerning the coming of our Lord Jesus Christ and our being gathered together to him, we ask you, brothers, not to be quickly shaken in mind or alarmed, either by* a spirit *or a* spoken word, *or a* letter seeming to be from us, *to the effect that the day of the Lord has come. Let no one deceive you in any way."*** (2Thes 2:1-3 ESV) Fictional scriptures were a problem in Paul's day, and continue to be produced today. In his day, Paul contended with supposedly contemporary documents, claimed by forgers to be from him, or from another of the apostles or elders. Today, it is a parade of forged documents of purported antiquity, of a progressive revelation. All are false. All are instruments of deceit. All are satanic. Of their impact, Paul asked the Galatians, ***"O foolish Galatians! Who has bewitched you? It was before your*** *eyes that Jesus Christ was publicly portrayed as crucified."* (Gal 3:1 ESV) Who has lulled you into a stupor? Who has led you to drop your guard?

Peter, in his letter to those scattered throughout the provinces of the Roman Empire, assured them, *"For we did not follow cleverly devised myths when we made known to you the power and coming of our Lord Jesus Christ, but we were eyewitnesses of his majesty."* (2Pet 1:16 ESV) He contrasts the false teachings and their purveyors with the reality of the gospel of Christ, and Christ Himself. Paul does the same: *"But we have renounced disgraceful, underhanded ways. We refuse to practice cunning or to tamper with God's word, but by the open statement of the truth we would commend ourselves to everyone's conscience in the sight of God."* (2Cor 4:2 ESV) Oh, that those who use the Scriptures as an avenue to fame and fortune, to build for themselves a religious empire, would follow the example of Paul. In our day, though, the ticklers do not have to search for a following. As Paul writes to Timothy, *"For the time is coming when people will not endure sound teaching, but having itching ears they will accumulate for themselves teachers to suit their own passions, and will turn away from listening to the truth and wander off into myths."* (2Tim 4:3-4 ESV)

That time is now. Ear ticklers tamper with God's Word, modifying the message to appeal to the flesh, and feel that growth equals authenticity. In truth, those who refuse sound doctrine flock to the ones who tailor their teaching appease those wanting a form of godliness, while refusing the power.

Discernment is the cure. God supplies the needed wisdom and discernment by His Spirit, through His Word. Through Isaiah's pen, God admonishes, **To the teaching and to the testimony! If they will not speak according to this word, it is because they have no dawn."** (Isa 8:20 ESV) Through Paul's pen, *"Do your best to present yourself to God as* *one approved, a worker who has no need to be ashamed, rightly handling the word of truth.* (2Tim 2:15 ESV) *All Scripture is breathed out by God and profitable for teaching, for reproof, for correction, and for training in righteousness, that the man of God may be competent, equipped for every good work."* (2Tim 3:16-17 ESV) The written word, the Scriptures, and the Living Word they reveal, are to be our focus. Paul adds, *"Therefore, as you received Christ Jesus the Lord, so walk in him, rooted and built up in him and established in the faith, just as you were taught, abounding in thanksgiving."* (Col 2:6-7 ESV) Established in the faith, the Scriptures, abiding in Christ, responsive to the indwelling Holy spirit, we will be alert to messages that diminish our Lord Jesus Christ. Peter echoes Paul's admonition: *"And we have something more sure, the prophetic word, to which you will do well to pay attention as to a lamp shining in a dark place, until the day dawns and the morning star rises in your hearts, knowing this first of all, that no prophecy of Scripture comes from someone's own interpretation. For no prophecy was ever produced by the will of man, but men spoke from God as they were carried along by the Holy Spirit."* (2Pet 1:19-21 ESV) We stand on the solid, immoveable Rock, Christ Jesus. As Paul cautioned in closing his letter to the Hebrews, *"Jesus Christ is the same yesterday and today and forever. Do not be led away by diverse and strange teachings."* (Heb 13:8-9a ESV)

32

BRACKEN FERN

It was a ritual of spring. As boys growing up on a farm carved from the forest by Oregon pioneers, we were conscripted as combatants in the relentless struggle to hold the hay field against the annual onslaught of insurgents. Grass and clover grew slowly. Bracken fern grew quickly, raising fiddle heads to peek over the surrounding grass, then bursting into a towering army of raised fans that threatened to smother the hay crop. Our mission, and we had to accept it, was to march through the field, capture armloads of the invaders, and parole them in piles encamped along the border of the hay field, where they languished as noncombatants in the struggle.

Bracken fern is a prolific foe. We would seize the stem and pull, and the underground connection would snap. Then, where we had removed one fern, two or more would come up to take its place. Some of the first invaders of spring would reach a height of five feet, but their successors flared with a lower profile. Eventually, we had to remove clusters of short ferns concealed in the maturing hay. We grumbled as we worked.

Why all the concern over fern in the field? "It's poison. Get it out of there." That was all we were told. Centuries of farm folklore declared it so. Now, years later, research has confirmed it to be both toxic and carcinogenic. However, a controversy rages over the research results.

The fiddle-heads, succulent curling shoots reminiscent of the decoratively-carved head of a violin, as well as dry bracken sometimes found mixed in winter fodder, have a nasty impact on the inner workings of those who consume it. The toxins in the fern depresses bone-marrow function. This results in the reduction of white blood cells, vital to the immune system, and a severe reduction in platelet count, resulting in hemorrhagic syndrome, the tendency of hemorrhage, or bleeding, within tissues and organs. Add in its carcinogenic nature, causing intestinal and bladder tumors in grazing animals, and the ancient folk warning finds validation in research results. The fact that grazing animals pass about a tenth of the toxin into their milk, and thus to those who consume the milk, makes the warning even more urgent.

Bracken flourishes on six of the seven continents, in all habitable portions of the world. It shows up in the cuisine of various regions, with foragers gathering the young fiddle-heads, or new shoots, and either mixing them with other vegetables in soups, or preparing them in traditional dishes that feature bracken as the main ingredient. Asian countries, with Japan as the leading consumer, have the highest intake of bracken, with traditional recipes said to have a taste impossible to describe in English. In direct proportion to the bracken intake, but with vehement denials of any causative link, these countries have a spike in throat and stomach cancer.

Ptaquilocide, the toxin in bracken fern, is a carcinogen for which the acceptable intake level, which some refer to as the safe intake, is zero. The traditional method of preparation, said to remove the toxin, is to boil the fiddle-heads in a solution of water and wood ashes or baking soda, both alkaline. The resulting alkalizing of the toxin opens the molecular structure, accelerating its ability to attack DNA molecules, and thus heightening its carcinogenicity.

Foragers and international cuisine enthusiasts ignore or deny the research, minimize the hazard, and cite their own and others' presumed anecdotal immunity, with a scoffing I'm-still-here attitude, which belittles painstaking research by those more knowledgeable than they are. These self-styled experts not only place themselves at risk, but they also lead others to follow their risky behavior. From where does this willfulness spring?

In part, it is generational. Traditional cuisine is established over several lifetimes. In part, it is situational. The dishes are passed around the table, with the words, "Just try it." In part, it is personal. Choices are made in the light of the adage, "Rules are made to be broken!"

What about the rebellious willfulness that shapes the behavior of all humanity, apart from the intervention of God? The same factors are at work in the realm of spiritual things. Sin is, in part, generational. Dating back to our first parents, the saying, "Like father, like son," rings true in the life of the offspring, manifesting itself in so many ways. **"And Adam lived one hundred and thirty years and fathered a son in his own likeness, according to his image, and called his name Seth."** (Gen 5:3) That which is modeled as acceptable in the older generation is so often repeated in the succeeding ones. Seth inherited the fallen, rebellious nature from his father, a nature which he passed on to his children. As Seth grew, he was exposed to, and adopted, the ways of his father. He grew into both the likeness and image of Adam. We are startled to see ourselves mirrored in our children. This is a two-way surprise, though. Our granddaughter, serving as a nanny with quasi-parental responsibilities, observed, "I open my mouth, and my mother comes out!"

While the generational inheritance can include that which has good as its goal, the target is often disregarded, and Scripture concludes all as rebellious. Believers in the Lord Jesus Christ have been gathered by God out of that quagmire lifestyle Peter mentions: *"...knowing that not with corruptible things, silver or gold, were you redeemed from your worthless way of life handed down from your fathers..."* (1Pet 1:18) Paul described that lifestyle, and its spiritual impact: *"...and you being dead in deviations and sins, in which you formerly walked according to the course of this world, according to the ruler of the authority of the air, the spirit now working in the sons of disobedience, among whom we also all conducted ourselves in times past in the lusts of our flesh, doing the things willed of the flesh and of the understanding, and were by nature the children of wrath, even as the rest."* (Eph 2:1-3) The root of sin grew with each succeeding generation, blossomed in all its ugliness, and poisoned all humanity in its cumulative impact. However, when we sin, no one can say, "My parents made me do it." Nor can we brush sin aside, saying, "I was born that way. That's just the way I am."

Sin is, in part, situational. Opportunity and enticement interact with the nature within us. David writes, *"Blessed is the man who has not walked in the counsel of the ungodly, and has not stood in the way of sinners, and has not sat in the seat of scorners."* (Psa 1:1) We are bombarded by contrasting input into our lives. We are surrounded by would-be counselors. David places the state of blessedness opposite our tendencies. That nature within wants the counsel of the ungodly, because it resonates with our fleshly desires. Our nature wants to go along and watch the action of the sinners. Our nature wants to blend in, to partake of the activities. The reality of Paul's warning to believers, though it is equally true for the unregenerate, is mocked and rejected, often by both: *"Do not be led astray; bad companionships ruin good habits."* (1Cor 15:33) Just as bracken fern gives off allelopathic chemicals, evil-doers have an immense capacity to poison those around them.

Scripture speaks repeatedly of the assiduous nature of the efforts to subvert. Peter writes of those *"...intending to live ungodly."* (2Pet 2:6) Solomon's counsel is pointed. It seems hyperbolic, but underscores the enthusiasm for sin, and for the undermining of the testimony of those who by the working of God's grace in them find their own lives are a light in darkness: *"My son, if sinners lure you, do not be willing...Do not enter the path of the wicked, and do not go in the way of evildoers. Avoid it, do not pass by it; turn from it and pass on. For they do not sleep if they have done no evil, and their sleep is taken away unless they cause some to fall."* (Pro 1:10, 4:14-16) The arrogance of the fallen nature, and the lifestyle generated by it, is in focus when Paul writes of the enticers, *"...who knowing the righteous order of God, that those practicing such things are worthy of death, not only do them, but also approve those practicing them."* (Rom 1:32)

Who are these would-be counselors? Who are the ungodly of whom David speaks? Who are the bad companions bringing ruin? Paul expands the terms in writing to Timothy. He could have had our times in view, since his description portrays our era so aptly: *"But know this, that in the last days grievous times will be upon us. For men will be lovers of themselves, money-lovers, braggarts, arrogant, blasphemers, disobedient to parents, unthankful, unholy, without natural feeling, unyielding, slanderers, without self-control, savage, haters of good, betrayers, reckless, puffed up, lovers of pleasure rather than lovers of God, having a form of godliness, but denying the power of it; even turn away from these."* (1Tim 3:1-5) Repugnant in their portrayal as in their purposes, they yet attract because they are in masquerade. Wolves in sheep's clothing, pretended apostles, artificial lights, they entice with a syrupy "Just try it!" They lead sinners deeper into sin, even as they try to entice God's elect. Sin may be situational in part, but none can claim, "My friends made me do it."

Sin, in spite of contributing factors, is personal. Like the snaky, fibrous rhizome of the bracken that spreads beneath the surface, sending up poisonous fronds, the fruit of the desires of the flesh come from deep within. James describes the process: **"But each one is tempted by his own lusts, being drawn out and being seduced by them. Then having conceived lust brings forth sin. And sin being fully formed brings forth death."** (James 1:14-15) Human beings don't just sin. We contemplate sin. We decide to sin. The process may be long, or it may be brief, but, whether it is preceded by an Hamlet-esque soliloquy, "To (fill in your favorite sin) or not to...", with options carefully weighed, or whether it is a snap decision, it is still a decision. It is a short step from the contemplation to the action.

Remember that the carcinogen in bracken fern is a substance that has no acceptable intake level. What about sin? What is the allowable level for lies, or pride? What is the safe level of sexual sin, or blasphemy? We are prone to compare among sins, and among sinners. In ourselves, we are prone to minimize sin, to justify our behavior, to excuse our actions, and to brush aside the idea of guilt. God does not take the same view of evil doing.

Choosing to sin puts consequences into motion. Sometimes, they come on swift wings. Often, though, they plod inexorably on reluctant feet. Solomon noted that reality, and the tendency of humanity to adopt the daredevil attitude of the fiddle-head eaters: **"Where sentence on an evil work is not executed speedily, on account of this the heart of the sons of men is fully set in them to do evil."** (Ecc 8:11) They are like the boy who first tiptoed up to the beehive, gingerly tapped it, and ran. When nothing happened, he approached more boldly, and rapped on it, and backed away. Although it hummed, when no bees emerged, he stalked up to the hive, and pounded on it with both fists. When a guard bee landed on him, he crushed it. Consequences ensued.

The Apostle Paul seconded the description Solomon gave. *"Therefore, I say this, and testify in the Lord, that you no longer walk even as also the rest of the nations walk, in the vanity of their mind, having been darkened in the intellect, being alienated from the life of God through the ignorance which is in them because of the hardness of their heart, who, having cast off all feeling, gave themselves up to lust, to the working of all uncleanness with greediness."* (Eph 4:17-19) Sin captivates, captures, and enslaves.

What is God's view? Cartoonists depict Him as a bearded old man standing on the edge of a cloud, sometimes chuckling over the foibles of His creation, sometimes wringing His hands in despair. Scripture presents a far different picture. *"You have done these things, and I have kept silence; you thought that surely I would be like you; but I will rebuke you and set in order before your eyes. Now think of this, you who forget God, lest I tear, and there not be any to deliver..."* (Psa 50:21-22) Again and again in Scripture we see warnings of judgment given, and the judgment itself delayed. Noah spent one hundred twenty years working and warning, before God said to him and his, "Come into the ark." Prophets spent a similar period of time warning Judah to repent of their wickedness, or captivity would come. They were mocked and abused when judgment did not come immediately. It came. Paul writes, *"And all these things happened to those as examples, and it was written for our warning, on whom the ends of the ages have come."* (1Cor 10:11)

In our view, however, the consequences of behavior are for others, not for ourselves. We assure ourselves that we will get away with what we want to do, and then complain when we are ensnared in our own actions, and the plodding consequences catch up with us. Paul speaks of the foolishness of arrogant indulgence in the desires of the flesh, and the inevitability of the consequences, both temporally and eternally. To the sinner he says, *"Or do you despise the riches of His kindness, and the forbearance and the long-suffering, not knowing that the kindness of God leads you to repentance? But according to your hardness and your impenitent heart, do you treasure up to yourself wrath in a day of wrath, and revelation of a righteous judgment of God?"* (Rom 2:4-5)

Believers in the Lord Jesus Christ, we were all in that same reality. Our life was once a walking death. We were sons of disobedience, and children of wrath. The righteous wrath of God brooded over each one of us. Each of us, in our own besetting sin which we pursued with greediness, treasured up for ourselves judgment and condemnation. Paul writes, *"Or do you not know that unjust ones will not inherit the kingdom of God? Do not be led astray, neither fornicators, nor idolaters, nor adulterers, nor male prostitutes, nor homosexuals, nor thieves, nor covetous ones, nor drunkards, nor revilers, nor plunderers shall inherit the kingdom of God. And some of you were these things, but you were washed, but you were sanctified, but you were justified in the name of the Lord Jesus, and in the Spirit of our God."* (1Cor 6:9-11) His is not by any means a comprehensive list. Scripture contains several laundry lists of wickedness, and although we may pick through them and congratulate ourselves that we were "never one of those," we must confess that we were in there somewhere, probably more than once. Praise God for that past tense, "were." Some of of us *were* these things. But, as stated in the original rendition, we stand washed from wickedness, we stand sanctified, we stand justified in Christ Jesus our Lord and Savior.

Indeed it is out of that past-tense reality that God has gathered a remnant in this age of grace. He has presented believers as a cherished love-gift to His Son. His purpose is eternally sure. *"But God, being rich in mercy, because of His great love with which He loved us, even we being dead in deviations, He made us alive together with Christ (by grace you are being saved), and raised us up together and seated us together in the heavenlies in Christ Jesus, that He might demonstrate in the ages coming on, the exceeding great riches of His grace in kindness toward us in Christ Jesus."* (Eph 2:4-7)

33

GREATER GLORY

One of the most spectacular exhibits in our natural history museums is found in a darkened room. Daylight or artificial light illumine mostly drab-colored pieces of rock. Some have interesting colors and patterns, but most would not attract our attention as anything but gravel. A companion display contains an array of crystals in a palette of hues, beautiful in their natural state, and a collection of faceted gemstones, sparkling in polished splendor. Then, the light fades to darkness. After a moment, the same display of specimens blazes with vibrant colors that cover the color spectrum of the rainbow. The rocks appear to have a glowing aura of color radiating from their core, each different specimen manifesting its own color response to stimulation from an unseen energy source.

Fluorescence is the word used for the glowing response of some minerals to ultraviolet light. Fluorite was the first mineral discovered to manifest the glowing response, and its name was the basis for the term applied to the phenomenon. The mechanism of fluorescence is as fascinating as the glow itself. Not all minerals fluoresce. Not all specimens of the same mineral fluoresce, either. What we see requires the combination of two things we do not see.

First, consider the electromagnetic spectrum. It consists of an array of energy waves that include several forms of radiation, including gamma radiation, x-ray radiation, ultraviolet radiation, visible light radiation, infrared radiation, terahertz radiation, microwave radiation and radio waves. Long wave radiation at the low frequency end of the spectrum has waves, measured from the crest, through the trough, and to the next crest, of up to one thousand meters, or about a fifth of a mile. Gamma radiation, at the highest energy end of the spectrum, has a wavelength of about one ten-billionth of a meter, or one angstrom. The visible light we term white light is actually a blended segment of the spectrum, broken by a prism into its component color bands. It is a very narrow band, from between 760 nanometers for red, up to 400 nanometers for violet. A nanometer is one billionth of a meter. This energy level, reflected by objects, stimulates the retina of the human eye, and is interpreted by the brain as images, and we say that we see. It is only in this narrow fragment of the spectrum that the visual process functions. The other radiation frequencies are invisible to us without assistance.

Second, we must focus on the nature of the rocks themselves. Atoms of elements form a crystalline lattice, or combine to form molecular compounds that are arranged in a similar structure. The rock specimen may include several minerals within the same specimen, and within the structure may exist what are, geologically speaking, termed excitable inclusions. These, and the molecules of some minerals themselves, react to the impact of ultraviolet radiation. The invisible ultraviolet light transfers its energy to electrons in the atoms of the excitable portions of the specimen. Just as firing an on-board rocket will boost a space capsule to a higher orbit, the excited electron jumps to a higher shell, but only temporarily. It jumps back to its original orbit, and in so doing, it releases the energy absorbed from the invisible ultraviolet light as a visible light glow, in the color band typical of its mineral variety. While some minerals fluoresce in a specific color range, others, depending on the nature of the invisible inclusions, may fluoresce in a variety of colors from specimen to specimen, or even within the same specimen. A rock composed of a variety of minerals may manifest oceans of green, with islands of blue, red, yellow and violet that seem to pulsate as we gaze.

Some inclusions in the same variety of rocks have the opposite effect. If they exist within the specimen, they mute or block the fluorescing response. The same light impacts the specimens, but the response varies, revealing the nature of the inclusions.

Fluorescence also distinguishes between the authentic and the fake in gemstones. The gems may appear identical to the unaided eye, but the response to ultraviolet light reveals the reality beneath the appearance.

The unseen light from without interacting with the unseen excitable inclusions within reveal a glory at which we can only marvel. But, the unseen light with the power to reveal also has the power to destroy. The short wave UV that best reveals the hidden glory in the rocks is the most penetrating and most damaging to tissues, organs and DNA. It is the most antibiotic, and unfiltered, it would leave the landmass on Earth lifeless.

The astonishing beauty of the fluorescing rocks points us to an even higher glory. The first broad stroke of creation was light. *"In the beginning God created the heavens and the earth; and the earth being without form and empty, and darkness on the face of the deep, and the Spirit of God moving gently on the face of the waters, then God said, Let light be! And there was light. And God saw the light, that it was good..."* (Gen 1:1-4) He saw the light, all of it, in all of its aspects and influences. We do not. We see only in part, and a small part at that. But He who is Light gave light to reveal His creation, through which He in turn reveals His glory and His nature. *"And this is the message which we have heard from Him, and we proclaim to you: God is light, and no darkness is in Him, none!"* (1John 1:5)

This is a concept fascinating to contemplate. The message is as incomprehensible to us as the reality it contains. God uses a reality we can see to convey one we cannot. Habakkuk records, *"And His brightness is as the light; rays from His hand are His, and there was a covering of His strength."* (Hab 3:4) Even that covering of His strength is light, as the psalmist describes it: *"...covering Yourself with light like a cloak, and stretching out the heavens like a curtain..."* (Psa 104:2)

The rays, or outshining of His glory, veiled for our protection in our fallen estate, are declared rather than perceived. *"The heavens are recounting the glory of God, and the expanse proclaiming His handiwork."* (Psa 19:1) *"The heavens declare His righteousness and all the people see His glory."* (Psa 97:6) *"For the unseen things of Him from the creation of the world are clearly seen, being understood by the things made, both His eternal power and Godhead, for them to be without excuse."* (Rom 1:20)

My wife enjoys seeing the misty rays as the hidden sun shines through breaks in the clouds that conceal it. Sometimes a beam of sunlight illuminates a small circle of water on the ruffled surface of the bay in front of our house, a spotlight that sets the ripples aflame like dancing diamonds. What a picture of God's revealing work in the lives of believers. But, as the Apostle Paul wrote to the believers at Corinth, *"...we not considering the things seen, but the things not being seen; for the things being seen are not lasting, but the things not being seen are everlasting."* (2Cor 4:18)

Using an ultraviolet lamp, geologists search for mineral deposits that fluoresce because they have within themselves the ability to respond to that energy source. With humanity, there is no quest for people who harbor within themselves some spark of glory, some interest, some desire that will respond to God's heart of love. There are none. God's evaluation of all humanity, through the pen of the Apostle Paul, is a blanket indictment, and is all-inclusive: ***"...according as it has been written, There is not a righteous one, not even one! There is not one understanding; there is not one seeking God. All turned away, they became worthless together, not one is doing goodness, not so much as one!"*** (Rom 3:10-12)

His glory, like His general blessings, fall on all humanity, but only a remnant will respond, and that response is only by His purpose and His grace. Dull we are, drab and hardened against the reality of God. As rocks only fluoresce if they contain excitable inclusions, so we only respond to His power, His love and His grace as He prepares that within us that will have the capacity to respond. All that He is remains foreign to us, absent His preparatory work. He is ***"...the only One having immortality, living in light that cannot be approached, whom no one of men saw, nor can see; to whom be honor and everlasting might."*** (1Tim 6:16) ***"But a natural man does not receive the things of the Spirit of God, for they are foolishness to him, and he is not able to know them, because they are spiritually discerned."*** (1Cor 2:14) As with ultraviolet radiation, we are incapable of perceiving or comprehending the pure light of His holiness and love. His nature is true light. Ours is not. Our mortal body is centered in and focused on this temporal realm in which we live, and our flesh, with its intrinsic desires, resonates to the values of this world. We revel in our drabness, and call it glory, the glory of man, and term the best of humanity luminaries of literature, of philosophy, of commerce and of philanthropy. Even at our self-proclaimed best, God calls us darkness, not light. The Light that He is reveals the darkness that we are, apart from His works of grace. In the worthless rebels we are, He determined to reveal His glory. To accomplish this, He must place within us the necessary excitable inclusions that will make the Light that He is visible.

Through Paul, He encapsulates the process: ***"But we ought*** *to thank God always concerning you, brothers, beloved by the Lord, because God chose you from the beginning to salvation in sanctification of the Spirit and belief of the truth, to which He called you through our gospel, to obtain the glory of our Lord Jesus Christ."* (2Thes 2:13-14) In the ones chosen to, or better termed, marked out for salvation, His miraculous work changes the condemned rebels we are into trophies of His grace, to be displayed in His presence eternally.

The first complex work of grace regenerates us, engendering within our mortal bodies a new creation in Christ Jesus. *"So that if anyone is in Christ, he is a new creation; the old things have passed away; behold, all things have become new!"* (2Cor 5:17) There is no reforming, no cleaning up the mess we are, no reconstituting. That which He creates within us is an entirely new being that inhabits this earthly tabernacle, or as my mother termed it, this husk, that is destined to be shed before we stand in His glorious presence. This regeneration, or salvation, is entirely His doing. God, by His Spirit, His love, His grace and His word, draws us to Christ Jesus. *"No one is able to come to Me unless the Father who sent Me draws him, and I will raise him up in the last day."* (John 6:44) Even in that initial drawing, we find the assurance of the purpose of God in the last phrase. The drawing of the Father assures the ultimate presentation in glory.

The sovereign working of God in salvation is intricate, while our thought processes are sequential. We try to arrange the work of salvation into steps that will fit our fixation on time. The creation of the new believer, or quickening, involves the Holy Spirit sensitizing the dead heart of the natural man to the Word of God, opening the understanding of the foolish mind, applying the truth of the gospel to the heart, inclining the heart to believe the Truth, and applying the gift of faith to that heart. The one in whom this work is accomplished is made conscious of believing, and the new believer is placed by the Spirit *in Christ*. The entire process is wrought by God Himself. *"For by grace you are saved, through faith, and this not of yourselves; it is the gift of*

God..." (Eph 2:8) *"Because it is God who said, 'Out of darkness Light shall shine,' who shone in our hearts to give the brightness of the knowledge of the glory of God in the face of Jesus Christ."* (2Cor 4:6) *"But of Him, you are in Christ Jesus, who was made to us wisdom from God, both righteousness and sanctification and redemption..."* (1Cor 1:30) It is the new being of the heart, and the indwelling Spirit, and the abiding Word of Truth, and *"...Christ in you, the hope of glory..."* (Col 1:27), that comprise the excitable inclusions in believers, the elements within that resonate to the power of God's holy working of His good pleasure.

The on-going work of grace works to eliminate the quenching internal inclusions of sin, and their occluding external encrustations that obscure the revealing of the glory of His gift of life. This *"sanctification of the Spirit"* is the continuing process of eliminating the inward attitudes and meditations, as well as the outward behaviors, the habits of our former way of life. Paul assures us of the inevitability of that work of God: *"...being persuaded of this very thing, that the One having begun a good work in you will finish it until the day of Jesus Christ.."* (Php 1:6) He couples this assurance with the responsibility of submissive response to our new reality: *"...for you then were darkness, but are now light in the Lord; walk as children of light."* (Eph 5:8) It is the responsiveness to God's indwelling Holy Spirit, and His leading, that allows the light that God is to be made perceptible in the believer. *"But I say, Walk in the Spirit, and you will not fulfill the lust of the flesh. For the flesh lusts against the Spirit, and the Spirit against the flesh; and these are contrary to one another; lest whatever you may will, these things you do."* (Gal 5:16-17) The deep love, lavish grace and coordinated effort of the Godhead will accomplish the eternal purpose of God in each one He has marked out for salvation, in whom He works His perfect will: *"... for it is God who is working in you both to will and to work for the sake of His good*

pleasure." (Php 2:13)

The Apostle Paul, using himself as an example, tells us what constitutes that *good pleasure*: ***"But when God was pleased... having called me through His grace, to reveal His Son in me..."*** (Gal 1:15-16) The revelation of our Lord Jesus Christ in each believer is the fluorescing response of the responsive elements God has placed within us, the light of what He is performing within us manifesting the reality of Christ, and in turn revealing the glory of God, because ***"...in these last days He spoke to us in the Son, whom He appointed heir of all; through whom He indeed made the ages; who being the shining splendor of His glory, and the express image of His essence, and upholding all things by the Word of His power..."*** (Heb 1:2-3) All that He has wrought within the believer declares His glory, fluorescing in the darkness of this world in response to the invisible Light of God. As Paul writes, ***"But all things being exposed by the light are clearly revealed, for everything having been revealed is light."*** (Eph 5:13) To the degree He is effacing the opaqueness of the flesh, this residue of Adam we inhabit, the light He has made us reveals His Son in a perceptible fashion.

Positionally, we are light in Christ. ***"You are all sons of light and sons of day; we are not of night, nor of darkness."*** (1Thes 5:5) We look to God, ***"...giving thanks to the Father, who has made us fit for a share of the inheritance of the saints in light..."*** (Col 1:12) We anticipate the realization of what God sees as accomplished. That, though, is a heavenly reality awaiting us. It is heavenly. We are not, yet. As Paul points out, ***"And there are heavenly bodies, and earthly bodies. But the glory of the heavenly is truly different, and that of the earthly different; one glory of the sun, and another glory of the moon, and another glory of the stars; for star differs from star in glory."*** (1Cor 15:40-41) He uses the distinctions among the celestial bodies that proclaim the glory of the Lord to show the contrast between the veiled glory the light of God is revealing in our mortal lives to the glory he has prepared, that awaits us. We are in a progressive transition as He works in us. He has begun His sanctifying work that will bring into being all that He has declared, opened our understanding, and drawn us to yield to His Spirit as He uses His Word to conform us to the very character of His Son. *"But we all with our face having been unveiled, having beheld the glory of the Lord in a mirror, are being changed into the same image from glory to glory, as from the Lord Spirit."* (2Cor 3:18)

God's purpose for this dispensation places believers in the darkness of this world, where His revealed glory shows more brightly, as Christ is revealed in us. Paul tells us that God's purpose for us is *"...that you may be blameless and harmless, children of God, without fault in the midst of a crooked generation, even having been perverted, among whom you shine as luminaries in the world, holding up the Word of Life..."* (Php 2:15-16) We are to serve as light-bearers God will use to reveal the Light of the world, and the light of the gospel of Christ.

The response to the light of the glory of Christ will be decidedly divergent. Some, the Spirit will draw, leading them to an opportunity to hear the gospel of salvation in Christ Jesus. *"But sanctify the Lord God in your hearts, and always be ready to give an answer to everyone asking you a reason concerning the hope in you, with meekness and fear..."* (1Pet 3:15) Others will back away. In the words of our Lord, *"And this is the judgment, that the Light has come into the world, and men loved the darkness more than the Light, for their works were evil. For everyone practicing wickedness hates the Light, and does not come to the Light, that his works may not be exposed."* (John 3:19-20) Still others, perhaps the majority, will respond with animosity: *"And, indeed, all desiring to live godly in Christ Jesus will be persecuted."* (2Tim 3:12) The words of our Savior to His own underscore this reality: *"I have spoken these things to you that you may have peace in Me. You have distress in the world; but be encouraged, I have overcome the world."* (John 16:33) In Him, we are overcomers, as well: *"But in all these things we more than conquer through Him loving us."* (Rom 8:37) This statement, true of every true believer in the Lord Jesus Christ, looks beyond our earthly pilgrimage, to the inheritance reserved in Heaven.

The trials and troubles of this journey are trivial in two comparisons. They fade to insignificance when the sufferings of Christ are juxtaposed with the most severe earthly distress. In addition, as Paul assures us, *"For I calculate that the sufferings of the present time are not worthy to compare to the coming glory to be revealed in us."* (Rom 8:18) *"...according as it has been written, Eye has not seen, and ear has not heard, nor has it risen up into the heart of man, the things which God has prepared for those that love Him."* (1Cor 2:9)

That greater glory is the purpose of of the Father for every believer He has chosen out of the world, cleansed, justified, sanctified and purified, and presented as a cherished love gift to His Son. It is the earnest purpose of the Son, Who prayed, *"Father, I desire that those whom You have given Me, that where I am, they may be with Me also, that they may behold My glory which You gave Me, because You loved Me before the foundation of the world."* (John 17:24) When our mortal body, plagued by the quenching inclusions and matrix of sin, is shed for our immortal, incorruptible body, the glory of His abundant grace will be freely displayed. *"Now to Him being able to keep you without stumbling, and to set you before His glory without blemish, with unspeakable joy; to the only wise God, our Savior, be glory and majesty and might and authority, even now and forever. Amen."* (Jude 1:24-25)

Michael J. Leamy

ABOUT THE AUTHOR

Michael J. Leamy was raised on a 160-acre pioneer homestead, under the sequential admonition from his father, "See everything there is to see. See everything about what you see. Remember what you see!" He brings this early training to the study of God's Word, and looks for the depth of the Scriptures, revealed by the One sent to lead us into all truth. Trained as a teacher, he has for years looked to the example of the greatest Teacher, our Lord Jesus Christ, who used elements from daily life to carry home the points of spiritual truth He was placing before His disciples, and through the Scriptures, to us. No longer teaching school, the author employs the same techniques in Bible studies, sermons and writing. He lives with Lynda, his wife of 43 years (and counting!) on a quiet knoll overlooking Youngs Bay, just south of Astoria, Oregon. This setting provides vistas of flaming sunsets and boisterous storms, and is home to many varieties of wildlife. His yard is visited by chipmunks, rabbits, raccoons and opossums, and his bird feeder is frequented by flocks of songbirds, including the rare and audacious Oregon Blacktail Warbler (a three-point buck) that empties the feeder in the wee hours of the morning. The warbler is a three point out west. For you out east, that would be a six-pointer.

Wander down the meandering paths of memory with the author, and share in the varied adventures and experiences, personal and otherwise, but most of all, meditate on the truths they lead us to discover in God's precious Word.

Made in the USA
Middletown, DE
04 August 2024